DATE DUE

AP 14 '97			
NO 20 '97			
SE 8 '98			
NO 10 '98			
DE 18 '98			
NO 12 '99			
JY 20 '00			
NO 12 '02			
NV 12 '04			
DE 2 '04			

2000 YEARS OF DISBELIEF

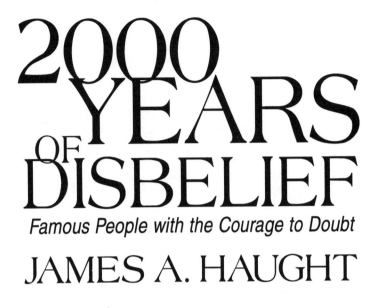

2000 YEARS OF DISBELIEF

Famous People with the Courage to Doubt

JAMES A. HAUGHT

 **Prometheus Books**

59 John Glenn Drive
Amherst, NewYork 14228-2197

For Nancy, Joel, Jake, Jeb, and Cass

Published 1996 by Prometheus Books

00 99 98 97 96   5 4 3 2 1

Library of Congress Cataloging-in-Publication Data

Haught, James A.
    2000 years of disbelief : famous people with the courage to doubt / James A. Haught.
        p.   cm.
    Includes bibliographical references and index.
    ISBN 1–57392–067–3 (alk. paper)
    1. Atheists—Biography. 2. Agnostics—Biography. I. Title. II. Title: Two thousand years of disbelief
BL2785.H38   1996
211'.8'0922—dc20   96–8175
                                                                      CIP

Printed in the United States of America on acid-free paper

Contents

Part Three: The European Enlightenment

Part Four: The American Rationalists

Part Five: The Nineteenth Century
(and the Turn of the Twentieth)

Part Six: The Early Twentieth Century

Part Seven: The Mid- and Late Twentieth Century

Acknowledgments

The more than one thousand quotations in this volume have been gathered over three decades from scores of books and other sources. Where possible, I cite original sources. Many quotes, however, were drawn from existing anthologies and collections, and their help is gratefully acknowledged.

Edward M. and Michael E. Buckner, *Quotations That Support the Separation of Church and State* (The Atlanta Freethought Society, 1993).

Charles Q. Bufe, ed., *The Heretic's Handbook of Quotations: Cutting Comments on Burning Issues* (Tucson, Ariz.: See Sharp Press, 1992).

Ira D. Cardiff, *What Great Men Think of Religion* (Christopher Publishing House, 1945; reprint New York: Arno Press, 1972).

Carole Gray, designer of the 1992 Atheist Desk Calendar and the 1993 and 1994 Women of Freethought Calendars, Columbus, Ohio.

Rev. Roger E. Greeley, ed., *The Best of Humanism* (Amherst, N.Y.: Prometheus Books, 1988).

H. L. Mencken, *A New Dictionary of Quotations* (New York: Alfred A. Knopf, 1966).

Rufus K. Noyes, *Views of Religion* (Boston: L. K. Washburn, 1906).

Laurence J. Peter, *Peter's Quotations: Ideas for Our Time* (New York: William Morrow & Co., 1977).

George Seldes, ed., *The Great Quotations* (New York: Lyle Stuart, 1960).

Thomas S. Vernon, *Great Infidels* (Fayetteville, Ark.: M&M Press, 1989).

Laird Wilcox and John George, eds., *Be Reasonable: Selected Quotations for Inquiring Minds* (Amherst, N.Y.: Prometheus Books, 1994).

In this book, quotations from these collections are marked (Cardiff), (Seldes), (Vernon), and so on.

For more than two thousand years, at different times and places, from ancient Greece to strict Muslim lands today, doubters of prevailing religious dogmas have risked jailing, flogging, banishment—or worse. (Engraving by Jan Luyken from *Martyrs Mirror,* The Netherlands, 1685)

Introduction

The Freedom
to Doubt

Intelligent, educated people tend to doubt the supernatural. So it is hardly surprising to find a high ratio of religious skeptics among major thinkers, scientists,
writers, reformers, scholars, champions of democracy, and other world changers—
people usually called great.

The advance of Western civilization has been partly a story of gradual victory
over oppressive religion. The rise of humanism slowly shifted society's focus
away from obedience to bishops and kings, onto individual rights and improved
living conditions. Much of the progress was impelled by men and women who
didn't pray, didn't kneel at altars, didn't make pilgrimages, didn't recite creeds.

Since disbelief remains a taboo topic, this pattern is rarely mentioned. Churchmen generally contend that great figures in history, such as America's founders,
were conventional worshipers. That's untrue.

"One of the embarrassing problems for the early nineteenth-century champions of the Christian faith was that not one of the first six presidents of the United
States was an orthodox Christian," philosopher-educator Mortimer Adler and a
team of *Encyclopedia Britannica* writers said.[1]

Most of the founders were Deists, roughly equivalent to Unitarians, who
doubted that Christ was a god, yet praised his message of compassion. They
spoke of God as the power behind nature, as discerned by science.

Other pioneers in many fields in many centuries included nonconformists of
all sorts, from mild dissidents to outright atheists.

Western culture has traveled an erratic journey. Ancient Greece and Rome
teemed with intellectual inquiry, amid polytheism. Then the Christian Age of
Faith brought darkness for centuries. The Renaissance revived individualism and

---

1. *The Annals of America: Great Issues in American Life: A Conspectus,* Mortimer J. Adler, ed-
itor-in-chief (Chicago: Encyclopedia Britannica, 1968), vol. 2, p. 420.

free thinking, which soared in the Age of Reason and the Enlightenment. With the flowering of science in the nineteenth century, many thinkers assumed that mystical religion would vanish. Among intellectuals, it largely has done so. But dogma and fundamentalism have resurfaced in society at large.

Disbelief always has remained partly hidden, because it entails risk. Believers can inflict terrible punishments on doubters. During eras when religion was supreme, nonconformists lived in peril. Here are some examples:

• In 399 B.C.E., Socrates was condemned by a 500-man Athenian jury on vague charges, including an accusation that he was guilty of "not worshiping the gods whom the state worships." His predecessor, Anaxagoras, likewise was sentenced to death for teaching that the sun and moon are natural objects, not deities, but he fled into exile. Protagoras was banished from Athens for saying he didn't know if the gods exist. His books were burned, and he perished at sea.

• In the year 385, the Spanish ascetic Priscillian was executed for holding an unorthodox view of the Trinity and other variant beliefs.

• In 415, the great woman scientist Hypatia, head of the renowned Alexandrian Library, was beaten to death by Christian monks who considered her a pagan.

• Around 550 at Constantinople, the Byzantine Emperor Justinian executed multitudes to impose Christian orthodoxy.

• After the turn of the millennium, the killing of nonconformists soared in Europe. Popes waged gory "internal crusades" against "heretical" Christians such as the Albigenses, Waldensians, and Apostolic Brethren. This led to establishment of the Inquisition, which tortured and burned the unorthodox. St. Thomas Aquinas declared that if it was proper to execute counterfeiters, "there is much more reason for excommunicating and even putting to death one convicted of heresy."[2]

• After the Reformation, both Catholic and Protestant authorities killed "blasphemers" such as the physician Michael Servetus, who discovered the pulmonary circulation of blood. He was burned alive in John Calvin's Geneva in 1553 for doubting the Trinity.

• Matthew Hamount went to the stake in 1579 at Norwich, England, after priests accused him of saying that the Bible "is but foolishness, a mere fable; that Christ is not God or the savior of the world, but a mere man. . . ."

• The Roman Inquisition burned philosopher Giordano Bruno in 1600 for contending that the earth circles the sun, and that the universe is infinite. A generation later, the Inquisition sentenced Galileo to life confinement for writing his belief that the earth moves.

• In 1697, a young man was burned at Edinburgh for ridiculing the Bible.

---

2. Thomas Aquinas, *Summa theologiae,* ca. 1265.

• In 1766, a French teenager, Chevalier de La Barre, was beheaded on charges that he had marred a crucifix, sung irreligious songs, and worn his hat while a religious procession passed.

For every nonconformist executed, hundreds were jailed, tortured, fined, flogged, censured, banished, or ostracized. Understandably, few people dared voice skepticism. However, by the eighteenth century, with a slight loosening of the church's grip, a few bold French and English rebels—especially thinkers allied with Voltaire—ventured into dangerous water. They promulgated Deism and Unitarianism, denying the divinity of Jesus and rejecting miracles, while contending that God can be seen in patterns of nature and the universe. A brazen few expressed outright atheism.

Their innovation wasn't without hazard. Thomas Woolston, who wrote treatises questioning Christ's resurrection and other miracles, was convicted in 1729 and kept under house arrest until he died. Denis Diderot, chief creator of the first encyclopedia, was imprisoned in 1749 for writing that knowledge comes only through sense impressions. Scientist Joseph Priestley, the discoverer of oxygen, also a Unitarian clergyman, caused a public outrage with his writings, precipitating a 1791 riot in which his home, church, and laboratory were burned. In 1819, British author-journalist Richard Carlile, whose writings questioned Christianity, was jailed for six years for "blasphemous libel."

Deism, Unitarianism, and the Enlightenment spread to America, influencing the radical thinkers who launched modern democracy: Thomas Jefferson, John Adams, James Madison, Benjamin Franklin, Thomas Paine, Ethan Allen, and others. Paine's skeptical writings caused controversy, and Englishmen who sold his books were jailed for blasphemy.

When Jefferson entered Virginia's House of Delegates in 1776, state laws still decreed death for heresy and three years in prison for doubting the Trinity. Along with Madison, George Mason, and other rebels, Jefferson succeeded in halting tax support of the Anglican Church and passing a statute of religious freedom, eliminating punishments for disapproved beliefs. Eventually, their efforts gave the world a new principle—separation of church and state—ending government enforcement of religion.

Religious dissent has many levels, from doctrinal nitpicking, to general uncertainty, to unabashed atheism. In medieval times, the label "atheist" was hurled at many who were believers, but of the wrong faith. No American writing before 1800 actually denied the existence of God, historian James Turner says. Various categories of skepticism took form: British scientist Thomas Henry Huxley coined the word "agnostic" for people who feel that it's impossible to know whether a spirit realm exists. The designation "freethinkers" derived from French freethought groups of the eighteenth century.

Slowly, as scientific thinking grew and religion retreated, freedom to doubt emerged in the West. But not without setbacks: In the 1830s, Abner Kneeland, a founder of the Universalist Church, was jailed for blasphemy in Massachusetts because he questioned miracles and the divinity of Jesus. In the mid-1800s, George Jacob Holyoake gave London lectures containing declarations such as "I do not believe there is such a thing as a god." He was jailed for atheism, and his small daughter died of malnutrition while he was unable to support his family. British editor Charles Bradlaugh was elected to Parliament repeatedly in the 1880s, but was refused admittance because he would not take a religious oath. In 1883, George William Foote of London was imprisoned for publishing satirical sketches of Bible stories. In Sweden near the turn of the twentieth century, Viktor Lennstrand was jailed and fined for criticizing Christianity. Woodrow Wilson's uncle, Professor James Woodrow, was fired by Presbyterian Theological Seminary in South Carolina in 1884 for defending evolution.

Eventually, the right to disbelieve was established. Freethought blossomed among intellectuals in Europe and America, reaching a heyday at the end of the nineteenth century and the beginning of the twentieth. Doubters such as Robert Ingersoll conducted speaking tours to challenge supernaturalism. Newspaper writers such as H. L. Mencken openly assailed "superstition."

But the heyday passed, and conformity prevailed. Today, skeptics remain misfits in much of American society. No politician could be elected if he admitted atheism. Newspapers and mainstream magazines rarely print agnostic articles. Television programs seldom contain direct denials of God. In France in 1988, Catholic mobs burned two movie theaters showing *The Last Temptation of Christ,* which hinted that Jesus wasn't divine.

The freedom to doubt has not reached the Islamic world, where disbelief remains punishable by death. Muslim holy men still issue *fatwas* (religious edicts) ordering the murder of "blaspheming" writers. In Saudi Arabia in 1992, a man was beheaded in the marketplace at Qatif after being convicted of "insulting Allah, the Holy Koran and Muhammad the Prophet."

It is a strange contradiction: The majority of people around the globe still worship unseen gods, and sometimes even kill for them—yet most Western thinkers, scientists, writers, and other intellectuals generally reject the supernatural.

For anyone scanning the past and surveying the current world scene, it is nearly impossible to find any outstanding person—except for popes, archbishops, kings, and other rulers seeking popular support—who says the purpose of life is to be saved by an invisible Jesus and to enter an invisible heaven. But it is easy to find many among the great who doubt this basic dogma.

This book describes renowned people, past and present, who have challenged religion to one degree or other and who have bravely voiced their doubts. It utilizes the most reliable evidence—their own words. The purpose of this book is to assure thinking people that they needn't apologize if they can't believe mystical claims. They are in the company of giants.

Part One

The Beginnings
of Rationalism

1

The Ancients

Socrates

Zeus and Hera, Jupiter and Juno, Ares and Mars, Athena and Minerva, Aphrodite and Venus, Eros and Cupid, Pluto, Saturn, Apollo, Neptune, Vulcan, Mercury, Diana, Bacchus, and so on and so on.

The assembly of gods and goddesses worshiped in ancient Greece and Rome seems childish today, rather like cartoon characters, akin to Batman and Robin. But they were so real to their devotees twenty centuries ago that doubters sometimes were put to death. Impiety was a capital offense in Athens, even in the Golden Age of philosophers and early scientists.

In addition to Socrates, Protagoras, and Anaxagoras, others also faced criminal charges of impiety. Stilpo of Megara, charged with saying that Athena was "not a god," joked at his trial that Athena was a goddess instead. He was exiled. Theophrastos, head of Aristotle's school, made the error of questioning animal sacrifice, and was arrested. Even Aspasia, beloved mistress of the Athenian statesman Pericles, was accused.

Despite the risk, some thinkers and writers of the classical era revealed their skepticism, overtly or covertly. *Sisyphus,* the lost play by Critias, reportedly contended that religion is a fabrication by governments to keep subjects submissive. Plato's *Symposium* concludes that there is no personal immortality. Thales of Miletos, often called the first scientific thinker, was reported to have "lost belief in the gods." The Greek philosophers Theodoros and Diagoras were called atheists by the Roman Cicero. Several historians record that Julius Caesar scoffed at the gods.

The renowned Greek teacher Epicurus was a skeptic. He didn't deny that gods exist, but asserted that they neither work miracles nor reward and punish humans. He, too, rejected an afterlife. His followers were expelled from Crete and Messene on charges of atheism. The modern view of Epicureanism as wanton self-indulgence is false; Epicurus actually taught that simple enjoyment of nature and friendship is the best route to a rewarding life. Two centuries later, the scientific-minded Roman poet Lucretius hailed Epicurus as a giant of thought.

In addition, some Greek and Roman thinkers claimed to see evidence of a single god in nature, which repudiated the official array of many gods. A sampling of ancient skepticism follows.

*   *   *

"Open your mouth and shut your eyes, and see what Zeus shall send you."
—Aristophanes (448–380 B.C.E.), Athenian comic poet (Cardiff)

"Shrines! Shrines! Surely you don't believe in the gods. What's your argument? Where's your proof?"—Aristophanes (Noyes)

"Prayers and sacrifices to the gods are of no avail."—Aristotle (384–322 B.C.E.), Greek philosopher (Cardiff)

"A tyrant must put on the appearance of uncommon devotion to religion. Subjects are less apprehensive of illegal treatment from a ruler whom they consider god-fearing and pious. On the other hand, they do less easily move against him, believing that he has the gods on his side."—Aristotle, *Politics*

"Men create gods after their own image, not only with regard to their form but with regard to their mode of life."—Aristotle (Noyes)

"Zeus rains, not that corn may be increased, but from necessity."—Aristotle, ibid.

"Suns may rise and set; we, when our short day has closed, must sleep on during one perpetual night."—Catullus (84–54 B.C.E.), Roman poet (Peter)

"Without the hope of immortality, no one would ever face death for his country."
—Cicero (106–43 B.C.E.), Roman orator and philosopher

"What old woman is so stupid now as to tremble at those tales of hell which were once so firmly believed in?"—Cicero (Cardiff)

"When men became less credulous, the power of the Pythian Oracle vanished."
—Cicero (Noyes)

"The life of the dead rests in the remembrances of the living."—Cicero, ibid.

". . . There are no miracles."—Cicero, quoted in *Time,* April 10, 1995, p. 67

"Not knowing life, how can we know death? Why talk of spirits when you do not understand men?"—Confucius (sixth century B.C.E.), Chinese philosopher (Cardiff) (Noyes)

"It was man who first made men believe in gods."—Critias (ca. 480–403 B.C.E.), Athenian orator and politician, fragment (Mencken)

"We believe whatever we want to believe."—Demosthenes (384–322 B.C.E.), Athenian orator and statesman, *Third Olynthiac*

"The myths about Hades and the gods, although they are pure invention, help to make men virtuous."—Diodorus Siculus (fl. first century C.E.), Greek historian, *Bibliotheca historica*

"It is to the interest of states to be deceived in religion."—Diodorus Siculus (Cardiff)

"Thus does Diogenes sacrifice to all the gods at once."—Diogenes (412–323 B.C.E.), Greek Cynic philosopher, upon cracking a louse on the altar rail of a temple (Cardiff)

"When I look upon seamen, men of physical science, and philosophers, man is the wisest of all beings. When I look upon priests, prophets, and interpreters of dreams, nothing is so contemptible as man."—Diogenes (Noyes)

"None of the gods has formed the world, nor has any man; it has always been."—Empedocles (495–435 B.C.E.), Greek philosopher and statesman (Noyes)

"Where are you going? It cannot be to a place of suffering; there is no hell." —Epictetus (50–135 C.E.), Greek Stoic philosopher (Noyes)

"Either God wants to abolish evil, and cannot; or he can, but does not want to. . . . If he wants to, but cannot, he is impotent. If he can, but does not want to, he is wicked. . . . If, as they say, God can abolish evil, and God really wants to do it, why is there evil in the world?"—Epicurus (341–270 B.C.E.), Greek philosopher, *Aphorisms*

". . . Men, believing in myths, will always fear something terrible, everlasting punishment as certain or probable. . . . Men base all these fears not on mature opinions, but on irrational fancies, so that they are more disturbed by fear of the unknown than by facing facts. Peace of mind lies in being delivered from all these fears."—Epicurus (Greeley)

". . . You should accustom yourself to believing that death means nothing to us, since every good and every evil lies in sensation; but death is the privation of sensation."—Epicurus, ibid.

"Fabulous persuasion in faith is the approbation of feigned ideas or notions; it is credulous belief in the reality of phantoms."—Epicurus (Noyes)

"Do we, holding that the gods exist, deceive ourselves with unsubstantial dreams and lies, while random careless chance and change alone control the world?"—Euripides (484–406 B.C.E.), Athenian dramatist, *Hecuba*

"Men make their choice: one man honors one god, and one another."—Euripides, *Hippolytus,* 428 B.C.E.

"What is god, what is not god / What is between man and god / Who shall say?" —Euripides, *Helen,* 412 B.C.E.

"We serve the gods—whatever the gods may be."—Euripides, *Orestes*

"He was a wise man who originated the idea of God."—Euripides (Seldes)

"Religion is a disease, but it is a noble disease."—Heraclitus (fl. ca. 500 B.C.E.), Greek philosopher, fragment (Mencken)

"The universe has been made neither by gods nor by men, but it has been, and is, and will be eternally."—Heraclitus (Noyes)

"Too often in time past, religion has brought forth criminal and shameful actions. . . . How many evils has religion caused!"—Lucretius (99–55 B.C.E.), Roman Epicurean philosopher, *On the Nature of Things,* remarking on King Agamemnon's sacrifice of his daughter to the gods to ensure success of a military campaign

"The nature of the universe has by no means been made through divine power, seeing how great are the faults that mar it."—Lucretius, ibid.

"Long time men lay oppress'd with slavish fear / Religion's tyranny did domineer . . . / At length a mighty one of Greece [Epicurus] began / To assert the natural liberty of man, / By senseless terrors and vain fancies led / To slavery. Straight the conquered phantoms fled."—Lucretius, ibid., verse translation by Creech

"Rest, brother, rest. Have you done ill or well / Rest, rest, There is no God, no gods, who dwell / Crowned with avenging righteousness on high / Nor frowning ministers of their hate in hell."—Lucretius, ibid.

"All religions are equally sublime to the ignorant, useful to the politician, and ridiculous to the philosopher."—Lucretius (Cardiff)

"Fear was the first thing on earth to make gods."—Lucretius, ibid.

"Not they who reject the gods are profane, but those who accept them."—Lucretius (Noyes)

"Nature is seen to do all things spontaneously of herself, without meddling of the gods."—Lucretius, ibid.

"We, peopling the void air, make gods to whom we impute the ills we ought to bear."—Lucretius, ibid.

"There is no murky pit of hell awaiting anyone. . . . Mind cannot arise alone without body, or apart from sinews and blood. . . . You must admit, therefore, that when the body has perished, there is an end also of the spirit diffused through it. It is surely crazy to couple a mortal object with an eternal. . . ."—Lucretius (Greeley)

"The world holds two classes of men—intelligent men without religion, and religious men without intelligence."—Abū al-'Alā' Ahmad ibn 'Abd Allāh al-Ma'arri (973–1057), Syrian poet (Cardiff)

"I learned from Diognetus not to give credit to what was said by miracle-workers, and about the driving away of demons and such things."—Marcus Aurelius (121–180 C.E.), Roman emperor and philosopher (Noyes)

"It is expedient that gods should exist; since it is expedient, let us believe they do."—Ovid (43 B.C.E.–A.D. 17), Roman poet, *Ars amatoria*

"It was fear that first brought gods into the world."—Petronius Arbiter (d. 66 C.E.), Roman novelist, *Satyricon*

"He was a wise man who invented God."—Plato (ca. 429–347 B.C.E.), *Sisyphus*

"It is ridiculous to suppose that the great head of things, whatever it may be, pays any regard to human affairs."—Pliny the Elder (ca. 23–79 C.E.), Roman scholar, *Natural History*

"From the moment of death onward, the body and soul feel as little as they did before birth."—Pliny (Noyes)

"The ancient cabalists, religionists, magicians, orphies, etc., led into errors of considerable magnitude, not only individuals, but kings and nations."—Plutarch (46–120 C.E.), Greek biographer (Noyes)

"The superstitious man wishes he did not believe in gods, as the atheist does not, but fears to disbelieve in them."—Plutarch, ibid.

"Since the masses of the people are inconstant, full of unruly desires, passionate, and reckless of consequence, they must be filled with fears to keep them in order. The ancients did well, therefore, to invent gods, and the belief in punishment after death."—Polybius (ca. 203–120 B.C.E.), Greek historian, *Histories*

"As to the gods, I have no means of knowing either that they exist or do not exist, or what they are like. Many things prevent our knowing: the subject is obscure, and brief is the span of mortal life."—Protagoras (ca. 481–ca. 411 B.C.E.), Greek philosopher, quoted by Diogenes Laertius in *Lives of Eminent Philosophers*

"Man is the measure of all that is / All loves and lives and gods are his."—Protagoras (Cardiff)

"Religion is regarded by the common people as true, by the wise as false, and by the rulers as useful."—Seneca (4 B.C.E.–65 C.E.), Roman philosopher and dramatist (Cardiff)

"After death, nothing is. . . . Let the ambitious zealot lay aside his hope of heaven, whose faith is but his pride. . . . Naught's after death, and death itself is naught. . . . Then may the saints lose all their hope of heaven, and sinners quit their racky fears of hell."—Seneca (Cardiff)

"The longer I consider the subject of God, the more obscure it becomes."—Simonides (556–468 B.C.E.), Greek poet (Noyes)

— "The race of mortals has forged images of God of stone, wood, gold, and ivory; we dedicate to them festival days, and we call that religion."—Sophocles (496–406 B.C.E.), Athenian dramatist (Noyes)

"It was fear in the world that created the gods."—Statius (ca. 45–96 C.E.), Roman poet, *Thebaid*

"Christianity is a pestilent superstition."—Tacitus (55–120 C.E.), Roman historian (Noyes)

"It is for the good of states that men should be deluded by religion."—Varro (116–27 B.C.E.), Roman scholar and antiquarian, *Antiquitatum divinarum*

"The Ethiopians say that their gods are snub-nosed and black, the Thracians that theirs have light blue eyes and red hair."—Xenophanes (ca. 560–478 B.C.E.), Greek philosopher, fragment, quoted in the *Macmillan Dictionary of Quotations,* p. 475.

". . . Men imagine gods to be born and to have raiment and voice and body, like themselves. . . . Oxen, lions, and horses, if they had hands wherewith to grave images, would fashion gods after their own shapes and make them bodies like to their own."—Xenophanes, fragment quoted in *Encyclopedia Britannica*

"No man has perceived certainty, nor shall anyone perceive it, about the gods and all whereof I speak; for, however perfect what he says may be, yet he does not know it; all things are matters of opinion."—Xenophanes, ibid.

"Temples are not to be built to the gods."—Zeno (334–261 B.C.E.), Greek Stoic philosopher (Noyes)

2

Omar Khayyam (1048?–1131)

Courtesy Bibliotheca Persica, Center for Iranian Studies, Columbia University

Today, in much of the Muslim world, a writer who casts doubt on heaven and holy men is likely to be jailed or targeted by a religious death decree.

Yet nine hundred years ago, a brilliant Persian scientist dared to voice eloquent agnosticism in the most famous poem ever to come from an Islamic land. The *Rubaiyat* of Omar Khayyam scoffs at theologians, laments the unknowability of the hereafter, and hails worldly pleasure as the only tangible goal.

"Here with a loaf of bread beneath the bough / A flask of wine, a book of verse—and thou / Beside me singing in the wilderness—/ And wilderness is Paradise enow."

The poet advised seekers to stop pondering contradictory religious dogmas, and escape with a flagon of wine—"The grape that can with logic absolute / The two-and-seventy jarring sects confute."

Abu ol-Fath Omar ibn Ibrahim was called Khayyam (tentmaker), perhaps because his ancestors had practiced that trade. Omar was educated in science and philosophy in his native Nishapur, then went to Samarkand, where he wrote a treatise on algebra. Sultan Malik Shah commissioned him to help build an observatory in Isfahan and make astronomical observations to reform the calendar. After the death of his patron in 1092, Omar returned to Nishapur as a teacher and served the ruling court through his knowledge of mathematics, medicine, history, law, philosophy, and other subjects.

Omar wrote quatrains expressing his wistful musings on the meaninglessness of life. After his death in 1131, copies were made, and evidently embellished with improvisations by other poets. For centuries, the old manuscripts were forgotten—until chance turned them into a literary sensation.

In 1856, a librarian at Oxford University sent an aged Persian manuscript to a talented English poet, Edward FitzGerald, who was studying Persian. The skeptical-minded FitzGerald was captivated by the existential tone of the verses, which reminded him of the ponderings of Epicurus. FitzGerald wrote to Alfred, Lord Tennyson, who had been his classmate at Cambridge:

"I have . . . got hold of an old Epicurean so desperately impious in his recommendations to live only for today that the good Mahometans have scarcely dared to multiply manuscripts of him."

FitzGerald rewrote the quatrains into English—not as direct translations, but as poetic creations based on Omar. Publishing them was risky, because blasphemy was a crime in Victorian England, and skepticism was taboo. *Fraser's Magazine* refused to print the *Rubaiyat.* FitzGerald finally paid to have five hundred copies printed privately in 1859, without his name attached.

The small books lay unnoticed for two years at a London bookstore, and some were sold as wastepaper. Remaining copies were put in a bargain bin for a penny each. A young man bought one and gave it to the painter Dante Gabriel Rossetti, who was fascinated and bought copies for the poets Robert Browning and Algernon Charles Swinburne. But the public remained unaware.

FitzGerald produced enlarged versions in 1868 and 1872. The anonymous book began drawing public attention. The translator's identity became known, and FitzGerald was pleased by the "little craze" caused by his work.

FitzGerald's eyesight failed, and he died in 1883. He never knew that his *Rubaiyat* went on to become a world classic that sold millions of copies in hundreds of editions.

Subsequently, researchers have found as many as 1,391 ancient quatrains attributed to Omar, and have attempted to separate the genuine ones from derivative concoctions, with little success.

Segments from the Rubaiyat, *translated by Edward FitzGerald*

"Myself when young did eagerly frequent / Doctor and saint, and heard great argument / About it and about: but evermore / Came out by the same door as in I went.

"With them the seed of wisdom did I sow / And with my own hand labored it to grow / And this is all the harvest that I reaped—/ 'I came like water, and like wind I go.'

"Into this universe, and why not knowing / Nor whence, like water willy-nilly flowing / And out of it, as wind along the waste / I know not whither, willy-nilly blowing."

"Alike for those who for today prepare / And those that after a tomorrow stare / A muezzin from the tower of darkness cries / 'Fools! Your reward is neither here nor there.'

"Why, all the saints and sages who discussed / Of the two worlds so learnedly, are thrust / Like foolish prophets forth; their words to scorn / Are scattered, and their mouths are stopped with dust.

"Oh, threats of hell and hopes of paradise! / One thing at least is certain—*this* life flies; / One thing is certain, and the rest is lies; / The flower that once has blown forever dies."

"The moving finger writes, and having writ / Moves on: nor all thy piety nor wit / Shall lure it back to cancel half a line / Nor all thy tears wash out a word of it.

"And that inverted bowl we call the sky / Whereunder crawling coop'd we live and die / Lift not your hands to it for help—for it / Rolls impotently on as thou and I."

"Ah, Love, could thou and I with fate conspire / To grasp this sorry scheme of things entire / Would we not shatter it to bits, and then / Remold it nearer to the heart's desire!"

"The revelations of the devout and learned / Who rose before us and as prophets burned / Are all but stories, which, awoke from sleep / They told their comrades, and to sleep returned."

Part Two

The Renaissance

3

Michel
de Montaigne
(1533–1592)

The Renaissance—three centuries of reawakening, from around 1300 to 1600—is commonly acknowledged as the European epoch when the oppressive Age of Faith began losing ground to humanism and the desire to improve people's earthly lives.

Yet religious torture and killing continued amid the bloom of the Renaissance. The Holy Inquisition burned thousands of nonconforming "heretics" and more thousands of suspected witches. The Reformation sent Protestant and Catholic armies into gory wars that laid nations waste. Christians killed Jews in numerous pogroms. Doubters could be jailed or executed for "blasphemy."

Under such conditions, it would seem advisable for skeptics to stay quiet. Yet some brave rebels voiced unorthodox thoughts.

Michel de Montaigne's mother came from a Spanish-Jewish family that had been forcibly converted to Catholicism, and had fled to France to escape the Spanish Inquisition. His father was a wealthy merchant whose family had bought the feudal territory of Montaigne, with its noble title.

Although the son came of age in an era when the Inquisition had been torturing and burning doubters for three centuries, and it was not a propitious time to voice any religious thought that might lead to the rack, nonetheless the brilliant Montaigne took the risk of writing candidly about religion and morals, not always conforming to official dogma. He created the literary form of the essay: a personal commentary which he said was "concerned with my own self, an integral part of my life." Some of Montaigne's essays included witty jabs at religion. University of Washington scholar Abraham Keller has said the essays "show so much skepticism that some critics have questioned whether he was really a Christian."[1]

Montaigne's first publication was a translation of a thousand-page book by Spanish theologian Raimond Sebond, who contended that Christian doctrines

---

1. *World Book Encyclopedia* (1978 ed.), p. 619.

could be proved by scientific logic. Later, when Montaigne published his book of essays, the longest was a skeptical "Apology for Raimond Sebond," which argued that human logic is too swayed by cultural and psychological factors to be reliable. Acceptance of religion must be by faith alone, he said.

His family was officially Catholic, although a brother and sister became Protestants. Montaigne served in the Parliament of Bordeaux for thirteen years, and was mayor of Bordeaux for four years. In the hideous wars between French Catholics and Protestant Huguenots, he attempted to be a peacemaker. At one point he was jailed briefly by Protestants, at another by Catholics. Montaigne urged King Henry IV to issue the Edict of Nantes which gave each sect the right to worship.

Debate still occurs over whether Montaigne was a believer or a secret atheist. If the latter, he was wise to keep it secret.

Montaigne's Comments on Religion

"Man is certainly stark mad; he cannot make a worm, yet he will make gods by the dozen."—*Essays*, 1580

"Men of simple understanding, little inquisitive and little instructed, make good Christians."—ibid.

"How many things that were articles of faith yesterday are fables today."—ibid.

"Nothing is so firmly believed as what we least know."—ibid.

"How many things do we name miraculous and against nature? Each man and every nation doth it according to the measure of his ignorance. . . . Miracles are according to the ignorance wherein we are by nature, and not according to nature's essence."—ibid.

"Philosophy is doubt."—ibid.

"Everyone's true worship was that which he found in use in the place where he chanced to be."—ibid.

"To know much is often the cause of doubting more."—ibid.

"The gross imposture of religions, wherewith so many worthy and sufficient men have been besotted. . . ."—(Cardiff)

"Diagoras and Theodorus flatly deny that there were ever any gods at all." —(Noyes)

"It is setting a high value upon our opinions to roast men and women alive on account of them."—ibid.

"Men make themselves believe that they believe."—ibid.

"What do I know?"—his personal motto

4

Christopher Marlowe (1564–1593)

Portrait assumed to be of Marlowe, courtesy of the Master and Fellows of Corpus Christi College, Cambridge, England

Playwrights Christopher Marlowe and William Shakespeare were born in the same year—a year when people still were executed for their religious beliefs, or lack thereof.

Christianity was enforced by law in Elizabethan England. Church attendance was mandatory, under penalty of prosecution. Schoolchildren were indoctrinated in the official creeds. The public was taxed to support the official church.

It was the time of the Reformation, and England had seesawed through decades of gore. When King Henry VIII was a Catholic, he wrote a pamphlet denouncing Martin Luther and decreed death to any who doubted the Roman church. Several Lollard Protestants were jailed, tortured, or burned at the stake. The pope proclaimed Henry "Defender of the Faith." But when the pope would not let Henry divorce and remarry, the king split with Rome in 1533 and created the Church of England. Thereafter, it was a capital offense to doubt Anglicanism. Henry executed unconverted Catholics such as Sir Thomas More and others.

Henry was succeeded briefly by his ten-year-old son, then in 1553 by Mary, his daughter by his first wife. Intensely Catholic, she became "Bloody Mary," striving to restore Catholicism by force. She burned three hundred Protestants, including Henry's top bishops.

Then Mary was followed in 1558 by Elizabeth, Henry's daughter by his second wife, and the seesaw tipped back to Anglicanism. At first Elizabeth attempted to tolerate all faiths, but mutiny by Catholics and ferment by hidebound Puritans caused Parliament to outlaw both beliefs. Elizabeth executed two hundred Catholics and three Puritans, but both faiths remained stubbornly alive.

Doubters fared no better. In 1579, Matthew Hamount was burned at Norwich for saying the Bible "is but foolishness, a mere fable" and that Jesus was only a human, not a god.

In 1588, Spain's Catholic king sent the Spanish Armada to force England's return to Catholicism, but failed.

These were the religious perils during Marlowe's brief life—and he himself became a victim of them.

Son of a Canterbury shoemaker, Marlowe was a gifted student who entered Cambridge University at sixteen. Soon he was writing verse, Latin translations, and plays that changed English theater. His *Tamburlaine* and *Doctor Faustus* are considered the first English tragedies. Researchers say Marlowe was amazingly learned for a man in his twenties.

Although Marlowe, like other citizens, was required to attend church, accusations of atheism rose against him. Rival playwright Robert Greene denounced "scoffing poets" and "that Atheist *Tamburlaine.*" In a deathbed tract, Greene rebuked an unnamed dramatist—clearly meaning Marlowe—for saying "There is no God."

In *Tamburlaine,* Marlowe has the conqueror burn a Koran on stage and challenge Muhammad to materialize, "if thou have any power . . . and work a miracle." In *Doctor Faustus,* the doomed protagonist concludes that "hell's a fable."

In 1593, officers raided the lodging of Marlowe's former roommate and seized papers which an interrogator called "vile hereticall conceipts denyinge the deity of Jhesus Christ our Savior." Under torture, the ex-roommate confessed that the agnostic papers were Marlowe's, and that the playwright once read "an atheist lecture" and was inclined "to jest at the divine scriptures."

An informant filed a charge with the Privy Council saying of Marlowe: ". . . Almost into every company he cometh, he persuades men to atheism, willing them not to be afeard of bugbears and hobgoblins." The charge accused Marlowe of saying that "the first beginning of religion was only to keep men in awe" and that "all Protestants are hypocritical asses." It concluded: "All men in Christianity ought to endeavor that the mouth of so dangerous a member may be stopped."

The playwright was arrested, then freed on bail and ordered to appear before the Privy Council each day until the grave accusation was resolved.

But the charge never was tried. A few days later, Marlowe was stabbed to death in a tavern quarrel. His gifted life ended at age twenty-nine.

Some among the devout wrote that Marlowe's murder was God's vengeance for his disbelief.

Marlowe's Comments on Religion

"I count religion but a childish toy, and hold there is no sin but ignorance."—*The Jew of Malta,* 1590

"Religion hides many mischiefs from suspicion."—ibid., Act 1, Scene 2

"Both law and physic are for petty wits / Divinity is basest of the three / Unpleasant, harsh, contemptible, and vile."—(Cardiff)

5

William Shakespeare (1564–1616)

Courtesy British Information Services

Of course, Shakespeare was a Christian. It was a crime to be otherwise, in a time when church attendance was enforced by law. But whether he believed the supernatural dogmas remains a topic of debate.

Although there are few records of his life, Shakespeare undoubtedly received Anglican indoctrination as a schoolboy at Stratford, eighty miles northwest of London. All pupils were required to memorize and recite long segments of scripture.

Shakespeare married, but evidently left his wife and children behind in Stratford when he went to London in the 1590s. He began writing poetry, and became involved in theater, both as actor and playwright.

His plays contain references to God, as well as to ghosts, fairies, and witches. What he personally believed seems impossible to learn. Obviously, Shakespeare did not share the beliefs of England's Puritans, who sought everywhere to stamp out play-acting and theater-going as wicked. For a time, he lived in the bawdy Bankside district of London, hotbed of prostitution and carousal; yet some researchers say Shakespeare lived more sedately than Christopher Marlowe, Ben Jonson, and other theater colleagues.

Near his death, after Shakespeare had grown wealthy and returned to his family in Stratford, he wrote a traditional Christian testimonial into his last will. Authorities disagree over whether it was sincere, or a formality. A half century after his death, an Oxford chaplain wrote that Shakespeare "died a papist"—but most scholars doubt this assertion. Perhaps, like many people, the bard wavered in matters of religion. A definite answer seems unknowable.

In Shakespeare's plays, believers tend to see evidence of faith, and skeptics signs of doubt. At the height of the Enlightenment, freethinker Joseph Ritson wrote that Shakespeare was free from "the reigning superstition of his time" and subscribed to no "temporary religion," neither "Papish or Protestant, Paganism or Christianity."

34

Atheistic philosopher George Santayana wrote an essay titled "Absence of Religion in Shakespeare," commenting on the bard's "strange insensibility to religion." Santayana said it is remarkable that "we should have to search through all the works of Shakespeare to find half a dozen passages that have so much as a religious sound, and that even these passages, upon examination, should prove not to be the expression of any deep religious conception." At another time, Santayana remarked: "For Shakespeare, in the matter of religion, the choice lay between Christianity and nothing. He chose nothing."

Playwright George Bernard Shaw observed: "Shakespeare had no conscious religion."

Although voicing doubt could bring prosecution in Elizabethan England, Shakespeare's plays contain several lines that seem to lampoon believers.

As for the meaning of life, in all his profound passages, Shakespeare never says that the purpose of human existence is to be saved by the mystical Jesus and go to heaven. Instead, in Macbeth's great lament (Act 5, Scene 5), he bitterly contends that each life proceeds to oblivion, without ultimate meaning. The soliloquy is a classic of existentialism:

> Tomorrow, and tomorrow, and tomorrow
> Creeps in this petty pace from day to day
> To the last syllable of recorded time;
> And all our yesterdays have lighted fools
> The way to dusty death. Out, out, brief candle!
> Life's but a walking shadow, a poor player
> That struts and frets his hour upon the stage
> And then is heard no more; it is a tale
> Told by an idiot, full of sound and fury
> Signifying nothing.

Shakespeare's Comments on Religion

"In religion, what damned error but some sober brow will bless it, and approve it with a text, hiding the grossness with fair ornament?"—*The Merchant of Venice*, Act 3, Scene 2

"Thrust your head into the public street, to gaze on Christian fools with varnish'd faces."—ibid, Act 2, Scene 5

"Methinks sometimes I have no more wit than a Christian. . . ."—*Twelfth Night*, Act 1, Scene 3

"It is an heretic that makes the fire, not she which burns in it."—*The Winter's Tale*, Act 2, Scene 3

"Thou villain, thou art full of piety."—*Much Ado About Nothing,* Act 4, Scene 2

"His worst fault is, he's given to prayer; he is something peevish that way."—*The Merry Wives of Windsor,* Act 1, Scene 4

"Scurvy jack-dog priest! By gar, me vill cut his ears."—ibid, Act 2, Scene 3

"I always thought it was both impious and unnatural that such immanity and bloody strife should reign among professors of one faith."—*I Henry VI,* Act 5, Scene 1

"What, cardinal, is your priesthood grown peremptory? *Tantaene animis caelestibus irae?** Churchmen so hot? Good uncle, hide such malice. With such holiness can you do it?"—*II Henry VI,* Act 2, Scene 1

"Modest doubt is call'd the beacon of the wise."—*Troilus and Cressida,* Act 2, Scene 2

"Thou art a proud traitor, priest . . . gleaning all of the land's wealth into one, into your own hands, cardinal, by extortion. . . . I'll startle you worse than the sacring bell, when the brown wench lay kissing in your arms, lord cardinal."—*King Henry VIII,* Act 3, Scene 2

"We are such stuff as dreams are made of, and our little life is rounded with a sleep."—*The Tempest,* Act 4, Scene 1

"I tell thee, churlish priest, a ministering angel shall my sister be, when thou liest howling."—*Hamlet,* Act 5, Scene 1

"I commend my soul unto the hands of God my Creator, hoping, and assuredly believing through the merits of Jesus Christ, my Savior, to be made partaker of life everlasting."—opening paragraph of Shakespeare's will

---

*"Is there such wrath in heavenly minds?"

6

Other Renaissance Figures

Ferdinand Magellan: Library of Congress Print Collection

In addition to the historic figures already profiled, here is a sampling of other nonconformity during the Renaissance.

* * *

"The greatest vicissitude of things amongst men is the vicissitude of sects and religions."—Sir Francis Bacon (1561–1626), English scientist, philsopher, and essayist, "Of Vicissitude of Things," 1597

"In every age, natural philosophy had a troublesome adversary and hard to deal with; namely, superstition, and the blind and immoderate zeal of religion." —Bacon, *Novum Organum,* 1620

"It addeth deformity to an ape to be so like a man, so the similitude of superstition to religion makes it the more deformed."—Bacon, "Of Superstition"

"Atheism leaves a man to sense, to philosophy, to natural piety, to laws, to reputation: all of which may be guides to an outward moral virtue, though religion were not; but superstition dismounts all these and erecteth an absolute monarchy in the minds of men."—Bacon, ibid.

"The general root of superstition is that men observe when things hit, and not when they miss, and commit to memory the one, and pass over the other."—Bacon (Wilcox/George)

"The trinitarian believes a virgin to be the mother of a son who is her maker." —Bacon (Noyes)

"The more contrary to reason the divine mystery, so much the more must it be believed for the glory of God."—Bacon, ibid.

"The foolish renounce this world and pursue an imaginary world to come."—Giordano Bruno (1548–1600), Italian philosopher burned at the stake by the Holy Inquisition (Noyes)

"Nothing appears to be really durable, eternal and worthy of the name of principle, save matter alone."—Bruno, ibid.

"What excellent fools religion makes of men."—Ben Jonson (1572–1637), English poet and playwright, *Sejanus,* Act 5, 1603

"Hood an ass with reverend purple, so you can hide his two ambitious ears, and he shall pass for a cathedral doctor."—Jonson, *Volpone,* Act 1, Scene 2, 1605

"Take no miracles on trust; always look for causes."—Leonardo da Vinci (1452–1519), Italian artist and inventor (Cardiff)

"It is therefore the duty of princes and heads of republics to uphold the foundations of the religion of their countries, for then it is easy to keep their people religious, and consequently well conducted and united."—Niccolo Machiavelli (1467–1527), Italian political philosopher, *Discourses on the First Ten Books of Livy,* 1517

"The church says the earth is flat, but I know that it is round, for I have seen the shadow on the moon, and I have more faith in a shadow than in the church."—Ferdinand Magellan (1480–1521), Portuguese navigator, quoted by Robert Ingersoll (Seldes)

"Go tell the Church it shows what's good, and doth no good."—Sir Walter Raleigh (1554–1618), English poet and navigator, *The Lie* (Raleigh was accused of atheism by Jesuits.)

Part Three

The European Enlightenment

7

Thomas Hobbes (1588–1679)

Library of Congress Collection

Immanuel Kant's maxim, *Sapere aude!*—Dare to know!—symbolizes the era which historians have labeled the Age of Reason or the Enlightenment, which spanned the seventeenth and eighteenth centuries.

Intellectuals of that era relished the adventure of using their minds in an unfettered search for knowledge. Subtly, the process undermined religion's contention that ultimate knowledge was revealed in the Bible and creeds, and must be accepted on faith.

Although doubt could bring brutal prosecution, enlightened thinkers of the time increasingly questioned the church. Many in the late eighteenth century scorned it outright and the number of skeptical writings multiplied immensely.

Thomas Hobbes was a pioneer among logical thinkers who gave rise to the Age of Reason. He was branded an atheist, and repeatedly fled into exile, but nonetheless gained wide renown and lived a long life.

Hobbes was the son of a fiery English vicar who got into a brawl at his church door and disappeared, abandoning his wife and three children. The son went to church schools and to Oxford, then became tutor to a young nobleman who took him traveling in Europe. New scientific advances on the Continent enchanted him.

Hobbes had been born in the year that Catholic Spain sent an armada in a doomed attempt to crush Protestantism in England. He matured in the time when Puritans were dragging England toward a ghastly civil war. Because of the prevailing hate and danger, he said he and fear were twins.

Obsessed with the need for safety and civil order, Hobbes evolved the concept of the social contract: that people, fearing each other, willingly grant power to a ruler or assembly wielding force enough to ensure peace.

When he wrote this concept in a 1640 essay, it angered both sides in England's growing unrest. Monarchists felt it denied the divine right of kings; Puritans thought it handed too much power to the monarch. Hobbes fled to Paris and lived eleven years in exile, while Puritans conquered England and beheaded the king.

In Paris, Hobbes wrote scientific treatises on matter and motion, contending that spirit has little to do with the universe. And there he also wrote his political masterpiece, *Leviathan,* reiterating the social contract. The book took a pragmatic approach to religion, saying a ruler may dictate whatever worship the people should follow. It observed that Aristotle, "fearing the fate of Socrates," compromised with religion.

Hobbes attacked the papacy, which angered French Catholics, so he returned in flight to England to take his chances under the Puritans.

In a written exchange, Hobbes debated free will with the bishop of Londonderry. Their dispute deepened, and the bishop publicly accused him of atheism.

In 1660, the monarchy was restored, and the new king Charles II, who had been a pupil of Hobbes, welcomed him to court. But his presence scandalized the clergy. "Hobbism" was denounced as dangerous freethinking. The bishop of Derry wrote that "the Hobbian principles are destructive to Christianity and to all religion."

In 1666, Parliament moved against atheism and heresy, and ordered an investigation of *Leviathan.* Hobbes, then nearly eighty, hastily burned incriminating manuscripts. He wrote a defense saying he wasn't guilty of heresy because he had not contradicted the Nicene Creed.

Parliament later dropped the atheism action, but the public censor thereafter banned publication of any Hobbes writings on human conduct.

Philosopher Corliss Lamont said Hobbes lived precariously, "some of the more intolerant bishops wishing to have him burned as a heretic."[1]

In his final years, although reviled by English enemies, the old philosopher was esteemed abroad, and foreign intellectuals visited him.

Hobbes's Comments on Religion

"Fear of power invisible, feigned by the mind or imagined from tales publicly allowed, [is] religion; not allowed, superstition."—*Leviathan*

"Fear of things invisible, is the natural seed of that which every one in himself calleth religion."—ibid.

"They that approve a private opinion, call it opinion; but they that dislike it, heresy; and yet heresy signifies no more than private opinion."—ibid.

"Theology is the kingdom of darkness."—(Noyes)

---

1. Corliss Lamont, *The Philosophy of Humanism* (New York: Continuum, 1988), p. 41.

"Opinion of ghosts, ignorance of second causes, devotion to what men fear, and taking of things casual for prognostics, consisteth the natural seeds of religion." —ibid.

"Religions are like pills, which must be swallowed whole without chewing." —ibid.

"Immortality is a belief grounded upon other men's sayings, that they knew it supernaturally; or that they knew those who knew them that knew others that knew it supernaturally."—ibid.

"They define God's nature as spirit incorporeal and then confess their definition to be unintelligible."—ibid.

"The papacy is the ghost of the departed Roman Empire, sitting crowned on its grave."—ibid.

8

Baruch Spinoza (1632–1677)

Many philosophers in the Age of Reason were denounced as apostates to Christianity. Spinoza was different—he was expelled from Judaism.

Spinoza was born in Amsterdam of Jewish families who had fled the Inquisition in Spain and Portugal. Both his grandfather and father had been compelled to convert to Christianity to save their lives, until they reached the tolerant Netherlands, where they resumed their original faith.

As a young man, Spinoza's unorthodox beliefs disturbed synagogue leaders, who offered him an annuity in hope of buying his conformity. After he refused, he was excommunicated from Judaism at age twenty-four and was briefly banished from Amsterdam. Thereafter, he supported himself as a lens grinder, and plunged into philosophical study and writing.

Spinoza contended that God is not personal, or even conscious, but is the underlying substance of nature. He also asserted that people have no life after death, and that nothing in nature is either good or evil. And the Bible is not a scientifically factual record, but consists of "imaginational" writings for moral guidance. Further, Spinoza argued that civil governments should not attempt to enforce approved theology, but should permit unfettered discussion of ideas.

Despite Holland's relative tolerance, religious persecution occurred. Spinoza was called an atheist. He was defended by intellectual Dutchmen such as statesman Jan de Witt. One of Spinoza's dissertations was denounced as a work "forged in hell by a renegade Jew and the devil, and issued with the knowledge of Mr. Jan de Witt." Soon afterward, de Witt was killed by an enraged Dutch mob during a war with France. Spinoza planned to post placards denouncing the "barbarians" who killed his friend, but his landlord forcibly stopped him, probably saving his life.

Never married, Spinoza died at age forty-four of tuberculosis, aggravated by inhaling glass dust from his lens-grinding work.

His writings are a maze of abstruse philosophical logic. Professor Corliss Lamont has remarked:

> The truth is that Spinoza did not believe in either God or immortality as usually defined; but subject as he was to persecution by both church and state on account of his unorthodox ideas, it may be that he stayed out of jail and preserved his life through his highly intellectualized redefinitions of God and immortality.[1]

Spinoza's Comments on Religion

"Philosophy has no end in view save truth; faith looks for nothing but obedience and piety."—*Tractatus Theologico-Politicus,* 1670, chap. 14

"How blest would our age be if it could witness a religion freed from all the trammels of superstition!"—ibid., chap. 11

". . . The theologians were everywhere lying in wait for me."—letter to a friend, explaining his delay in publishing a new treatise, quoted by Corliss Lamont in *The Philosophy of Humanism,* p. 35

"A miracle signifies nothing more than an event . . . the cause of which cannot be explained by another familiar instance, or . . . which the narrator is unable to explain."—*Ethica ordine geometrica demonstrata*

"[Believers] are but triflers who, when they cannot explain a thing, run back to the will of God; this is, truly, a ridiculous way of expressing ignorance."—(Gray)

"Those who wish to seek out the cause of miracles, and to understand the things of nature as philosophers, and not to stare at them in astonishment like fools, are soon considered heretical and impious, and proclaimed as such by those whom the mob adores as the interpreters of nature and the gods. For these men know that, once ignorance is put aside, that wonderment would be taken away, which is the only means by which their authority is preserved."—*Ethics,* 1677, appendix

"Popular religion may be summed up as a respect for ecclesiastics."—quoted by Eugene Brussell in *The Dictionary of Quotable Definitions* (Englewood Cliffs, N.J.: Prentice-Hall, 1970), p. 490

"I do not know how to teach philosophy without becoming a disturber of established religion."—in 1670, upon being offered a Heidelberg professorship

"Final causes are nothing but human figments."—(Noyes)

---

1. Corliss Lamont, *The Philosophy of Humanism* (New York: Continuum, 1988), p. 35.

9

John Locke
(1632–1704)

Today, the divine right of kings seems a laughable notion; but nobody laughed in the seventeenth century, when challenging the concept could lead to the gibbet. The disappearance of this and other lethal doctrines was partly wrought by thinkers of the Age of Reason, such as English philosopher-scientist-moralist John Locke.

Locke came of age amid holy horror. While he was young, fanatical English Puritans under Oliver Cromwell waged civil war against the Anglican establishment of King Charles I. Cromwell won, and beheaded Charles. The Puritans banned entertainments, closed theaters, and even decreed death for sex outside marriage.

After Cromwell died, an Anglican backlash brought the restoration of the monarchy. Cromwell's body was unearthed, and his head was mounted on a pole. Anglicans banned non-Anglican worship, and eventually decreed death for attending a nonconformist service.

Surrounded by absolutism, Locke cautiously advocated tolerance. His liberalism was shared by the Earl of Shaftesbury, and the two became outspoken colleagues. Shaftesbury, who opposed the possible ascension of Catholic James II to the throne, was forced to flee to Holland, where he died. Locke likewise fled, and was accused of treason in absentia.

When James was crowned in 1685, Locke reportedly joined English Protestants in urging Holland's Protestant William of Orange to invade England and drive James from power. This "Glorious Revolution" of 1688 succeeded, and it was safe for Locke to return home.

At last free to write, he published the treatises that left his mark on the world. Regarding epistemology, the study of how knowledge is obtained, he denied the premise that God implants morality and piety in people's minds. Locke contended that all ideas arise from observation and logic, not from divine insertion.

Locke urged religious toleration and minimized the need for fixed dogmas.

This caused him to be denounced as a Socinian, after Faustus Socinus, a medieval Italian who rejected the Trinity.

In science, he embraced the "corpuscular" theory that matter is composed of atoms.

Most importantly, Locke advocated democracy, contending that government should rest on the consent of the governed, not on the divine authority of kings. Particularly, he recommended separation of church and state, as well as the separation of powers within government. Locke's ideas later were adopted in America's great experiment in popular rule.

Locke cannot be called a disbeliever, for he declared himself a Christian. Yet his championing of logic and tolerance helped make it possible for many in the Age of Reason to question supernaturalism.

Locke's Comments on Religion

"Religion, which should most distinguish us from beasts, and ought most peculiarly to elevate us, as rational creatures, above brutes, is that wherein men often appear most irrational, and more senseless than beasts themselves."—*An Essay Concerning Human Understanding,* 1690

"Faith, on the other side, is the assent to any proposition not thus made out by the deductions of reason, but upon the credit of the proposer, as coming from God, in some extraordinary way of communication."—ibid.

"Nothing that is contrary to, and inconsistent with, the clear and self-evident dictates of reason, has a right to be urged or assented to as a matter of faith, wherein reason hath nothing to do."—ibid.

"Every sect, as far as reason will help them, make use of it gladly; and where it fails them, they cry out, 'It is a matter of faith, and above reason.' "—ibid.

". . . The literati, or learned, keeping to the old religion of China, and the ruling party there, are all of them atheists."—ibid.

"However, that some may not color their spirit of persecution and un-Christian cruelty with a pretense of care of the public weal . . . I esteem it above all things necessary to distinguish exactly the business of civil government from that of religion, and to settle the just bounds that lie between the one and the other."—*A Letter Concerning Toleration,* 1689

"Possibly if a true estimate were made of the morality and religions of the world, we should find that the far greater part of mankind received even those opinions and ceremonies they would die for, rather from the fashions of their countries and the constant practice of those about them than from any conviction of their reasons."—*On Education*

"How many men have no other ground for their tenets than the supposed honesty, or learning, or number of those of the same profession."—(Noyes)

"People who are born to orthodoxy imbibe the opinions of their country or party and never question their truth."—ibid.

"How any man who should inquire and know for himself can content himself with a faith or belief taken upon trust, is to be astonishing."—ibid.

10

Baron de Montesquieu (1689–1755)

Charles-Louis de Secondat, baron de Montesquieu, was another wealthy French noble who devoted many years to reformist writing, some of it incurring the wrath of the church.

Educated in prestigious Catholic schools, Montesquieu inherited great estates while young, married a wealthy Protestant, and largely left her to manage the farms and children while he pursued science, philosophy, and the social gaiety in Paris and elsewhere.

At age thirty-two, he anonymously published the *Persian Letters,* a spoof of Parisian life as seen by two fictional Persian visitors. The popular book mocked the recent reign of Louis XIV, satirized Roman Catholic doctrine, and brimmed with iconoclastic wit. The author's identity became known. Montesquieu grew famous among the liberated elite—and infamous to the clergy.

Later, when he sought admission to the French Academy, he was opposed by a cardinal, but Montesquieu managed to appease him.

Montesquieu traveled through Europe and England, scoffing at religious miracles and becoming an advocate of human rights. Late in life, he produced his masterpiece, *The Spirit of Laws,* a 1,086-page treatise supporting the radical concept of a democratic republic, with power separated into executive, legislative, and judicial branches of government. This concept later became reality in America's new democracy. The book also treated religion as a social phenomenon, to be examined clinically.

Montesquieu was hailed by the irreverent "philosophes" of the Enlightenment and was denounced by the French Catholic clergy. The pope put *The Spirit of Laws* on the Index of banned books.

Montesquieu's Comments on Religion

"No kingdom has ever suffered as many civil wars as the kingdom of Christ."
—*Persian Letters,* 1721

"If triangles made a god, they would give him three sides."—ibid.

"History is full of religious wars; but, we must take care to observe, it was not the multiplicity of religions that produced these wars, it was the intolerating spirit which animated that one which thought she had the power of governing."—ibid.

"Churchmen are interested in keeping the people ignorant. I call piety a malady of the heart. The false notion of miracles comes of our vanity, which makes us believe we are important enough for the Supreme Being to upset nature on our behalf."—(Cardiff)

"All pagans do not merit eternal damnation."—(Noyes)

"The religion of Confucius denies the immortality of the soul, and the sect of Zeno did not believe in it."—ibid.

11

Voltaire
(1694–1778)

François Marie Arouet—"that consuming fire called Voltaire," as Will Durant described him—helped bring human rights and democratic freedoms to the world.

His name is synonymous with the Enlightenment and the Age of Reason, the tumultuous era when Western people gained the right to think independently, to follow the revelations of science, and to question religious dogmas, without being executed or jailed for it.

After attaining fame and wealth as a witty writer, Voltaire became a fierce crusader against cruelties of the church and the aristocracy. He roused international outcries in behalf of victims killed or jailed for their religious beliefs. In a sense, Voltaire was the modern world's first civil rights activist. His demands for freedom of speech and of worship spread across the Atlantic and helped formulate America's budding democracy.

Born in Paris, son of a lawyer, Voltaire was sent to Jesuit schools with children of the aristocracy. His sparkling wit and clever writing made him popular among the fashionable set. But when he wrote a poem mocking a dissolute regent, he was thrown into the Bastille for a year.

While in prison, he adopted the pen name Voltaire and finished his first play, which became a success after his release. He poured forth writings, including an epic poem honoring King Henry IV, who decreed religious tolerance and temporarily ended France's Wars of Religion, until he was assassinated by a fanatic. The poem was banned because it was seen as an attack on Christianity.

In 1726, Voltaire insulted an aristocrat, who had him beaten and thrown into the Bastille again. To gain release, the writer agreed to go to England. While there, he was impressed by England's growing personal freedoms. It is sometimes said that Voltaire went into exile a poet and came back a philosopher.

He returned to Paris, only to encounter trouble a third time. His writings in praise of England's freedoms were taken as condemnation of France's lack thereof.

Authorities issued a warrant for his arrest, and he fled to Cirey, where he became the lover of a sophisticated noblewoman.

Voltaire's plays, poems, novels, essays—and especially his *Philosophical Dictionary*—jabbed church dogmas and aristocratic tyranny. His works were condemned and occasionally he was forced to flee. After the death of his mistress, Voltaire went to Berlin as a guest of Frederick the Great, and eventually settled on a large estate on the Swiss border—from where he could escape into France if pursued by Swiss Calvinists, or into Switzerland if menaced by French Catholics.

As he aged, Voltaire grew increasingly hostile to Christianity, and sought justice for victims of religious bigotry. Here is a famous case:

A teenage youth, Chevalier de La Barre, was convicted of marring a crucifix, singing irreverent songs, and wearing his hat while a religious procession passed. He was sentenced to have his tongue torn out and be burned to death. Horrified, Voltaire helped appeal the sentence to Parliament. The clergy clamored for a painful death, but Parliament showed "mercy" by giving the youth a swift execution by beheading. His body was burned, along with a copy of Voltaire's *Philosophical Dictionary*.

Voltaire was infuriated and sickened by this outrage and others. From his mountain estate, he bombarded Europe with letters and essays denouncing the injustices. He roused public ferment and won reversals in a few cases. Voltaire freed Jean Espinas, who had spent twenty-three years on a penal galley ship because he gave lodging to a Protestant minister for one night. He likewise freed Claude Chaumont from a galley bench, where he had been sentenced for attending a Protestant worship service.

From his crusades and literary works, Voltaire's fame spread worldwide. Renowned thinkers, scientists, and other luminaries visited his estate. He remained a provocateur until his death in 1778.

Thomas Paine wrote of Voltaire in *The Rights of Man*: "His forte lay in exposing and ridiculing the superstitions which priestcraft, united with statecraft, had interwoven with governments."

English writer Thomas Carlyle said of Voltaire: "He gave the death-stab to modern superstition. That horrid incubus, which dwelt in darkness, shunning the light, is passing away. . . . It was a most weighty service."

Many years later, in a New York speech, Robert Ingersoll summed it up: "Voltaire did more for human liberty than any other man who ever lived or died."

Voltaire's Views on Religion

"Christianity is the most ridiculous, the most absurd and bloody religion that has ever infected the world."—letter to Frederick the Great

"Doubt is not a pleasant condition, but certainty is a ridiculous one."—letter to Frederick, April 6, 1767

"For 1,700 years, the Christian sect has done nothing but harm."—ibid.

"Metaphysics consists of two parts: first, that which all men of sense already know, and second, that which they can never know."—letter to Frederick, April 17, 1737

"I wish that you would crush this infamy [the church]" (*Je voudrais que vous écrasassiez l'infâme*).—letter to Jean d'Alembert, June 23, 1760

"*Écrasez l'infâme!*" [crush the infamous thing—Christianity]—slogan with which Voltaire ended many letters and pamphlets

"You seem solicitous about that pretty thing called soul. I do protest I know nothing of it, nor whether it is, nor what it is, nor what it shall be. Young scholars and priests know all of that perfectly. For my part, I am but a very ignorant fellow."
—letter to James Boswell, February 11, 1765

"The truths of religion are never so well understood as by those who have lost the power of reasoning."—*Philosophical Dictionary*, 1764

"Among theologians, heretics are those who are not backed with a sufficient array of battalions to render them orthodox."—ibid.

"Atheism is the vice of a few intelligent people."—ibid.

"Most of the great men of this world live as if they were atheists."—ibid., quoted in the London edition, 1824

"Which is more dangerous, fanaticism or atheism? Fanaticism is certainly a thousand times more deadly; for atheism inspires no bloody passion, whereas fanaticism does. . . . Fanaticism causes crimes to be committed.—ibid.

"Christians have been the most intolerant of all men."—ibid.

"Nothing can be more contrary to religion and the clergy than reason and common sense."—ibid.

"Sect and error are synonymous."—ibid.

"With regard to the Christians, assuredly their greatest and most venerable saints were those whose brains had sustained the severest shock."—ibid.

"Whenever an important event, a revolution, or a calamity turns to the profit of the church, such is always signalized as the Finger of God."—ibid.

"Clergyman: A generic title under which is designated any Christian who consecrates himself to the service of God, and feels himself called upon to live without working at the expense of the rascals who work to live."—ibid.

"Superstition, born of paganism, and adopted by Judaism, invested the Christian Church from earliest times. All the fathers of the Church, without exception, believed in the power of magic."—ibid., under "Superstition"

"We offer up prayers to God only because we have made him after our own image. We treat him like a pasha, or a sultan, who is capable of being exasperated and appeased."—ibid., under "Prayer"

"Theological religion is the source of all imaginable follies and disturbances; it is the parent of fanaticism and civil discord; it is the enemy of mankind."—ibid., under "Religion"

"Every sensible man, every honest man, must hold the Christian sect in horror. But what shall we substitute in its place? you say. What? A ferocious animal has sucked the blood of my relatives. I tell you to rid yourselves of this beast, and you ask me what you shall put in its place?"—(Cardiff)

"The first divine was the first rogue who met the first fool."—ibid.

"Christianity must be divine since it has lasted 1,700 years despite the fact that it is so full of villainy and nonsense."—ibid.

"Theology: A science profound, supernatural and divine, which teaches us to reason on that which we don't understand and to get our ideas mixed up on that which we do."—ibid.

"Wars of religion: Copious and salutary blood-lettings prescribed by the physician of souls for the bodies of those nations whom God in his goodness desires to endow with a pure doctrine. They have been of frequent practice since the foundation of the Christian faith."—ibid.

". . . God is always on the side of the heaviest battalions."—letter to M. le Riche, February 6, 1770

"I have never made but one prayer to God, a very short one: 'O Lord, make my enemies ridiculous.' And God granted it."—letter to M. Damiliville, May 16, 1767

"When one man speaks to another man who doesn't understand him, and when the man who's speaking no longer understands, it's metaphysics."—*Candide,* 1759

"The man who says to me, 'Believe as I do, or God will damn you,' will presently say, 'Believe as I do, or I shall assassinate you.' "—(Seldes)

"If God created us in his own image, we have more than reciprocated."—*Le Sottisier*

"This agglomeration which was called and which still calls itself the Holy Roman Empire is neither holy, nor Roman, nor an empire."—*Essay on Morals and the Spirit of Nations*

"Would you believe that while the flames were consuming these innocent victims, the inquisitors and the other savages were chanting our prayers? These pitiless monsters were invoking the God of mercy . . . while committing the most atrocious crime."—*Sermon du Rabbin Akib,* 1765

"I know a man who is firmly persuaded that, at the death of a bee, its buzzing ceases."—(Noyes)

"Superstition sets the whole world in flames; philosophy extinguishes it."—ibid.

"Catechism: a collection of pious . . . instructions that priests take care to inculcate into little Christians to the end that they talk nonsense and rave for the rest of their lives."—ibid.

"Evil came into the world through the sin of Adam. If that idiot had not sinned, we should not have been afflicted with the smallpox, nor the itch, nor theology, nor the faith which alone can save us."—ibid.

"The word of God is the word of the priests; the glory of God is the pride of the priests; the will of God is the will of the priests; to offend God is to offend the priests; to believe in God is to believe all that the priests tell us."—ibid.

"On religion, many are destined to reason wrongly; others not to reason at all; and others to persecute those who do reason."—ibid.

12

David Hume
(1711–1776)

The Scottish philosopher David Hume loomed large in the Age of Reason. He applied the scientific method to explain how the mind acquires knowledge. He said morality derives from human experience, not from divine will.

It was an era when skepticism was still hazardous, as Hume discovered occasionally. But he was a thorough skeptic, from youth to death.

His father died when Hume was a baby, and he was raised by his mother. A. J. Ayer recounts: "She was an ardent Calvinist, and brought her children up in the faith, which David rejected, together with all other forms of Christianity, in his teens."[1]

At age eleven, Hume entered the University of Edinburgh. He studied three years, but obtained no degree. After returning home, he became so consumed with reading philosophy that his health faltered.

When a servant girl filed charges accusing Hume of fathering her baby, he went to Bristol and worked briefly in a merchant office. Then he went to France to study and write. He never married.

Returning to Scotland in 1737, Hume published *A Treatise of Human Nature,* containing hints of religious skepticism. But the book went unnoticed. "It fell dead-born from the press, without reaching such distinction as even to excite a murmur among the zealots," he later wrote.

When Hume applied to teach philosophy at Edinburgh, a protest was raised, the allegation being that his *Treatise* was atheistic. His application was duly rejected.

Hume wandered, worked as a tutor, and wrote. He applied to teach logic at Glasgow University—but again, accusations of disbelief ruined his chances.

Hume took the setbacks with humor. In a letter to a friend, he sardonically re-

---

1. A. J. Ayer, *Hume* (New York: Hill & Wang Past Masters Series, 1980), p. 1.

ferred to himself as "a sober, discreet, virtuous, frugal, regular, quiet, good-natured man, of a bad character."

Finally, he was appointed librarian at Edinburgh, a post which gave him freedom to research and write.

Hume's books gradually drew attention, and then he published a *History of England* that brought him fame. But the clergy considered him a dangerous doubter. The Vatican placed all his writings on the Index of forbidden works.

Hume wrote with sarcasm. In *An Enquiry Concerning Human Understanding,* he cited the ancient enigma of how an all-good, all-powerful God could create wicked people. "To defend absolute decrees, and yet free the Deity from being the author of sin, has been found hitherto to exceed all the power of philosophy," he said.

In another work, *On the Immortality of the Soul,* Hume's pen dripped irony: "Nothing could set in a fuller light the infinite obligations which mankind have to Divine revelation; since we find that no other medium could ascertain this great and important truth."

In *The Natural History of Religion,* Hume called the Old Testament God of the Calvinists "a most cruel, unjust, partial and fantastical being."

Personally, Hume was so warm and gracious that some Scots called him "Saint David." He had devoted friends, including economist Adam Smith and biographer James Boswell. The latter was flustered by Hume's cheerful refusal to accept Christianity.

When Hume finally lay dying, he was visited by Boswell, who hoped for a deathbed conversion. But none occurred. Hume was irreverent to the end. Boswell recorded the visit in his diary:

> He then said flatly that the morality of every religion was bad, and, I really thought, was not jocular when he said that when he heard a man was religious, he concluded that he was a rascal. . . . Speaking of his singular notion that men of religion were generally bad men, he said: "One of the men of the greatest honor that I ever knew is my Lord Marischal, who is a downright atheist. I remember I once hinted something as if I believed in the being of a God, and he would not speak to me for a week."

Hume's Comments on Religion

"Examine the religious principles which have, in fact, prevailed in the world, and you will scarcely be persuaded that they are anything but sick men's dreams."
—*The Natural History of Religion*

". . . The Roman Catholics are a very learned sect. . . . Of all religions, the most absurd and nonsensical is that whose votaries eat, after having created, their deity."—ibid., commenting on the doctrine of Transubstantiation, which teaches that the bread and wine miraculously turn into the "real presence" of Christ's body and blood during the mass.

". . . There is no tenet in all paganism which would give so fair a scope to ridicule as that of the 'real presence'; for it is so absurd, that it eludes the force of all argument."—ibid.

"The grosser pagans contented themselves with divinizing lust, incest, and adultery; but the predestinarian doctors have divinized cruelty, wrath, fury, vengeance, and all the blackest vices."—ibid.

". . . The Christian religion not only was at first attended with miracles, but even at this day cannot be believed by any reasonable person without one."—*An Enquiry Concerning Human Understanding,* 1748

"It forms a strong presumption against all supernatural and miraculous relations, that they are observed chiefly to abound among ignorant and barbarous nations; or if a civilized people has ever given admission to any of them, that people will be found to have received them from ignorant and barbarous ancestors."—ibid.

"There is not to be found, in all history, any miracle attested by a sufficient number of men, of such unquestioned good sense, education, and learning, as to secure us against all delusion in themselves; of such undoubted integrity, as to place them beyond all suspicion of any design to deceive others; of such credit and reputation in the eyes of mankind, as to have a great deal to lose in case of their being detected in any falsehood; and at the same time attesting facts, performed in such a public manner, and in so celebrated a part of the world, as to render the detection unavoidable."—ibid.

"The many instances of forged miracles and prophecies and supernatural events, which, in all ages, have been detected by contrary evidence, or which detect themselves by their absurdity, prove sufficiently the strong propensity of mankind to the extraordinary and marvelous, and ought reasonably to beget a suspicion against all relations of this kind."—ibid.

"Upon the whole, then, it appears that no testimony for any kind of miracle has ever amounted to a probability, much less to a proof."—(Cardiff)

"The Deity . . . is not the natural object of any passion or affection."—letter to William Mure, June 30, 1743

"What danger can ever come from ingenious reasoning and inquiry? The worst speculative skeptic ever I knew was a much better man than the best superstitious devotee and bigot."—letter to Gilbert Elliot, March 10, 1751

"By priests I understand only the pretenders to power and dominion, and to a superior sanctity of character, distinct from virtue and good morals."—*Essays Moral, Political and Literary*

"If we take in hand any volume of divinity, or school of metaphysics, let us ask, does it contain any abstract reasoning concerning quantity or matter? No. Does it contain any experimental reasoning concerning matter of fact, or existence? No. Commit it, then, to the flames, for it can contain nothing but sophistry and illusion."—(Noyes)

"If a religious spirit be ever mentioned in any historical narration, we are sure to meet afterwards with a denial of the miseries which attend it."—ibid.

"Why, then, eternal punishment for the temporary offenses of so frail a creature as man?"—ibid.

"Barbarity, caprice; these qualities, however nominally disguised, we may universally observe from the ruling character of the deity in all regular religions."—ibid.

"Miracles are really cases of human ignorance, rather than of divine interference."—ibid.

"If there be a soul, it is as mortal as the body."—ibid.

"Many of the votaries will seek the divine favor, not by virtue and good morals, but by frivolous observances, or by the belief of mysterious and absurd opinions."—ibid.

13

Denis Diderot
(1713–1784)

Religious doubters were still executed in eighteenth-century France. The skeptical-minded Diderot—father of the first major encyclopedia—was lucky to escape with mere imprisonment and the burning of his works.

Son of a provincial knife-maker, Diderot originally was destined to be a priest. At age thirteen, his head was shaved and he was titled "abbé." At fifteen, he entered the University of Paris. But the reading of science and philosophy turned him away from religion, and he became a bohemian writer and teacher.

As Diderot matured, he "progressed relatively slowly from faith to deism and to atheism," Exeter University scholar Robert Niklaus writes.[1]

In 1746, Diderot anonymously published *Pensées philosophiques,* expressing anti-Christian views. The book was condemned to be burned by the public executioner. Three years later, he wrote *An Essay on Blindness,* in which he raised questions about the existence of God. For this, Diderot was jailed three months in the prison at Vincennes. Thereafter, he allowed his skeptical writings to be distributed only privately among colleagues.

Meanwhile, Diderot had been hired to oversee the writing of an encyclopedia. He recruited a team of fellow reformers who tinged the project with rebukes against totalitarianism in church and state. As the volumes were published, trouble arose. Parliament ordered the work suppressed. Diderot later discovered, to his dismay, that the publisher secretly had excised many provocative portions.

Diderot also wrote plays and novels, and became the world's first major art critic. In his scientific writing, he theorized, a century before Darwin, that animal species had evolved from common ancestors. ·

Although married, Diderot had mistresses and was somewhat an apostle of free love. In one passage, he wrote:

---

1. Robert Niklaus, "Diderot," in *Encyclopaedia Britannica* (1974 ed.).

I have eyes and a heart and I like to look at a pretty woman, like to feel the curve of her breast under my hand, press her lips to mine, drink bliss from her eyes and die of ecstasy in her arms. Sometimes a gay party with my friends, even if it becomes a little rowdy, is not displeasing to me. But I must confess that I find it infinitely sweeter to . . . tell her whom I love something tender and true which brings her arms about my neck.[2]

At age seventy-one, as he lay dying, Diderot's last words were: "The first step toward philosophy is incredulity."

Diderot's Comments on Religion

"Men will never be free until the last king is strangled in the entrails of the last priest."—*Oeuvres complètes,* vol. 9, pp. 15–16, quoted by Corliss Lamont in *The Philosophy of Humanism*

"The Christian religion teaches us to imitate a God that is cruel, insidious, jealous, and implacable in his wrath."—(Gray)

"Fanaticism is just one step away from barbarism."—*Essay on Merit and Virtue,* 1746

"Skepticism is the first step toward truth."—*Pensées philosophiques*

"Considering the picture that is drawn for us of the Supreme Being, the most righteous soul must be tempted to wish that he did not exist."—(Cardiff)

"The man who first pronounced the barbarous word God ought to have been immediately destroyed."—(Noyes)

"The Christian religion: the most absurd in its dogmas, the most unintelligible, the most insipid, the most gloomy, the most Gothic, the most puerile."—ibid.

"I have not the hope of being immortal, because the desire of it has not given me that vanity."—ibid.

---

2. Roger E. Greeley, ed., *The Best of Humanism* (Amherst, N.Y.: Prometheus Books, 1988), pp. 156–57.

14

Edward Gibbon
(1737–1794)

English historian Edward Gibbon, renowned author of *The Decline and Fall of the Roman Empire,* wrestled with religion much of his life.

Born to affluence, son of a member of Parliament, Gibbon was a sickly youth who read voraciously, and was fascinated by history. At age sixteen, while at Oxford, he read theology and decided to convert to Catholicism. A London priest performed the conversion ritual.

Gibbon's Anglican father was horrified. In the 1750s, old laws remained on England's books making it "high treason" to return to the Roman church. Although the laws were rarely enforced, converts nonetheless could be deprived of property and inheritance. Conversion also meant expulsion from Oxford.

The father swiftly sent his errant son to Switzerland to live with a Calvinist pastor, to be "deprogrammed." It worked: a year later, young Gibbon renounced Catholicism. In his *Memoirs,* Gibbon recounted that he came to reject transubstantiation—the doctrine that the wafer and wine miraculously become the body and blood of Jesus during the mass—and "the various articles of the Romish creed disappeared like a dream." He added that Catholic monasteries and worship came to seem "the lively naked image of superstition."

Remaining in Switzerland, Gibbon plunged into study, relished the company of intellectuals, and attended parties hosted by Voltaire. The young man fell in love with a bright girl and proposed marriage; but upon his return to England, Gibbon's father forbade the marriage, and Gibbon remained forever a bachelor.

Gibbon became a military officer and member of Parliament, but his chief focus was history. As he began to write, he left behind whatever remained of his former supernatural beliefs.

In 1772, the first volume of *Decline and Fall* was published, with immediate success. Three printings were sold out in rapid succession. But the book caused an outcry among the clergy, because two chapters spoke contemptuously of Christianity as a debilitating factor that hastened Rome's decay.

"I have described the triumph of barbarism and religion," the author wrote. He said ancient wisdom from the schools of Athens was toppled by "the establishment of a new religion, whose ministers superseded the exercise of reason, resolved every question by an article of faith, and condemned the infidel or skeptic to eternal flames."

Despite his scorn, Gibbon did not deny any Christian creeds, which could have landed him in jail. Biographer Michael Joyce says Gibbon may have "adopted the ironic method in self-protection, and indeed he can scarcely have been ignorant of the case of Thomas Woolston, a fellow of Sidney Sussex, who had been deprived of his fellowship for his unorthodox writings, and had died in prison in 1733 after being prosecuted for his *Discourses on the Miracles of Our Saviour.*"[1]

An archdeacon accused Gibbon of writing sacrilege through "indirect machinations." Joyce notes: "It was open to Gibbon to reply that, if he had adopted the direct method and stated his case without ambiguity, he would have been liable to prosecution under the Blasphemy Act, and that it ill became a representative of the Church of England to reproach a fellow subject for keeping within the law."[2]

Gibbon wrote in his autobiography that the religious uproar surprised him. He said he had not foreseen that educated English people were "so fondly attached to the name and shadow of Christianity" that his book would offend "the pious, the timid, and the prudent."

The historian later left Parliament and moved to Switzerland, where he spent the rest of his life finishing his writings. He made a mark on scholarship by treating religion as a human movement, not a divine force.

John Henry Newman, the English scholar who became a Catholic and a cardinal, wrote: "It is melancholy to say it, but the chief, perhaps the only English writer who has any claim to be considered an ecclesiastical historian, is the unbeliever Gibbon."

Gibbon's Views on Religion

"The various modes of worship which prevailed in the Roman world were all considered by the people as equally true; by the philosopher as equally false; and by the magistrate as equally useful."—*The Decline and Fall of the Roman Empire*

"To a philosophic eye, the vices of the clergy are far less dangerous than their virtues."—ibid.

---

1. Michael Joyce, *Edward Gibbon* (New York: Longmans, Green & Co., 1953), p. 146.
2. Ibid., p. 148.

"A cruel unfeeling temper has distinguished the monks of every age and country; their stern indifference, which is seldom mollified by personal friendship, is inflamed by religious hatred; and their merciless zeal has strenuously administered the holy office of the Inquisition."—ibid.

"A state of skepticism and suspense may amuse a few inquisitive minds. But the practice of superstition is so congenial to the multitude that, if they are forcibly awakened, they still regret the loss of their pleasing vision. . . . So urgent on the vulgar is the necessity of believing, that the fall of any system of mythology will probably be succeeded by the introduction of some other mode of superstition."—ibid.

"The most serious charges were suppressed; the Vicar of Christ was accused only of piracy, murder, rape, sodomy, and incest."—ibid., describing the removal of Pope John XXIII in 1414

"Such is the connection between the throne and the altar, that the banner of the church has very seldom been seen on the side of the people."—ibid.

"Day and night they were incessantly busied either in singing hymns to the honor of their God, or in pillaging and murdering the servants of their prince. . . . Christians, in the course of their intestine dissensions, have inflicted far greater severities on each other, than they had experienced from the zeal of infidels."—ibid.

"Hitherto the weight of supernatural belief inclines against the Protestants; and many a sober Christian would rather admit that a wafer is God, than that God is a cruel and capricious tyrant."—ibid.

"Every friend to revelation is persuaded of the reality, and every reasonable man is convinced of the cessation, of miraculous powers."—ibid.

"The frequent repetition of miracles serves to provoke, where it does not subdue, the reason of mankind."—ibid.

"Every event, or appearance, or accident, which seems to deviate from the ordinary course of nature has been rashly ascribed to the immediate action of the Deity."—ibid.

"Is it incumbent on us to adore the mysterious dispensations of Providence, when we discover that the doctrine of the immortality of the soul is omitted in the law of Moses?"—(Cardiff)

"Religion is a mere question of geography."—ibid.

"The Christians, who, by the interposition of evil spirits, could so readily explain every preternatural appearance, were disposed and even desirous to admit the most extravagant fictions. . . ."—ibid.

"The evidence of the heavenly witnesses—the Father, the Word, and the Holy Ghost—would now be rejected in any court of justice."—(Noyes)

15

Other Figures in the Age of Enlightenment

Immanuel Kant: Library of Congress Collection

In addition to historic figures previously described, here is a survey of other non-conformist views in this age.

*   *   *

". . . Emancipate thy mind from the fears of superstition, and the wicked arts of priestcraft."—John Baskerville, English publisher, an epitaph he wrote for himself, 1775

"In matters of religion, it is very easy to deceive a man, and very hard to undeceive him."—Pierre Bayle (1647–1706), French philosopher and critic, *Dictionnaire historique,* 1697

"No nations are more warlike than those which profess Christianity."—Bayle, *Thoughts on the Comet,* 1682

"It is pure illusion to think that an opinion which passes down from century to century, from generation to generation, may not be entirely false."—Bayle, ibid.

". . . [T]he gods, by teaching us religion first, first set the world at odds."—Aphra Behn (1640–1689), English novelist, the first woman to support herself by writing, *The Golden Age,* stanza 4

"Prisons are built with stones of law, brothels with bricks of religion."—William Blake (1757–1827), English poet and artist, *Proverbs of Hell,* 1790

"Can such bitterness enter into the heart of the devout?"—Nicholas Boileau (1636–1711), French critic and poet, *Le Lutrin*

"The religion of one seems madness unto another."—Sir Thomas Browne (1605–1682), English physician and author, *Hydriotaphia,* chap. 2

"As for those wingy mysteries in divinity, and airy subtleties in religion, which have unhinged the brains of better heads, they never stretched the *pia mater* of mine."—Browne, *Religio Medici,* 1642

". . . All this superstitious folly, ecclesiastical nonsense and holy tyranny hold a reverend place in the estimation even of those who are otherwise enlightened." —Edmund Burke (1729–1787), English statesman, *A Vindication of Natural Society,* 1756

"The miseries derived to mankind from superstition under the name of religion, and of ecclesiastical tyranny under the name of church government, have been clearly and usefully exposed. We begin to think and to act from reason and from nature alone."—Burke, ibid.

"It is hard to say whether the doctors of law or divinity have made the greater advances in the lucrative business of mystery."—Burke, ibid.

"Religious persecution may shield itself under the guise of a mistaken and overzealous piety."—Burke, address, February 17, 1788

"One religion is as true as another."—Robert Burton (1577–1640), English clergyman and author, *The Anatomy of Melancholy,* 1621

"So 'ere the storm of war broke out, religion spawn'd a various rout / Of petulant capricious sects, the maggots of corrupted texts."—Samuel Butler (1612–1680), English satirical poet, *Hudibras*

". . . And prove their Doctrine Orthodox, by Apostolick Blows and Knocks / Call Fire and Sword and Desolation a godly-thorough-Reformation."—Butler, ibid.

"What makes all doctrines plain and clear? / About two hundred pounds a year. / And that which was prov'd true before / Prove false again? Two hundred more." —Butler, ibid., on high-paid clergy

"A credulous mind . . . finds most delight in believing strange things, and the stranger they are, the easier they pass with him."—Butler, *Characters*

"Until Christianity is dead and buried we shall never get the burning questions that lie beyond approached in a spirit of sobriety and common sense."—Butler (Cardiff)

"Religion is in the interest of churches / That sell in other worlds in this to purchase."—Butler, ibid.

"Christ was only crucified once, and for a few hours. Think of the thousands he has been crucifying in a quiet way ever since."—Butler (Gray)

"Faith is a necessary fraud at best."—Charles Churchill (1731–1764), English poet and satirist, *Gotham,* 1763

"Persecution, religious pride, the love of contradiction, are the food of what the world commonly calls religion."—Michel de Crèvecoeur, (1735–1813), French-born American essayist, *Letters from an American Farmer,* 1782

"In regard to religious matters, there is an intellectual cowardice instilled into the minds of the people from their infancy; to inquire or exert their reason is denounced as sinful."—Erasmus Darwin (1731–1802), English physician and poet, and grandfather of Charles Darwin (Noyes)

"Whores and priests will never want excuse."—Daniel Defoe (1660–1731), English journalist and novelist, *The True-Born Englishman,* 1701

"Of all the plagues with which mankind are cursed / Ecclesiastic tyranny's the worst."—Defoe, ibid.

"In pious times, ere Priest-craft did begin / Before Polygamy was made a Sin." —John Dryden (1631–1700), English poet and playwright, *Absalom and Achitophel* (1681)

"The smiles of courtiers and the harlot's tears, the tradesman's oaths, and mourning of an heir, are truths to what priests tell."—John Dryden and Nathaniel Lee (1653?–1692), *Oedipus,* 1679

"No man has ever sat down calmly unbiased to reason out his religion, and not ended by rejecting it."—Henry Fielding (1707–1754), English novelist (Cardiff)

"Theologians are all alike, of whatever religion or country they may be. Their aim is always to wield despotic authority over men's consciences. They therefore persecute all of us who have the temerity to unveil the truth."—Frederick the Great (1712–1786), King of Prussia, letter to Voltaire, November 4, 1736

"Religion is the idol of the mob; it adores everything it does not understand. . . . We know the crimes that fanaticism in religion has caused. . . ."—Frederick the Great, letter to Voltaire, July 6, 1737

"If the philosophers were to form a government, the people, after 150 years, would forge some new superstition, and would either pray to little idols, or to the graves in which the great men were buried, or invoke the sun, or commit some similar nonsense. Superstition is the weakness of the human mind, which is inseparably tied up with it; it has always existed, and always will."—Frederick the Great, letter to Voltaire, 1766

"The imbecile priests! The best destiny they can look for is that they and their vile artifices will forever remain buried in the darkness of oblivion."—Frederick the Great (Noyes)

"There are so many things to be said against religion that I wonder they do not occur to everyone."—Frederick the Great, ibid.

"A broad hat does not always cover a venerable head."—Thomas Fuller, physician, *Gnomologia,* 1732

"He who reads ecclesiastical history reads nothing but the roguery and folly of bishops and churchmen."—Hugo Grotius (1583–1645), Dutch scholar and statesman (Noyes)

"A man who believes that he eats his God we do not call mad; a man who says he is Jesus Christ, we call mad."—Claude Adrien Helvétius (1715–1771), French philosopher

"Religion can bear no jesting."—George Herbert (1593–1633), English poet, *Jacula Prudentum*

". . . What has been said of [God] is either unintelligible or perfectly contradictory; and for this reason must appear impossible to every man of common sense." —Paul-Henri-Dietrich, Baron d'Holbach (1723–1789), French philosopher, *Good Sense,* 1772

"If we go back to the beginning of things, we shall always find that ignorance and fear created the gods; that imagination, rapture, and deception embellished or distorted them; that weakness worships them; that credulity nourishes them; that custom spares them; and that tyranny favors them in order to profit from the blindness of men."—Baron d'Holbach, *The System of Nature,* 1770

"The atheist is a man who destroys the chimeras which afflict the human race, and so leads men back to nature, to experience and to reason."—Baron d'Holbach, ibid.

"Ignorance of natural causes created the gods, and priestly impostures made them terrible."—Baron d'Holbach, ibid.

"All religions are ancient monuments to superstitions, ignorance, ferocity; and modern religions are only ancient follies rejuvenated."—Baron d'Holbach, *Le Bons sens, ou Idées naturelles*

"If the ignorance of nature gave birth to the gods, knowledge of nature is destined to destroy them."—Baron d'Holbach

"The Christian burns the Jew at what is called an auto-da-fe because he clings to the faith of his fathers; the Roman Catholic condemns the Protestant to the flames, and makes a conscience of massacring him in cold blood. . . . Sometimes the various sects of Christians league together against the incredulous Turk, and for a moment suspend their own bloody disputes that they may chastise the enemies of the True Faith."—Baron d'Holbach, *The System of Nature*

"There is no trusting to . . . crazy piety."—Samuel Johnson (1709–1784), English writer, lexicographer, and critic, *Boswell's Life of Dr. Johnson,* March 25, 1791

"When a man is determined to believe, the very absurdity of the doctrine does but confirm him in his faith."—"Junius," anonymous writer to a popular English newspaper, 1769–1772

"There is holy mistaken zeal in politics as well as religion. By persuading others, we convince ourselves."—ibid.

"Religion is too important a matter to its devotees to be a subject of ridicule. If they indulge in absurdities, they are to be pitied rather than ridiculed."—Immanuel Kant (1724–1804), German philosopher, lecture at Konigsberg, 1775

"The wish to talk to God is absurd. We cannot talk to one we cannot comprehend—and we cannot comprehend God; we can only believe in Him. The uses of prayer are thus only subjective."—Kant, ibid.

"The death of dogma is the birth of morality."—Kant (Noyes)

"Apart from moral conduct, all that man thinks himself able to do in order to become acceptable to God is mere superstition and religious folly."—Kant, ibid.

"Reason can never prove the existence of God."—Kant, ibid.

"He who has made great moral progress ceases to pray."—Kant, ibid.

"In theology we must consider the predominance of authority; in philosophy the predominance of reason."—Johannes Kepler (1571–1630), German astronomer who discovered that planetary orbits are ellipses, *Astronomia nova,* 1609

"When miracles are admitted, every scientific explanation is out of the question."—Kepler (Noyes)

"Men are superstitious in proportion as they are ignorant, and . . . those who know least of the principles of religion are the most earnest and fervent."—Richard Payne Knight (1750–1824), English antiquarian and classical scholar, *A Discourse on the Worship of Priapus,* 1786

"A sanctimonious man is one who under an atheist king would be an atheist." —Jean de La Bruyère (1645–1696), French moralist, *Les Caractères,* 1688

"To what excesses will men not go for the sake of a religion in which they believe so little and which they practice so imperfectly."—La Bruyère, ibid.

"Life is a purely physical phenomenon."—Chevalier de Lamarck (1744–1829), French naturalist (Noyes)

"Fanatic fools, that in those twilight times / With wild religion cloaked the worst of crimes!"—John Langhorne (1735–1779), English poet, *The Country Justice*

"There is not one command in all the Gospel for public worship. . . . The frequent attendance at it is never so much as mentioned in all the New Testament." —William Law (1686–1761), English writer, *A Serious Call to a Devout and Holy Life,* 1728

"There is a sort of transcendental ventriloquy through which men can be made to believe that something which was said on earth came from heaven."—Georg Christoph Lichtenberg (1742–1799), German physicist, *Aphorisms*

"As nations improve, so do their gods."—Lichtenberg, *Reflections,* 1799

"After all, is our idea of God anything more than personified incomprehensibility?"—Lichtenberg, ibid.

"Many a man who is now willing to be shot down for the sake of his belief in a miracle would have doubted, if he had been present, the miracle itself."—Lichtenberg, ibid.

"Probably no invention came more easily to man than when he thought up heaven."—Lichtenberg (Peter)

"People have no security against being priest-ridden but by keeping all imperious bishops and other clergymen who love to 'lord it over God's heritage' from getting their foot into the stirrup at all. Let them be once fairly mounted, and their 'beasts, the laity,' may prance and flounce about to no purpose; and they will at length be so jaded and hacked by these reverend jockeys that they will not even have spirits enough to complain that their backs are galled."—Jonathan Mayhew, *A Discourse Concerning Unlimited Submission and Non-Resistance to the Higher Powers,* 1750

"Let us next consider the subject of metaphysics. Alas, what an immensity of nonsense awaits us!"—J. B. Mencken (1674–1715), German writer and historian, *De charlanteria eruditorum,* 1715

"The greatest burden in the world is superstition, not only of ceremonies in the church, but of imaginary and scarecrow sins at home."—John Milton (1608–1674), English poet, *A Complete Collection of the Historical, Political, and Miscellaneous Works of John Milton,* vol. 1, p. 277

"Romanism is less a religion than a priestly tyranny armed with the spoils of civil power which, on the pretext of religion, it hath seized against the command of Christ himself."—Milton, *Treatise on Civil Power in Ecclesiastical Causes,* 1659

"Tolerated popery, as it extirpates all religious and civil supremacies, so itself should be extirpated."—Milton, *Aeropagitica: A Speech for the Liberty of Unlicensed Printing,* 1644

"Others apart sat on a hill retir'd / In thoughts more elevate, and reasoned high / Of Providence, foreknowledge, will and fate / Fixed fate, free will, foreknowledge absolute / And found no end, in wand'ring mazes lost."—Milton, *Paradise Lost,* 1667

". . . The finical goosery of your neat sermon actor."—Milton, *An Apology for Smectymnuus,* 1642

"Priests can lie, and the mob believe, all over the world."—Lady Mary Wortley Montagu (1689–1762), English writer (Cardiff)

"I have a firm belief in the Author of Nature, but only a disdain of creeds and theological whimsies. Every honest person must condemn the quackery of all the churches."—Lady Montagu, ibid.

"Either the papists are guilty of idolatry or the pagans never were so."—Lady Montagu (Noyes)

"If we do but observe how our wit grows up by degrees, flourishes for a time, and at last decays, keeping the same pace with the changes that age and years bring into our body, which observes the same laws that flowers and plants do; what can we suspect, but that the soul of man, which is so magnificently spoken of amongst the learned, is nothing else but a temperature of body, and that it grows and spreads with it, both in bigness and virtues, and withers and dies as the body does, or at least that it does wholly depend on the body for its operations, and that therefore there is no sense nor perception of anything after death?"—Henry More (1614–1687), English philosopher and poet, *The Immortality of the Soul,* 1659

"The orthodoxy of my youth is all over, and will never come back."—Wolfgang Amadeus Mozart (1756–1791), Austrian musician and composer (Cardiff)

"Men never do evil so completely and cheerfully as when they do it from religious conviction."—Blaise Pascal (1623–1662), French scientist and philosopher, *Pensées*

"The metaphysical proofs of God are so remote from the reasoning of men, and so complicated, that they make but little impression; and even were this to serve some persons, it would be only during the instant of their seeing the demonstration, and an hour afterward they would fear they had been deceived."—Pascal, ibid.

"We need a religion of humanity. The only true divinity is humanity."—William Pitt (1708–1778), English statesman (Cardiff)

"Know then thyself, presume not God to scan / The proper study of mankind is man."—Alexander Pope (1688–1744), English poet, *An Essay on Man*

"For modes of faith, let graceless zealots fight / He can't be wrong whose life is in the right."—Pope, ibid.

"For virtue's self may too much zeal be had / The worst of madmen is a saint run mad."—Pope, *Horace,* "To Murray"

"The less reasonable a cult is, the more men seek to establish it by force."—Jean-Jacques Rousseau (1712–1778), French philosopher and author (Wilcox/George)

"Religions are the cradles of despotism."—Marquis de Sade (1740–1814), French writer, *Philosophy in the Bedroom,* 1795

"Men show no mercy and expect no mercy, when honor calls, or when they fight for their idols or their gods."—Friedrich von Schiller (1759–1805), German poet and historian, *The Maid of Orleans*

"A healthy nature needs no God or immortality. There must be a morality which suffices without this faith."—Schiller (Noyes)

"*Scrutamini scripturas* [Let us examine the scriptures]. These two words have undone the world."—John Selden (1584–1654), English scholar, jurist, and politician, 1689

"The clergy would have us believe them against our own reason, as the woman would have had her husband against his own eyes."—Selden, *Table-Talk,* "Clergy," 1689

"Who gave you the privilege of calling yourself ambassador and vice-regent of a ghost-begotten God?"—Charles Maurice de Talleyrand (1754–1838), French statesman, to a high church official (Noyes)

"No! it is not man's fault, but the impostures of priests and kings, which have everywhere destroyed truth; they alone have invented the worship of a God or gods."—Talleyrand, ibid.

"A little, round, fat, oily man of God."—James Thomson (1700–1748), Scottish poet, *The Castle of Indolence,* 1748

"Metaphysics, rightly shown / But teach how little can be known."—John Trumbull (1750–1831), American lawyer and poet, *The Progress of Dulness,* 1773

"A Gothic church or a convent fills one with romantic dreams—but for the mysterious, the church in the abstract, it is a jargon that means nothing, or a great deal too much, and I reject it and its apostles."—Horace Walpole (1717–1797), English man of letters, letter to William Cole, July 12, 1778

"What can be more ridiculous than to suppose that Omnipotent Goodness and Wisdom created [a heaven] and will select the most virtuous of its creatures to sing His praises to all eternity? It is an idea that I should think could never have entered but into the head of a king, who might delight to have his courtiers sing birthday odes forever."—Walpole, letter to William Mason, November 8, 1783

"The Bishop of Derry has renounced all religions to qualify himself for being a cardinal."—Walpole, letter to the Countess of Upper Ossory, December 30, 1783

"Religion, oh, how it is commedled with policy! The first bloodshed in the world happened about religion."—John Webster (ca. 1580–ca. 1625), English dramatist, *The White Devil,* 1608

"What unheard-of misery have thousands suffered to purchase a cardinal's hat for an intriguing obscure adventurer who longed to be ranked with princes, or lord it over them by seizing the triple crown!"—Mary Wollstonecraft (1759–1797), English author and feminist, *A Vindication of the Rights of Women,* 1792

"[Clergy are] idle vermin who two or three times a day perform in the most slovenly manner a service which they think useless, but call their duty."—Wollstonecraft, ibid.

"We must get entirely clear of all the notions drawn from the wild traditions of original sin, the eating of the apple . . . and the other fables, too tedious to enumerate, on which priests have erected their tremendous structures of imposition."—Wollstonecraft, *An Historical and Moral View of the Origin and Progress of the French Revolution,* 1794

"The itch of disputing will prove the scab of churches."—Henry Wotton (1568–1639), English poet and diplomat, *A Panegyric to King Charles*

"He has the canonical smirk and the filthy clammy palm of a chaplain."—William Wycherly (1640–1716), English dramatist, *The Country Wife,* 1673

"His Majesty is not disposed to rest the security of his state upon the stupidity of his subjects."—Baron von Zedlitz, Prussian minister of religion under Frederick the Great, replying to an assertion by the Breslau Consistory that "those who believe most are the best subjects," 1785

Part Four

The American Rationalists

16

Benjamin Franklin (1706–1790)

Dover

Like most of the Founding Fathers, the irrepressible, science-minded Franklin wasn't a conventional Christian. He called himself "a thorough Deist," but he veered somewhat in belief at different times.

Born in Boston, Franklin was apprenticed at twelve to work with his older brother, James, a printer. Four years later, when James created the weekly *New England Courant,* Franklin wrote irreverent essays tweaking Harvard divinity students and sectarian schisms in Christianity.

"His brother was jailed for the blasphemies, for which no doubt Benjamin was responsible," freethought leader Joseph Lewis said in a 1925 radio address.[1] Church leaders protested that the *Courant* "mocked religion, brought the Holy Scriptures into contempt, and profanely abused the faithful ministers of God."

Franklin later wrote that the controversy caused him to be "pointed at with horror by good people as an Infidel or Atheist"; it was one of the reasons he moved to Philadelphia the next year. Later Franklin went to London, worked as a printer, and wrote a Deist pamphlet denying immortality and depicting God as the laws of nature. When he returned to Philadelphia, he modified his views. For his private use, Franklin wrote what he titled "Articles of Belief and Acts of Religion." It affirmed a supreme, perfect being, "Author and Father of the Gods themselves," and spoke of subservient gods.

Franklin was a bit of a libertine, and fathered a son by an unknown woman. Then he married a former sweetheart and raised the illegitimate son along with their own children.

He bought the *Pennsylvania Gazette* in 1729; began printing *Poor Richard's Almanack* in 1732; won a contract to print Pennsylvania's paper money; became Philadelphia's postmaster and clerk of the Pennsylvania legislature and helped or-

---

1. Joseph Lewis, *Atheism and Other Addresses* (New York: Arno Press, 1972), n. pag.

ganize the first public police department, fire brigade, library, insurance company, and academy.

Intrigued by science, Franklin studied electricity and made his famous kite-and-lightning experiment. He also invented the lightning rod, the Franklin stove, and bifocal eyeglasses. And he started a discussion group that later became the American Philosophical Society.

Franklin was both affluent and renowned by the time the snowballing Revolution propelled him into his historical role in the birth of the new nation.

Today, every schoolchild knows of the colorful Franklin—but few are taught that he was a maverick who both eschewed Christianity and was fascinated by it. *National Geographic* magazine notes: "Franklin drank deep of the Protestant ethic and then, discomfited by church constraints, became a freethinker. All his life he kept Sundays free for reading, but would visit any church to hear a great speaker."[2]

Dr. Joseph Priestley, the discoverer of oxygen—himself a Unitarian minister who suffered mob attacks for his unorthodoxy—felt Franklin was too radical for his taste. Priestley wrote: "It is much to be lamented that a man of Dr. Franklin's general good character and great influence, should have been an unbeliever in Christianity, and also have done so much as he did to make others unbelievers."[3]

Franklin's Comments on Religion

"My parents had early given me religious impressions, and brought me through my childhood piously in the Dissenting way. But I was scarcely fifteen when, after doubting by turns of several points, as I found them disputed in the different books I read, I began to doubt of Revelation itself. Some books against Deism fell into my hands. . . . They wrought an effect on me quite contrary to what was intended by them; for the arguments of the Deists, which were quoted to be refuted, appeared to me much stronger than the refutations; in short, I became a thorough Deist."—from Franklin's autobiography, published posthumously

"He [the Rev. Mr. Whitefield] used, indeed, sometimes to pray for my conversion, but never had the satisfaction of believing that his prayers were heard."—ibid.

"Revelation had indeed no weight with me."—ibid.

"Many a long dispute among divines may be thus abridged: It is so; It is not so. It is so; it is not so."—*Poor Richard's Almanack,* 1743

"The way to see by faith is to shut the eye of reason."—*Poor Richard's Almanack,* 1758

---

2. Alice J. Hall, "Philosopher of Dissent: Benjamin Franklin," *National Geographic* July 1975, p. 94.

3. Quoted by Peter McWilliams in *Ain't Nobody's Business If You Do* (Los Angeles: Prelude Press, 1993), p. 165.

"Lighthouses are more helpful than churches."—(Cardiff)

"Wise men wonder at the present growth of infidelity. They should have consider'd, when they taught people to doubt the authority of newspapers and the truth of predictions in almanacs, that the next step might be a disbelief in the well-vouch'd acts of ghosts, witches, and doubts even of the truths of the Creed."—letter to a London newspaper, May 20, 1765

"I imagine it great vanity in me to suppose that the Supremely Perfect does in the least regard such an inconsiderable nothing as man. More especially, since it is impossible for me to have any positive, clear idea of that which is infinite and incomprehensible, I cannot conceive otherwise than that He, the Infinite Father, expects or requires no worship or praise from us. . . ."—*Articles of Belief and Acts of Religion,* November 20, 1728

"When a religion is good, I conceive it will support itself; and when it does not support itself, and God does not take care to support it so that its professors are obliged to call for help of the civil power, 'tis a sign, I apprehend, of its being a bad one."—letter to Richard Price, October 9, 1780

"If we look back into history for the character of the present sects in Christianity, we shall find few that have not in their turns been persecutors, and complainers of persecution. The primitive Christians thought persecution extremely wrong in the pagans, but practiced it on one another. The first Protestants of the Church of England blamed persecution in the Romish Church, but practiced it upon the Puritans. These found it wrong in the bishops, but fell into the same practice themselves both here [in England] and in New England."—*An Essay on Toleration*

"When I traveled in Flanders . . . in the afternoon on a Sunday, both high and low went to the play and to the opera, where there was plenty of singing and dancing. I looked around for God's judgments, but saw no signs of them."—(Noyes)

"You desire to know something of my religion. . . . Here is my creed. I believe in one God, creator of the universe. That he governs it by his providence. That he ought to be worshiped. That the most acceptable service we render to him is doing good to his other children. That the soul of man is immortal, and will be treated with justice in another life. . . . As to Jesus of Nazareth, my opinion of whom you particularly desire, I think his system of morals and his religion, as he left them to us, the best the world ever saw or is like to see; but I apprehend it has received various corrupting changes, and I have, with most of the present Dissenters in England, some doubts as to his divinity; though it is a question I do not dogmatize upon, having never studied it, and think it needless to busy myself with it now, when I expect soon an opportunity of knowing the truth with less trouble. . . . I have ever let others enjoy their religious sentiments, without reflecting on them for those who appeared to me unsupportable and even absurd. . . ."—letter to President Ezra Stiles of Yale University, March 9, 1790, just before Franklin's death

17

John Adams (1735–1826)

Dover

Another non-Christian president of the United States was John Adams, a radical who was greatly responsible for America's independence.

He was the son of a Massachusetts farmer-deacon, who sent him to Harvard College and pressured him to become a clergyman. But Adams chose law. He told a friend that he respected lawyers, but saw in the clergy the "pretended sanctity of some absolute dunces."[1]

When Britain imposed the Stamp Act on the colonies in 1765, Adams joined the irate opposition and became a leader of colonial resistance to Britain. After his election to the Massachusetts legislature, he attacked British policies. Then he went to Philadelphia in 1774 as a delegate to the First Continental Congress, where he became one of the chief advocates of independence. Adams proposed creation of a Continental Army, with George Washington as commander.

Two years later, he seconded the motion to break with Britain, and was named to the committee to write a Declaration of Independence. Adams worked with his younger colleague from Virginia, Thomas Jefferson, who called him "the colossus of that debate," to win passage of the declaration.

Adams served as envoy to France and Britain, and helped negotiate an end to the Revolution in 1783. In the first elections in 1788 and 1792, he received the second-highest number of electoral votes, and was vice president under President Washington. In the 1796 election, he got three more votes than his fellow radical from Virginia, so he became president and Jefferson vice president.

In the 1790s, political parties took shape. Populist-minded Jefferson and James Madison led the incipient Democrats. Aristocratic Alexander Hamilton and half-aristocratic Adams headed the Federalists. Hamilton turned the 1800 election vicious. He half-heartedly supported Adams as the Federalist nominee for presi-

---

1. Letter to Charles Cushing, October 19, 1756.

dent while leading a Federalist slander campaign that branded Jefferson an atheist. Jefferson narrowly won, and Adams bitterly went home to retirement.

Years later, after President Jefferson also had retired to his farm, a remarkable thing happened: The two men who had been young radical friends, then split as political enemies, reconciled and entered a long period of warm correspondence.

Their letter writing focused repeatedly on religion. Both were Deists who rejected the divinity of Christ, but felt they could perceive evidence of God as the designer of the cosmos. As in politics, Adams tended to be more conventional, and Jefferson more radical—yet they concurred in their scorn for Christianity.

Again and again in their letters, Adams and Jefferson pondered the ultimate questions of life and the possibility of an afterlife. When Adams's daughter, and then his wife, died, the grief-stricken old man turned to a hope of meeting them in heaven. Jefferson consoled him with a letter full of assurances of a hereafter.

"Adams pathetically clutched the branch extended to him," biographer Gilbert Chinard comments. Adams responded with an even stronger letter of hope that a kindly God would reunite his family after death. Chinard continues:

> This was a most consoling belief, which Jefferson, for the time being, pretended to share, but which he fought with all his might as soon as he thought that Adams was able again to look at the question rationally instead of emotionally.[2]

For the remainder of their twilight years, Adams and Jefferson kept up their fond letters. Finally, on July 4, 1826—the fiftieth anniversary of the Declaration of Independence—the dying Adams spoke his final words: "Thomas Jefferson still lives." He did not know that Jefferson had died a few hours earlier.

Adams's Views on Religion

"The frightful engines of ecclesiastical councils, of diabolical malice, and Calvinistical good-nature never failed to terrify me exceedingly whenever I thought of preaching."—letter to his brother-in-law, Richard Cranch, October 18, 1756, explaining why he rejected the ministry

"Numberless have been the systems of iniquity. . . . The most refined, sublime, extensive, and astonishing constitution of policy that ever was conceived by the mind of man was framed by the Romish clergy for the aggrandizement of their own order. . . . They even persuaded mankind to believe, faithfully and undoubtingly, that God Almighty had entrusted them with the keys of heaven, whose gates they might open and close at pleasure . . . with authority to license all sorts of sins and crimes . . . or withholding the rain of heaven and the beams of the sun; with the

---

2. Gilbert Chinard, *Honest John Adams* (Boston: Little, Brown & Co., 1933), p. 340.

management of earthquakes, pestilence, and famine; nay, with the mysterious, awful, incomprehensible power of creating out of bread and wine the flesh and blood of God himself. All these opinions they were enabled to spread and rivet among the people by reducing their minds to a state of sordid ignorance and staring timidity, and by infusing into them a religious horror of letters and knowledge. Thus was human nature chained fast for ages in a cruel, shameful, and deplorable servitude."—"A Dissertation on the Canon and the Feudal Law," printed in the *Boston Gazette,* August 1765

". . . Of all the nonsense and delusion which had ever passed through the mind of man, none had ever been more extravagant than the notions of absolutions, indelible characters, uninterrupted successions, and the rest of those fantastical ideas, derived from the canon law, which had thrown such a glare of mystery, sanctity, reverence, and right reverend eminence and holiness around the idea of a priest as no mortal could deserve . . . the ridiculous fancies of sanctified effluvia from episcopal fingers. . . ."—ibid.

"The United States of America have exhibited, perhaps, the first example of governments erected on the simple principles of nature. . . . [In] the formation of the American governments . . . it will never be pretended that any persons employed in that service had interviews with the gods, or were in any degree under the influence of heaven. . . . These governments were contrived merely by the use of reason and the senses."—*A Defense of the Constitutions of Government of the United States of America,* 1788

". . . The government of the United States is not, in any sense, founded on the Christian religion. . . ."—treaty with Tripoli, passed unanimously by the U.S. Senate and signed by President Adams on June 10, 1797

"Indeed, Mr. Jefferson, what could be invented to debase the ancient Christianism which Greeks, Romans, Hebrews and Christian factions, above all the Catholics, have not fraudulently imposed upon the public? Miracles after miracles have rolled down in torrents."—letter to Thomas Jefferson, December 3, 1813

". . . Cabalistic Christianity, which is Catholic Christianity, and which has prevailed for 1,500 years, has received a mortal wound, of which the monster must finally die. Yet so strong is his constitution, that he may endure for centuries before he expires."—letter to Thomas Jefferson, July 16, 1814

"The question before the human race is, whether the God of nature shall govern the world by his own laws, or whether priests and kings shall rule it by fictitious miracles."—letter to Thomas Jefferson, June 20, 1815

"I do not like the reappearance of the Jesuits. If ever there was a body of men who merited damnation on earth and in Hell, it is this society of Loyola's. Nevertheless, we are compelled by our system of religious toleration to offer them an asylum."—letter to Thomas Jefferson, May 5, 1816

"Let the human mind loose. It must be loose. It will be loose. Superstition and dogmatism cannot confine it."—letter to his son, John Quincy Adams, November 13, 1816

"As I understand the Christian religion, it was, and is, a revelation. But how has it happened that millions of fables, tales, legends, have been blended with both Jewish and Christian revelation that have made them the most bloody religion that ever existed?"—letter to F.A. Van der Kamp, December 27, 1816

"Twenty times, in the course of my late reading, have I been on the point of breaking out, 'This would be the best of all possible worlds, if there were no religion in it!' But in this exclamation I should have been as fanatical as Bryant or Cleverly [minister and tutor to Adams's son]. Without religion, this world would be something not fit to be mentioned in polite company, I mean hell. . . . The most abandoned scoundrel that ever existed, never yet wholly extinguished his conscience, and while conscience remains there is some religion. Popes, Jesuits and Sorbonists and inquisitors have some conscience and some religion. . . ."—letter to Thomas Jefferson, April 19, 1817

"Can a free government possibly exist with the Roman Catholic religion?"—letter to Thomas Jefferson, May 19, 1821

"There exists, I believe, throughout the whole Christian world, a law which makes it blasphemy to deny or doubt the divine inspiration of all the books of the Old and New Testaments, from Genesis to Revelations. In most countries of Europe it is punished by fire at the stake, or the rack, or the wheel. In England itself, it is punished by boring through the tongue with a red-hot poker. In America it is not better; even in our own Massachusetts, which I believe, upon the whole, is as temperate and moderate in religious zeal as most of the states, a law was made in the latter end of the last century, repealing the cruel punishments of the former laws, but substituting fine and imprisonment upon all those blasphemers upon any book of the Old Testament or New. Now, what free inquiry, when a writer must surely encounter the risk of fine or imprisonment for adducing any argument for investigating the divine authority of those books?"—letter to Thomas Jefferson, January 23, 1825

"I almost shudder at the thought of alluding to the most fatal example of the abuses of grief which the history of mankind has preserved—the Cross. Consider what calamities that engine of grief has produced!"—letter to Thomas Jefferson (Seldes)

"The priesthood have, in all ancient nations, nearly monopolized learning. . . . And, even since the Reformation, when or where has existed a Protestant or dissenting sect who would tolerate A FREE INQUIRY? The blackest billingsgate, the most ungentlemanly insolence, the most yahooish brutality is patiently endured, countenanced, propagated, and applauded. But touch a solemn truth in collision with a dogma of a sect, though capable of the clearest proof, and you will soon find you have disturbed a nest, and the hornets will swarm about your legs and hands, and fly into your face and eyes."—letter to John Taylor, 1814, quoted by Norman Cousins in *In God We Trust: The Religious Beliefs and Ideas of the American Founding Fathers* (New York: Harper & Brothers, 1958), p. 108

"What havoc has been made of books through every century of the Christian era? Where are fifty gospels condemned as spurious by the bull of Pope Gelasius? Where are forty wagon-loads of Hebrew manuscripts burned in France, by order of another pope, because of suspected heresy? Remember the *Index Expurgatorius,* the Inquisition, the stake, the axe, the halter, and the guillotine; and, oh! horrible, the rack! This is as bad, if not worse, than a slow fire. Nor should the Lion's Mouth be forgotten. Have you considered that system of holy lies and pious frauds that has raged and triumphed for 1,500 years. . . ."—ibid., p. 106–107

"God is an essence that we know nothing of. . . . Until this awful blasphemy [incarnation] is got rid of, there never will be any liberal science in the world." —(Cardiff)

"When philosophic reason is clear and certain by intuition or necessary induction, no subsequent revelation supported by prophecies or miracles can supersede it." —(Noyes)

18

Thomas Paine
(1737–1809)

In the early 1900s, President Theodore Roosevelt wrote that Paine—the fiery voice of the American Revolution—was a "filthy little atheist." Many others throughout American history have shared this evaluation.

Actually, Paine was a Deist, who felt he could sense God in the immensity of nature, and who once wrote, "I hope for happiness beyond this life."

However, he deemed Christianity and all other organized religions to be frauds sustained by priests and kings. This view, plus his crusading for people in need, kept Paine in trouble much of his life.

Paine was born in England, the son of a Quaker corset-maker. As a young man, he failed to find a suitable role for himself: he went through two brief marriages and several unsatisfactory jobs. Then, in London, Paine met Benjamin Franklin, who urged him to seek a career in America and gave him letters of introduction.

In 1774, Paine arrived in Philadelphia, where he became a writer for the *Pennsylvania Magazine.* Revolutionary fever was growing, and he joined the cry for independence and democracy. His fifty-page booklet, *Common Sense,* sold 500,000 copies in early 1776 and helped set the stage for the Declaration of Independence. The following winter, as the Colonial forces suffered, Paine wrote the first of sixteen *Crisis* pamphlets, opening with the renowned words: "These are the times that try men's souls." Washington ordered it read to his freezing soldiers at Valley Forge.

Throughout the War of Independence, Paine refused to take money from his pamphleteering, and led relief drives to aid the Colonial troops. After the victory, he was given a New York farm.

He returned to England in 1787 to promote construction of a Philadelphia bridge, but was once more drawn into politics and wrote an attack on Prime Minister William Pitt. When Edmund Burke denounced the French Revolution, Paine replied with his famous *Rights of Man* and a sequel, assailing monarchy and championing democracy. He proposed public education, opportunity for the poor, pensions for the aged, public works for the jobless, and other such reforms. England's rulers called it an incitement to "bloody revolution." The writer was charged with treason and his writings were seized.

Paine narrowly escaped to France, where the revolutionaries already had elected him to the National Convention. But he plunged into trouble again by opposing the guillotining of aristocrats. He was imprisoned, and a mark designating execution was chalked on the door of his cell, but mistakenly on the wrong side, so that it could not be seen when the door was closed.

While Paine was in prison, his *Age of Reason,* an assault upon Christianity and the Bible, was published, sending a shock wave through much of the world. He was denounced in America and England as a blasphemer and disbeliever.

In 1794, when the Reign of Terror in France ended, Paine was released, but in broken health. In 1801, he grew homesick for America. His friend President Thomas Jefferson offered to send a warship to fetch him. But Paine knew that Jefferson, too, was being denounced as an infidel, and declined the offer, to avoid adding further stigma to Jefferson.

Paine returned quietly to America in 1802, where found himself widely hated. He lived in poverty, and died in New York City in 1809.

Paine's Views on Religion

"All national institutions of churches, whether Jewish, Christian or Turkish, appear to me no other than human inventions, set up to terrify and enslave mankind, and monopolize power and profit."—*The Age of Reason,* 1794

"Priests and conjurors are of the same trade."—ibid.

"Whenever we read the obscene stories, the voluptuous debaucheries, the cruel and tortuous executions, the unrelenting vindictiveness, with which more than half of the Bible is filled, it would be more consistent that we call it the word of a demon than the word of God. It is a history of wickedness that has served to corrupt and brutalize mankind."—ibid.

"I do not believe in the creed professed by the Jewish church, by the Roman church, by the Greek church, by the Turkish church, by the Protestant church, nor by any church that I know of. My own mind is my own church. . . . Each of those churches accuses the other of unbelief; and for my own part, I disbelieve them all."—ibid.

"What is it the New Testament teaches us? To believe that the Almighty committed debauchery with a woman engaged to be married; and the belief of this debauchery is called faith."—ibid.

"Take away from Genesis the belief that Moses was the author, on which only the strange belief that it is the word of God has stood, and there remains nothing of Genesis but an anonymous book of stories, fables, and traditionary or invented absurdities, or of downright lies."—ibid.

"The most detestable wickedness, the most horrid cruelties, and the greatest miseries that have afflicted the human race have had their origin in this thing called revelation, or revealed religion."—ibid.

"The adulterous connection of church and state. . . ."—ibid.

"The study of theology, as it stands in Christian churches, is the study of nothing; it is founded on nothing; it rests on no principles; it proceeds by no authorities; it has no data; it can demonstrate nothing. . . ."—ibid.

"The world is my country, all mankind are my brethren, and to do good is my religion."—ibid.

"Toleration is not the opposite of intoleration, but is the counterfeit of it. Both are despotisms. The one assumes to itself the right of withholding liberty of conscience, and the other of granting it. The one is the pope, armed with fire and fagot, and the other is the pope selling or granting indulgences."—*The Rights of Man,* 1791

"Whence arose all the horrid assassinations of whole nations of men, women, and infants, with which the Bible is filled; and the bloody persecutions, and tortures unto death, and religious wars, that since that time have laid Europe in blood and ashes; whence arose they, but from this impious thing called religion, and this monstrous belief that God has spoken to man?"—(Cardiff)

"Of all the systems of religion that ever were invented, there is none more derogatory to the Almighty, more unedifying to man, more repugnant to reason, and more contradictory in itself than this thing called Christianity. Too absurd for belief, too impossible to convince, and too inconsistent for practice, it renders the heart torpid or produces only atheists or fanatics. As an engine of power, it serves the purpose of despotism, and as a means of wealth, the avarice of priests, but so far as respects the good of man in general it leads to nothing here or hereafter."—ibid.

"Belief in a cruel God makes a cruel man."—(Seldes)

"One good schoolmaster is of more use than a hundred priests."—ibid.

"The Bible has been received by the Protestants on the authority of the Church of Rome. . . . We do not admit the authority of that church with respect to its pretended infallibility, its manufactured miracles, its setting itself up to forgive sins. . . . It was by propagating that belief and supporting it by fire and fagot that she kept up her temporal power."—unsigned contribution to *The Prospect,* 1804

"The age of ignorance commenced with the Christian system."—(Peter)

"If thou trusteth to the book called the Scriptures, thou trusteth to the rotten staff of fables and of falsehood."—(Noyes)

"Prophesying is lying professionally."—ibid.

"Paris, February 21st, 1802, since the fable of Christ."—dating a letter, ibid.

19

Ethan Allen (1738–1789)

Ethan Allen, a reckless hero of the American Revolution, was just as reckless in attacking Christianity, which he called "superstition" in an unruly book.

A New England resident, Allen actually rebelled before the Revolution. A 1770 dispute over land grants threatened settlers with loss of their farms. They raised a defense regiment called the Green Mountain Boys, with Allen its colonel. The British governor of New York declared him an outlaw and put a price on his head. The settlers held the governor's forces at bay.

When the Revolution broke out, the Green Mountain Boys joined the action and overwhelmed the British garrison at Fort Ticonderoga. Then Allen made a foolhardy attempt to capture Montreal, but was captured himself and sent to England as a prisoner. Later, he was released.

Allen was a freethinker. At his wedding, the ritual required him to pledge "to live with Fanny Buchanan agreeable to the laws of God." Allen halted the ceremony in protest. Only after it was specified that his pledge meant the god of nature, as envisioned by Deists, did he proceed.

Before the war, Allen had worked with a fellow skeptic, Dr. Thomas Young, in drafting a book. But Young died, leaving the work unfinished. After the war, Allen revised the manuscript and published it under his name alone as *Reason, the Only Oracle of Man.* It was a scathing assault on Calvinist Christianity. The clergy seethed in anger. One minister published a verse rebuke:

> Behold, inspired from Vermont dens
> The seer of Antichrist descends
> To feed new mobs with Hell-born manna
> In gentle lands of Susquehanna.

When on his deathbed Allen was told by a minister, "General, I fear the angels are waiting for you," the old soldier replied: "Waiting, are they? Waiting, are they? Well, goddam 'em, let 'em wait."[1]

Allen's Comments on Religion

"I have generally been denominated a Deist, the reality of which I have never disputed, being conscious that I am no Christian, except mere infant baptism makes me one; and as to being a Deist, I know not, strictly speaking, whether I am one or not."—*Reason, the Only Oracle of Man,* 1784, preface

". . . The doctrine of the Trinity is destitute of foundation, and tends manifestly to superstition and idolatry."—ibid., p. 124

"That Jesus Christ was not a god is evident from his own words, where, speaking on the day of judgment, he says, 'Of that day and hour, knoweth no man, not the angels which are in heaven, neither the son.' This is giving up all pretension to divinity, acknowledging in the most explicit manner that he did not know all things."—ibid., p. 125

"There is not any thing, which has contributed so much to delude mankind in religious matters, as mistaken apprehension concerning supernatural inspiration or revelation."—ibid., p. 200

"In those parts of the world where learning and science has prevailed, miracles have ceased; but in those parts of it as are barbarous and ignorant, miracles are still in vogue."—ibid., p. 265

". . . They are blind with respect to their own superstition, yet they can perceive and despise it in others. Protestants very readily discern and expose the weak side of Popery, and papists are as ready and acute in discovering the errors of heretics."—ibid., p. 337

---

1. Quoted in Stewart H. Holbrook, *Ethan Allen* (New York: Macmillan, 1940), p. 251.

20

Thomas Jefferson (1743–1826)

Dover

Popular history avoids mentioning that Jefferson, the chief creator of American democracy, was a skeptic who wrote many attacks on the clergy, and who was denounced as a "howling atheist," a "hardened infidel," and an "enemy of religion."

Jefferson was born into the Anglican Church and remained a lifelong member, nominally. Yet he came to reject his church's supernatural dogmas, such as the belief that Jesus was divine. Jefferson concluded that Jesus was simply a human advocate of compassion and forgiveness—the finest such in history. Jefferson even compiled the moral maxims of Jesus into a condensation later called the "Jefferson Bible," from which he omitted what he called the "superstitions, fanaticisms and fabrications" that perverted the gospels.

As a Virginia legislator and governor, Jefferson led efforts to separate church and state. He succeeded in disestablishing his Anglican denomination as the official state church, and wrote the Virginia Act for Religious Freedom outlawing religious tests for citizens.

Jefferson befriended English Unitarian leaders, deniers of the Christian Trinity, and called himself a Unitarian. He also was ranked among Deists, the Enlightenment-era thinkers who rejected mystical Christianity but felt they perceived God in the vastness and intricacies of nature.

Publicly, Jefferson was reticent about his disbelief, but he expressed it boldly in dozens of private letters to friends. He also revealed hints of doubt in his only full-length book, *Notes on the State of Virginia* published in London in 1787. In this work, Jefferson noted that Christian conflicts had killed millions, and that it did no harm for a person "to say there are twenty gods, or no god."

Jefferson's colleagues were well aware of his disbelief. President John Quincy Adams wrote of Jefferson in his diary (January 11, 1831): "If not an absolute atheist, he had no belief in a future existence. All his ideas of obligation or retribution were bounded by the present life."

Biographer Fawn Brodie concurs: "No other statesman of his time could match Jefferson in his hatred of the established faith. . . . His distrust of clergymen as factionalists, schismatizers, and imprisoners of the human spirit continued to his death."[1]

During the presidential campaign of 1800, ministers and Federalist political opponents called Jefferson an atheist. He was denounced so frequently, and with such vehemence, that many historians regard the 1800 campaign as the cruelest in U.S. history.

Although he narrowly won the election, accusations of atheism continued until Jefferson's death and for decades afterward. Gradually they faded, supplanted by the sanitized popular view that he was a conventional believer.

Today, Jefferson's immortal vow of "eternal hostility against every form of tyranny over the mind of man" is engraved upon his memorial in Washington— but few who read it know that he was speaking of the clergy.

Jefferson's Views on Religion

Private Letters

"The day will come when the mystical generation of Jesus, by the supreme being as his father in the womb of a virgin, will be classed with the fable of the generation of Minerva in the brain of Jupiter."—letter to John Adams, April 11, 1823

"On the dogmas of religion, as distinguished from moral principles, all mankind, from the beginning of the world to this day, have been quarreling, fighting, burning and torturing one another, for abstractions unintelligible to themselves and to all others, and absolutely beyond the comprehension of the human mind."—letter to Archibald Cary, 1816

"In every country and in every age, the priest has been hostile to liberty. He is always in alliance with the despot, abetting his abuses in return for protection to his own."—letter to Horatio Gates Spafford, March 17, 1814

". . . I am not afraid of the priests. They have tried upon me all their various batteries, of pious whining, hypocritical canting, lying and slandering, without being able to give me one moment of pain."—letter to Horatio Gates Spafford, 1816

"I promised you a letter on Christianity, which I have not forgotten. . . . The clergy [had] a very favorite hope of obtaining an establishment of a particular form of Christianity throughout the United States; and as every sect believes its own form

---

1. Fawn M. Brodie, *Thomas Jefferson: An Intimate History* (New York: W. W. Norton & Co., 1974), p. 55.

the true one, every one perhaps hoped for his own, but especially the Episcopalians and Congregationalists. The returning good sense of our country threatens abortion to their hopes, and they believe that any portion of power confided to me will be exerted in opposition to their schemes. And they believe rightly: for I have sworn upon the altar of God eternal hostility against every form of tyranny over the mind of man."—letter to Dr. Benjamin Rush, September 23, 1800

"History, I believe, furnishes no example of a priest-ridden people maintaining a free civil government. This marks the lowest grade of ignorance, of which their political as well as religious leaders will always avail themselves for their own purposes."—letter to Baron Alexander von Humboldt, December 6, 1813

"Question with boldness even the existence of a God; because, if there be one, he must more approve of the homage of reason than that of blindfolded fear."—letter to his nephew, Peter Carr, August 10, 1787

"It is too late in the day for men of sincerity to pretend they believe in the Platonic mysticisms that three are one, and one is three; and yet that the one is not three, and the three are not one. . . . But this constitutes the craft, the power and the profit of the priests. Sweep away their gossamer fabrics of factitious religion, and they would catch no more flies."—letter to John Adams, August 22, 1813

"To talk of immaterial existences is to talk of *nothings*. To say that the human soul, angels, god, are immaterial, is to say they are nothings, or that there is no god, no angels, no soul. I cannot reason otherwise . . . without plunging into the fathomless abyss of dreams and phantasms. I am satisfied, and sufficiently occupied with the things which are, without tormenting or troubling myself about those which may indeed be, but of which I have no evidence."—letter to John Adams, August 15, 1820

"In our Richmond there is much fanaticism, but chiefly among the women. They have their night meetings and praying parties, where, attended by their priests, and sometimes by a hen-pecked husband, they pour forth the effusions of their love to Jesus, in terms as amatory and carnal, as their modesty would permit them to use to a mere earthly lover."—letter to Dr. Thomas Cooper, November 2, 1822

"I have ever judged of the religion of others by their lives. . . . But this does not satisfy the priesthood. They must have a positive, a declared assent to all their interested absurdities. My opinion is that there would never have been an infidel, if there had never been a priest."—letter to Mrs. M. Harrison Smith, August 6, 1816

"But a short time elapsed after the death of the great reformer of the Jewish religion [Jesus], before his principles were departed from by those who professed to be his special servants, and perverted into an engine for enslaving mankind and aggrandizing their oppressors in church and state. . . . The purest system of morals ever before preached to man has been adulterated and sophisticated by artificial constructions into a mere contrivance to filch wealth and power to themselves."—letter to Samuel Kercheval, January 19, 1810

"My aim [in compiling Christ's humanitarian maxims] was to justify the character of Jesus against the fictions of his pseudo-followers . . . the follies, the falsehoods and the charlatanisms which his biographers father upon him. . . . That Jesus did not mean to impose himself on mankind as the son of God, physically speaking, I have been convinced."—letter to William Short, August 4, 1820

"The hocus-pocus phantasm of a god like another Cerberus, with one body and three heads, had its birth and growth in the blood of thousands and thousands of martyrs."—letter to James Smith, December 8, 1822

"What a conspiracy this, between church and state! Sing Tantarara, rogues all, rogues all! Sing Tantarara, rogues all!"—letter to English radical John Cartwright, June 25, 1824

"[Creeds] have been the bane and ruin of the Christian church, its own fatal invention, which, through so many ages, made of Christendom a slaughterhouse, and at this day divides it into castes of inextinguishable hatred to one another."—letter to Thomas Whittemore, June 5, 1822

"Of publishing a book on religion, my dear sir, I never had an idea. I should as soon think of writing for the reformation of Bedlam, as of the world of religious sects. Of these there must be, at least, ten thousand, every individual of every one of which believes all wrong but his own."—letter to the Rev. Charles Clay, rector of Jefferson's parish church in Albemarle County, Va., January 29, 1815

"I am anxious to see the doctrine of one god commenced in our state. But the population of my neighborhood is too slender, and is too much divided into other sects to maintain any one preacher well. I must therefore be contented to be an Unitarian by myself, although I know there are many around me who would become so, if once they could hear the questions fairly stated."—letter to Dr. Benjamin Waterhouse, January 8, 1825

"I trust there is not a young man now living in the United States who will not die a Unitarian."—letter to Waterhouse, June 26, 1822

"I am of a sect by myself, as far as I know."—letter to the Rev. Ezra Stiles, president of Yale University, June 25, 1819

"I concur with you strictly in your opinion of the comparative merits of atheism and demonism, and really see nothing but the latter in the being worshiped by many who think themselves Christians."—letter to Richard Price from Paris, January 8, 1789*

---

*Jefferson was responding to a letter from Richard Price of October 26, 1788, which said: ". . . There has been in almost all religions a melancholy separation of religion from morality. Popery teaches a method of pleasing God without forsaking vice, and of getting into heaven by penances, bodily mortifications, pilgrimages, saying masses, believing mysterious doctrines, burning heretics, aggrandizing priests, &c. Mahometans expect a paradise of sensual pleasures. Pagans worship'd lewd, revengeful and cruel deities, and thus sanctify'd to themselves some of the worst passions. The religion likewise of many Protestants is little better than a compromise with the deity for wrong practices

"A professorship of theology should have no place in our institution [the University of Virginia]."—letter to Thomas Cooper, October 7, 1814

"I have recently been examining all the known superstitions of the world, and do not find in our particular superstition [Christianity] one redeeming feature. They are all alike, founded upon fables and mythologies."—letter to Dr. Woods (Cardiff) (Noyes)

"Calvin's religion was demonism. If ever a man worshiped a false god, he did. The God is a being of terrific character—cruel, vindictive, capricious, and unjust."—(Cardiff)

"We discover [in the gospels] a groundwork of vulgar ignorance, of things impossible, of superstition, fanaticism and fabrication."—ibid.

"It has been fifty and sixty years since I read the Apocalypse, and I then considered it merely the ravings of a maniac."—ibid.

"Gouverneur Morris had often told me that General Washington believed no more of that system [Christianity] than he did himself."—in his private journal, February 1800.

"Christianity neither is, nor ever was, a part of the common law."—letter to Dr. Thomas Cooper, February 10, 1814

"The priests of the different religious sects . . . dread the advance of science as witches do the approach of daylight, and scowl on the fatal harbinger announcing the subdivision of the duperies on which they live."—letter to Correa de Serra, April 11, 1820

Public Writings

". . . No man shall be compelled to frequent or support any religious worship, place, or ministry whatsoever. . . ."—Virginia Act for Religious Freedom, 1786

". . . The impious presumption of legislators and rulers, civil as well as ecclesiastical, who, being themselves but fallible and uninspired men, have assumed dominion over the faith of others, setting up their own opinions and modes of thinking as the only true and infallible, and as such endeavoring to impose them on others, hath established and maintained false religions over the greatest part of the world and through all time."—ibid.

---

by fastings, sacraments, hearing the word, &c. Would not society be better without such religions? Is atheism less pernicious than demonism? And what is the religion of many persons but a kind of demonism that delights in human sacrifices and causes them to look with horror on the greatest part of mankind? Plutarch, it is well known, has observed very justly that it is better not to believe in a god than to believe him to be a capricious and malevolent being."

"Millions of innocent men, women, and children, since the introduction of Christianity, have been burnt, tortured, fined, imprisoned; yet we have not advanced one inch toward uniformity. What has been the effect of coercion? To make one half of the world fools and the other half hypocrites. To support roguery and error all over the earth."—*Notes on the State of Virginia,* 1787

"It does me no injury for my neighbor to say there are twenty gods, or no God. It neither picks my pocket nor breaks my leg."—ibid.

"A single zealot may commence persecutor, and better men be his victims."—ibid.

"Every state, says an inquisitor, has established some religion. No two, say I, have established the same. Is this a proof of the infallibility of establishments?"—ibid.

"The way to silence religious disputes is to take no notice of them."—ibid.

"No man complains of his neighbor for ill management of his affairs, for an error in sowing his land or marrying his daughter, for consuming his substance in taverns. . . . In all these he has liberty; but if he does not frequent the church, or then conform in ceremonies, there is an immediate uproar."—ibid.

21

James Madison (1751–1836)

Dover

S till another non-Christian American president was James Madison, who fought skirmishes with religion throughout his life.

Born into a wealthy Virginia family, Madison was a brilliant student. He chose to ride horseback to New Jersey to attend what is now Princeton University—"selected for its hostility to episcopacy," according to historian Irving Brant. Madison completed the four-year course in just two years, which still left him enough spare time to demonstrate against England and write ribald poetry ridiculing members of a literary club at the school.

"Madison never became a church member, but in maturity he expressed a preference for Unitarianism," Brant writes. The historian adds that the young Virginian engaged in "furious denunciation of the imprisonment of nearby dissenters from the established Anglican Church."[1]

In 1776, Madison was elected to Virginia's Revolutionary Convention, where he drafted a guarantee of religious freedom, to prevent such jailings for nonconformity. After the convention turned into a state legislature, he and Thomas Jefferson succeeded in having the Anglican Church "disestablished," i.e., cut off from tax support and denied exclusive legal status.

In 1784, the clergy attempted to recoup, by persuading Patrick Henry and George Washington to support "a bill establishing a provision for teachers of the Christian religion," which would have given tax money to all churches. Henry called it a convenient compromise, but Jefferson and Madison called it government-enforced religion. Madison wrote a *Memorial and Remonstrance* against the bill and they defeated the legislation. Subsequently, the legislature passed Jefferson's Religious Freedom Act, affirming separation of church and state. Later, this principle was written into America's Bill of Rights, in the First Amendment to the U.S. Constitution.

---

1. Irving Brant in the 1974 *Encyclopedia Britannica.*

When Madison succeeded Jefferson as president in 1809, he affronted the clergy by vetoing two bills: one to give Mississippi land to a Baptist church, another to incorporate an Episcopal church in the District of Columbia. Each measure violated the separation of church and state, he said. Madison also criticized the employment of chaplains to pray at sessions of Congress.

Even in matrimony, Madison displayed an irreverent streak. He married Dolley Todd, a buxom, vivacious, lapsed Quaker who ignored church strictures and relished parties.

Madison's Comments on Religion

"Religious bondage shackles and debilitates the mind and unfits it for every noble enterprise, every expanded prospect."—letter to William Bradford, Jr., April 1, 1774

"That diabolical, hell-conceived principle of persecution rages among some; and to their eternal infamy, the clergy can furnish their quota of imps for such business. . . ."—letter to William Bradford, Jr., January 24, 1774

"Ecclesiastical establishments tend to great ignorance and corruption, all of which facilitate the execution of mischievous projects."—ibid.

". . . Freedom arises from the multiplicity of sects, which pervades America and which is the best and only security for religious liberty in any society. For where there is such a variety of sects, there cannot be a majority of any one sect to oppress and persecute the rest."—spoken at the Virginia convention on ratification of the Constitution, June 1778

"During almost fifteen centuries has the legal establishment of Christianity been on trial. What has been its fruits? More or less in all places, pride and indolence in the clergy; ignorance and servility in the laity; in both, superstition, bigotry, and persecution."—*A Memorial and Remonstrance,* addressed to the Virginia General Assembly, 1785

"What influence in fact have ecclesiastical establishments had on civil society? In some instances they have been seen to erect a spiritual tyranny on the ruins of civil authority; in many instances they have been seen upholding the thrones of political tyranny; in no instances have they been seen the guardians of the liberties of the people."—ibid.

"The purpose of separation of church and state is to keep forever from these shores the ceaseless strife that has soaked the soil of Europe in blood for centuries."—1803 letter objecting to the use of government land for churches

22

Other Early American Rationalists

George Washington: Dover

W hen America's founders wrote the nation's Constitution, they specified that "no religious test shall ever be required as a qualification to any office or public trust under the United States."[1]

This provision may seem innocuous today, but it was radical in the eighteenth century for a government to keep hands off religion, giving equal citizenship to believers and nonbelievers. Such a remarkable step was taken quite deliberately. The founders were familiar with Europe's horrors of religious coercion, and were determined to avoid the perils of state-enforced faith. Further, most of the founders themselves were nonconformists, Deists, Unitarians, non-Christians.

Although George Washington was close-mouthed about his religious views, he is generally deemed a Deist, like his colleagues. In February 1800, Thomas Jefferson wrote in his journal, *Anas,* this notation about Washington: "Gouverneur Morris, who pretended to be in his secrets & believed himself to be so, has often told me that Genl. Washington believed no more of that system [Christianity] than he himself did."

On one occasion, Christian chaplains in the army urged Washington to expel a Universalist chaplain who denied the existence of hell. But Washington refused.

Historian Barry Schwartz writes: "George Washington's practice of Christianity was limited and superficial because he was not himself a Christian. . . . He repeatedly declined the church's sacraments. Never did he take communion, and when his wife, Martha, did, he waited for her outside the sanctuary. . . . Even on his deathbed, Washington asked for no ritual, uttered no prayer to Christ, and expressed no wish to be attended by His representative."[2]

---

1. U.S. Constitution, Article 6, Section 3.

2. Barry Schwartz, *George Washington: The Making of an American Symbol* (New York: The Free Press, 1987), pp. 174–75.

And Paul F. Boller, Jr., states in his anthology on Washington, "There is no mention of Jesus Christ anywhere in his extensive correspondence."[3]

In fact, a half century after the nation's establishment, clergymen complained that no president to that date had been a Christian. In a sermon that was reported in newspapers, Episcopal minister Bird Wilson of Albany, New York, protested in October 1831: ". . . Among all our presidents from Washington downward, not one was a professor of religion, at least not of more than Unitarianism."[4]

Other Early American Rationalists' Comments on Religion

"There is in the clergy of all Christian denominations a time-serving, cringing, subservient morality, as wide from the spirit of the gospel as it is from the intrepid assertion and vindication of truth."—John Quincy Adams (1767–1848), in his diary, May 27, 1838

"The United States of America should have a foundation free from the influence of clergy."—Albert Gallatin (1761–1849), American statesman (Cardiff)

"Twelve centuries of moral and political darkness, in which Europe was involved, had nearly completed the destruction of human dignity. . . . During this long and doleful night of ignorance, slavery and superstition, Christianity reigned triumphant; its doctrines and divinity were not called in question. The power of the pope, the clergy and the church were omnipotent; nothing could restrain their frenzy, nothing could control the cruelty of their fanaticism; with mad enthusiasm they set on foot the most bloody and terrific crusades, the object of which was to recover the Holy Land. Seven hundred thousand men are said to have perished in the first two expeditions, which had been thus commenced and carried on by the pious zeal of the Christian church, and in the total amount, several million were found numbered with the dead: the awful effects of religious fanaticism presuming upon the aid of heaven."—Elihu Palmer, colleague of Thomas Paine, *Principles of Nature,* 3rd edition, 1806

"Religious controversies are always productive of more acrimony and irreconcilable hatreds than those which spring from any other cause."—George Washington, letter to Sir Edward Newenham, June 22, 1792

"Of all the animosities which have existed among mankind, those which are caused by difference of sentiments in religion appear to be the most inveterate and distressing, and ought most to be deprecated. I was in hopes that the enlightened

---

3. Paul F. Boller, Jr., *George Washington: A Profile* (New York: Hill & Wang, 1969), p. 166.

4. Recounted in Paul F. Boller, *George Washington & Religion* (Dallas: Southern Methodist University Press, 1963), pp. 14–15.

and liberal policy, which has marked the present age, would at least have reconciled Christians of every denomination so far that we should never again see the religious disputes carried to such a pitch as to endanger the peace of society."
—George Washington, letter to Sir Edward Newenham, October 20, 1792

Part Five

The Nineteenth Century
(and the Turn
of the Twentieth)

23

Johann Wolfgang
von Goethe
(1749–1832)

Dover

Goethe, a giant of world literature, was a troubled seeker who sometimes called himself a "heathen" and a "pagan," yet once dabbled in the occult, and wrote a masterpiece about Satan and salvation.

Son of a prosperous German lawyer, Goethe enjoyed a happy childhood and was sent to study law at the University of Leipzig. He fell in love with art, music, and culture—and with a comely barmaid, for whom he wrote songs.

Illness forced Goethe's return home, where he came under the influence of mystical Pietists. He also explored alchemy, astrology, and magical writings.

Upon recovery, Goethe went to school at Strassburg, and was drawn to scientific-minded scholars. He developed a second romantic passion, for a minister's daughter, and wrote rapturous poetry about her.

Goethe renounced Christianity, speaking disdainfully of "the fairy-tale of Christ." He identified with the pantheistic notions of Spinoza: that everything in the universe, including all people, are God. When a book labeled Spinoza an atheist, Goethe wrote that Spinoza "does not prove the existence of God. Being is God. If others denounce him as an atheist for this, I wish to exalt him. . . ."[1]

However, he was erratic. "Goethe is never consistent in his beliefs, and there is always some contradictory passage. . . ." Cambridge scholar Ronald Gray notes.[2] Like many people, the great German writer wavered in his religious thoughts.

Goethe's early writings were published to great acclaim. He became a Frankfurt lawyer, but neglected law to throw himself into writing, as well as into more doomed love affairs. He became infatuated with a girl engaged to another man; he

---

1. Gordon Stein, ed., *The Encyclopedia of Unbelief* (Amherst, N.Y.: Prometheus Books, 1985), p. 273.

2. Ronald Gray, *Goethe: A Critical Introduction* (Cambridge University Press, 1967), p. 104.

was engaged briefly to a banker's daughter; he entered a long-term liaison with a court official's wife. Out of his tumultuous romances, Goethe wrote *The Sorrows of Young Werther,* about a youth who kills himself out of hopeless love. The book became an international sensation, but was banned by Catholic authorities in Italy.

Finally, at age forty, Goethe moved an uneducated young woman into his home and found contentment, fathering several children by her. He finally married her as he neared sixty.

Goethe poured forth novels, poetry, and plays, and became world-renowned. He became fast friends with poet Friedrich Schiller, a fellow agnostic. Schiller wrote: "Which religion do I profess to follow? None! And why? Because of religion."[3] Some clergy accused Goethe of atheism.

Biographer H. G. Haile says that Goethe's "aversion to Roman Catholicism" impelled him to adopt "a thoroughly secular attitude toward the lot of man."[4] This lent intense human feeling to his works. Yet his greatest play, *Faust,* finally completed near his death, is a mystical tale of man who sells his soul to Satan, but finds salvation in heaven at the last moment.

Lord Byron called Goethe the "monarch of European letters." His life was tempestuous, and his rejection of religion was just one swirl of the storm.

Goethe's Comments on Religion

"The happy do not believe in miracles."—*Hermann und Dorothea,* 1797

"Mysteries are not necessarily miracles."—*Spruche in Prosa*

"We are so constituted that we believe the most incredible things: and, once they are engraved upon the memory, woe to him who would endeavor to erase them." —*Sorrows of Young Werther,* 1774

"The deepest, nay, the unique, theme of the history of the world, to which all other themes are subordinate, is the conflict of faith and unbelief."—*Wisdom and Experience*

"You say truly that Man is God and Satan, Heaven and Earth, all in one, for what else are these concepts but conceptions which Man has of his own nature."—letter to theologian Johann Lavater.

"Superstition is rooted in a much deeper and more sensitive layer of the psyche than skepticism."—(Wilcox/George)

---

3. *The Encyclopedia of Unbelief,* p. 288.

4. H. G. Haile, *Artist in Chrysalis: A Biographical Study of Goethe in Italy* (Urbana: University of Illinois Press, 1973), p. 190.

"The church alone beyond all question / Has for ill-gotten gains the right digestion."—*Faust,* Part 1, Scene 9

"Living will teach you to live better than preacher or Bible."—(Noyes)

"Great powers the mountains boast / There nature works, omnipotently free / The priest's dull mind blames it as sorcery."—ibid.

"I shall be well content that after the close of this life we should be blessed with another, but I would beg not to have there for companions any who have believed it here."—ibid.

"He who rises not high enough to see God and nature as one knows neither."—ibid.

"The sensible man leaves the future world out of consideration."—(Cardiff)

"Capacious is the Church's belly. Whole nations it has swallowed down."—ibid.

24

Napoleon
Bonaparte
(1769–1821)

AP/Wide World Photos

Whether you regard Napoleon as a brilliant hero (which he was) or an opportunistic egomaniac (which he also was), he remains a colossal figure in world history. He conquered most of Europe—until his lust for power brought him and a million Frenchmen to destruction.

Perhaps it's not surprising to learn that Napoleon was an agnostic during his years of triumph, but that as he neared death, broken by captivity, he uttered religious declarations.

Napoleon's rise began with the French Revolution, which was a rebellion against religion as well as against aristocratic greed. France's growing middle class came to disbelieve in the divine right of kings, and resented the parasitic luxury of the clergy and nobles. When the people's Assembly gained control in 1789, one of its first acts was to seize church property and order priests to swear loyalty to the new regime.

At that time, Napoleon was a young military officer who joined the radical Jacobin political club and made speeches against archbishops and aristocrats. After Jacobin zealotry produced the Reign of Terror, ending with the group's destruction, Napoleon was arrested briefly, but soon regained his army post.

When rioting royalists attempted to storm the National Convention in 1795, Napoleon ordered his troops to mow them down with grapeshot. Thus he saved the republic and became a public hero. Given ever larger military commands, he began to win victories for France.

Cynically, Napoleon used religion for power. While leading a French army in Egypt, he half declared himself a Muslim and an enemy of the pope to gain support of Egyptian potentates. When the Egyptian campaign bogged down, he slipped back to France, conspired with military colleagues, and staged a 1799 coup that installed him as First Consul, a dictator. Soon, he reached an accommodation with the Catholic Church, to the chagrin of freethinkers who had fought the church in the revolution.

"Among the Turks, I was a Mohammedan; now I shall become a Catholic," Napoleon told aides. To seal the agreement with the Vatican, he attended an extravagant mass in Notre Dame cathedral—but told confidants he would not take the sacrament "or participate in all the rest of the hocus-pocus that makes a man ridiculous."[1]

But Napoleon still defied the church. At his coronation as emperor in 1804, he seized the crown from the hands of Pope Pius VII and placed it upon his own head. Five years later, with Italy under French control, Napoleon demanded that Pius submit to his authority; but the pope replied by excommunicating the emperor. Napoleon laughed at the decree and told his lieutenants: "In these enlightened days, none but children and nursemaids are afraid of curses."[2] He had Pius seized and imprisoned temporarily.

Napoleon had two wives and several mistresses. He lived with a dazzling flair, leading armies in mighty conquests, setting up surrogate kingdoms with his brothers and sisters as rulers.

But Napoleon's self-aggrandizement eventually brought doom. He lost a half million troops in a futile attempt to conquer frozen Russia in the winter of 1812. Nations he had trampled united against him and forced him to abdicate in 1814. He was exiled to the Mediterranean island of Elba. But he escaped, returned to France, raised another army, and met final defeat at Waterloo. An exile once more, Napoleon was confined this time to the barren island of St. Helena, off the African coast, where he spent the final six years of his life.

Napoleon's Views on Religion

"I would believe in a religion if it existed ever since the beginning of time, but when I consider Socrates, Plato, Mahomet, I no longer believe. All religions have been made by men."—to Gaspard Gourgaud at St. Helena, January 28, 1817

"A soul? Give my watch to a savage, and he will think it has a soul. . . . If I have a soul, then pigs and dogs also have souls."—ibid., December 17, 1817

"If I had believed in a God of rewards and punishments, I might have lost courage in battle."—ibid., 1815

"I do not think Jesus Christ ever existed."—ibid.

"It remains an open question whether Christ ever lived."—to German novelist Christoph Wieland (Ludwig, p. 321)

---

1. Quoted by German historian Emil Ludwig in *Napoleon* (New York: Liveright Publishing Corp., 1926), pp. 120–21.
2. Ibid., p. 338.

"My firm conviction is that Jesus . . . was put to death like any other fanatic who professed to be a prophet or a messiah; there have been such persons at all times. . . . Besides, how could I accept a religion which would damn Socrates and Plato? . . . I cannot believe there is a god who punishes and rewards, for I see honest folk unlucky, and rogues lucky."—(Ludwig, p. 600)

"Oh well, my dear Gourgaud, when we are dead, we are simply dead."—(Ludwig, p. 602)

"The Society of Jesus is the most dangerous of orders, and has done more mischief than all the others."—to Barry O'Meara, St. Helena, November 2, 1816

"Fanaticism is always the child of persecution."—to O'Meara, St. Helena, January 27, 1817

"Last Sunday I was walking here alone when I heard the church bells of Ruel. I felt quite moved by the sound; so strong is the power of early association. I said to myself, 'If such a man as I am can be affected in this way, how deep must the impression be on simple believing souls?' What have your philosophers and ideologues to say to that? A nation must have a religion, and that religion must be under the control of the government."—to Count Antoine Thibaudeau, June 1801, recounted in Thibaudeau's book, *Bonaparte and the Consulate*

"Man's uneasiness is such, that the vagueness and the mystery which religion presents are absolutely necessary to him."—*Maxims,* 1804–1815

"The merit of Mahomet is that he founded a religion without an inferno."—ibid.

"Knowledge and history are the enemies of religion."—ibid.

"If I had to choose a religion, the sun as the universal life-giver would be my god."—(Cardiff)

"One of my grand objects was to render education accessible to everyone. . . . All my exertions were directed to illuminate the mass of the nation instead of brutifying them by ignorance and superstition."—ibid.

"Everything is more or less organized matter. To think so is against religion, but I think so just the same."—ibid.

"How can you have order in a state without religion? For, when one man is dying of hunger near another who is ill of surfeit, he cannot resign himself to this difference unless there is an authority which declares 'God wills it thus.' Religion is excellent stuff for keeping common people quiet."—quoted in *American Freeman*

"I am surrounded by priests who repeat incessantly that their kingdom is not of this world, and yet they lay hands on everything they can get."—(Noyes)

"Priests have everywhen and everywhere introduced fraud and falsehood."—ibid.

"The popes set Europe in flames. Perhaps it is yours to reestablish scaffolds and racks, but it shall be my care that you do not succeed."—to a high church official, ibid.

"All our religions are evidently the work of man."—ibid.

"The Christian creed is hostile to the perfect polity, for by bidding men look forward to another life it renders them submissive to the evils of the present."—ibid.

"I once had faith, but when I came to know something, I found my faith attacked. It is said that I am a papist; I am nothing."—ibid.

"I am neither an atheist nor a rationalist; I believe in God and am of the religion of my father. I was born a Catholic, and will fulfill all the duties of that church." —St. Helena, April 18, 1821, three weeks before his death (Seldes)

25

Arthur Schopenhauer (1788–1860)

One of the gloomiest figures of history was Arthur Schopenhauer, Germany's "philosopher of pessimism."

He had much to be gloomy about: His cold, distant father committed suicide. His mother, a popular novelist, sneered at her son's writing, and the two became estranged, never to see each other again. When Schopenhauer's philosophical books were printed, scholars and the public ignored them. After being appointed a professor at the University of Berlin, he scheduled his classes at the same hours as those of his idealist enemy, G. W. F. Hegel, in order to draw Hegel's students— but students ignored Schopenhauer and flocked to Hegel. Beaten, Schopenhauer withdrew from academia and lived on inherited money. He could not feel love for a woman, and never married. He was cranky, arrogant, suspicious, and obnoxious.

But Schopenhauer was brilliant, as the world eventually realized. Late in his life, he was recognized as a genius among modern thinkers, and his once-forgotten books became popular.

Like his predecessor Immanuel Kant, Schopenhauer agreed that it is impossible to find logical proofs of the existence of God. But unlike Kant, who said God should be assumed through blind faith, Schopenhauer said there is no God in which to have faith. It would be preposterous, he said, to think that a benevolent God created the world with all its horrors, disease, disasters, and cruelties.

Schopenhauer contended that "will" is the relentless driving force of life, impelling people and creatures onward in an ultimately meaningless competition for existence, which ends with death. During this sorry onrush, stress, suffering, and futility are the chief experience. As Columbia University philosopher Charles Larmore interprets Schopenhauer's philosophy: "Life is miserable and pointless, pushed along by a blind will-to-live." The only respite, Schopenhauer said, is to escape temporarily through the arts.

Near his death, however, the bitter thinker relented slightly and fondly quoted Petrarch: "If anyone who wanders all day arrives toward evening, it is enough."

Schopenhauer's Views on Religion

"Religions are like glowworms; they shine only when it is dark. A certain amount of general ignorance is the condition of all religions, the element in which alone they can exist. And as soon as astronomy, natural science, geology, history, and knowledge of countries and peoples have spread their light broadcast, and philosophy finally is permitted to say a word, every faith founded on miracles and revelation must disappear."—from "Religion—A Dialogue," reprinted in *The Works of Schopenhauer,* edited by Will Durant (New York: Frederick Ungar Publishing, 1955), p. 485

"You may always observe that faith and knowledge are related as the scales of a balance; when the one goes up, the other goes down."—ibid., p. 486

"Perhaps the time is approaching which has so often been prophesied, when religion will take her departure from European humanity, like a nurse which the child has outgrown; for the child will now be given over to the instructions of a tutor. For there is no doubt that religious doctrines which are founded merely on authority, miracles and revelations are only suited to the childhood of humanity." —ibid.

"The fruits of Christianity were religious wars, butcheries, crusades, inquisitions, extermination of the natives in America, and the introduction of African slaves in their place."—ibid., p. 490

"Almost every Spaniard in days gone by used to look upon an *auto da fe* as the most pious of all acts and one most agreeable to God. A parallel to this may be found in the way in which the Thugs (a religious sect in India, suppressed a short time ago by the English, who executed numbers of them) express their sense of religion and their veneration for the goddess Kali; they take every opportunity of murdering their friends and traveling companions. . . . The power of religious dogma, when inculcated early, is such as to stifle conscience, compassion, and finally every feeling of humanity."—ibid., p. 467–68

"Religion has always been and always will be in conflict with the noble endeavor after pure truth."—ibid., p. 474

"Man excels all the animals even in his ability to be trained. Muslims are trained to turn their faces toward Mecca five times a day and pray; they do so steadfastly. Christians are trained to cross themselves on certain occasions, to genuflect, etc.; while religion in general constitutes the real masterpiece in the art of training, namely the training of the mental capacities—which, as is well known, cannot be started too early. There is no absurdity so palpable that one could not fix it firmly in the head of every man on earth, provided one began to imprint it before his sixth year by ceaselessly rehearsing it before him with solemn earnestness."—In *Essays and Aphorisms* (Baltimore: Penguin Classics, 1970), p. 177

"The chief objection I have to pantheism is that it says nothing. To call the world God is not to explain it; it is only to enrich our language with a superfluous synonym for the word world."—*A Few Words on Pantheism,* 1851

"All religions promise a reward . . . for excellences of the will or heart, but none for excellences of the head or understanding."—*The World as Will and Idea,* 1819

"Astrology furnishes a splendid proof of the contemptible subjectivity of men. It refers the course of celestial bodies to the miserable ego; it establishes a connection between the comets in heaven and squabbles and rascalities on earth."—*Parerga und Paralipomena,* 1851

"That a god like Jehovah should have created this world of misery and woe, out of pure caprice, and because he enjoyed doing it, and should then have clapped his hands in praise of his own work, and declared everything to be very good—that will not do at all!"—(Cardiff)

"Whether one makes an idol of wood, stone, metal, or constructs it from absolute ideas, it is all the same; it is idolatry, whenever one has a personal being in view to whom one sacrifices, whom one invokes, whom one thanks."—(Noyes)

"The Catholic religion is an order to obtain heaven by begging, because it would be too troublesome to earn it. The priests are the brokers for it."—ibid.

"Any dogma, no matter how extravagantly absurd, inculcated in childhood, is sure to retain its hold for life."—ibid.

"Philosophy lets the gods alone, and asks in turn to be let alone by them."—ibid.

26

Percy Bysshe Shelley (1792–1822)

Dover

The Romantic age of poetry may seem quaint from today's viewpoint and the name Percy Bysshe Shelley may have a dainty tone, but, in truth, Shelley was a warrior. He fought ferociously against injustice, brutality, convention, conformity, and supernaturalism. The young poet who wrote "To a Skylark" was belligerent enough to defy the wrath of his entire society.

Born to wealth, son of a Parliament member, Shelley was radical from youth. At Eton College, classmates dubbed him "Mad Shelley." At Oxford, at age eighteen, he and a classmate were expelled for writing a freethought pamphlet, *The Necessity of Atheism* (1811), and distributing it to the clergy.

A year later, Lord Chief Justice Ellenborough sentenced an aging London publisher to prison and the stocks for selling Thomas Paine's anti-Christian classic, *The Age of Reason*. Shelley printed a pamphlet titled *A Letter to Lord Ellenborough* attacking this punishment of ideas. He also published a *Declaration of Rights* espousing freedom to write unpopular beliefs without reprisal.

In the next few years, Shelley wrote attacks on the death penalty, the British power elite, Britain's subjugation of Ireland, and of course Christianity. His radicalism caused his father to renounce him permanently.

Shelley's love-life was equally unconventional. He eloped with a tavern-keeper's daughter, fathered two children, lived by borrowing, grew in stature as a poet—and eloped again. His second love was Mary Wollstonecraft Godwin, daughter of philosopher William Godwin and pioneer feminist Mary Wollstonecraft. They lived a bohemian life among poets, philosophers, and the avant-garde, including Lord Byron, partly in England but increasingly abroad. After his abandoned first wife drowned herself, Shelley and Mary wed. She attained literary immortality of a different sort by writing the horror classic *Frankenstein*.

After the death of his grandfather, who left him a dependable income, Shelley became a permanent poet-in-exile in Italy, writing fervently and socializing with other expatriate British intellectuals.

In 1822, Shelley sailed his yacht across the gulf at Pisa to meet British writers whom Byron had invited to establish a new periodical, *The Liberal.* On the return trip, a sudden squall capsized the boat and Shelley drowned. His intense life was over at age twenty-nine.

Shelley's Views on Religion

"There is no God."—opening line of *The Necessity of Atheism,* 1811

"Mounting from cause to cause, mortal man has ended by seeing nothing; and it is in this obscurity that he has placed his God; it is in this darksome abyss that his uneasy imagination has always labored to fabricate chimeras. . . . It was on this debris of nature that man raised the imaginary colossus of the Divinity."—ibid.

"It is only by hearsay (by word of mouth passed down from generation to generation) that whole peoples adore the God of their fathers and of their priests. . . . They prostrate themselves and pray, because their fathers taught them to prostrate themselves and pray."—ibid.

"The being called God . . . bears every mark of a veil woven by philosophical conceit, to hide the ignorance of philosophers even from themselves. They borrow the threads of its texture from the anthropomorphism of the vulgar."—ibid.

"The crime of inquiry is one which religion never has forgiven."—*A Letter to Lord Ellenborough,* 1812

"If God has spoken, why is the universe not convinced?"—ibid.

"Earth groans beneath religion's iron age / And priests dare babble of a God of peace / Even whilst their hands are red with guiltless blood / Murdering the while, uprooting every germ / Of truth, exterminating, spoiling all, / Making the earth a slaughter-house."—*Queen Mab,* 1813

"I was an infant when my mother went / To see an atheist burned. She took me there. / The dark-robed priests were met around the pile. . . . His death pang rent my heart! The insensate mob / Uttered a cry of triumph, and I wept. / 'Weep not, child!' cried my mother, 'for that man / Has said, There is no God.' "—ibid.

"How ludicrous the priest's dogmatic roar! / The weight of his exterminating curse, how light! / And his affected charity, to suit the press of the changing times, / What palpable deceit!"—ibid.

"Let priest-led slaves cease to proclaim that man inherits vice and misery. . . ." —ibid.

"Frantic priests waved the ill-omened cross / O'er the unhappy earth; then shone the sun / On showers of gore from the upflashing steel / Of safe assassination, and all crime / Made stingless by the spirits of the Lord / And blood-red rainbows canopied the land."—ibid.

"The same means that have supported every other popular belief have supported Christianity. War, imprisonment, assassination, and falsehood; deeds of unexampled and incomparable atrocity have made it what it is."—Shelley's notes to *Queen Mab*

"It is easier to suppose that the universe has existed from all eternity than to conceive of a Being beyond its limits capable of creating it."—ibid.

"Every time we say that God is the author of some phenomenon, that signifies that we are ignorant of how such a phenomenon was caused by the forces of nature."—ibid.

". . . the impudent contradictions and stupendously absurd assertions which the teachers of the Christian religion pretend to deduce from the Old and New Testaments."—*On Miracles and Christian Doctrine*

". . . a formal Puritan, a solemn and unsexual man."—*Peter Bell the Third,* 1819

"Oh, that the wise from their bright minds would kindle / Such lamps within the dome of this dim world / That the pale name of priest might shrink and dwindle / Into the Hell from which it first was furled."—*Ode to Liberty,* 1820

"We owe the great writers of the Golden Age of our literature to that fervid awakening of the public mind which shook to dust the oldest and most repressive form of the Christian religion."—*Prometheus Unbound,* 1820

". . . the name of God and ghosts and heaven . . . poisonous names with which our youth is fed."—*Hymn to Intellectual Beauty,* 1816

". . . The Almighty God expressly commanded Moses to invade an unoffending nation; and, on account of the difference of their worship, utterly to destroy every human being it contained, to murder every infant and unarmed man in cold blood, to massacre the captives, to rip up the matrons, and retain the maidens alone for concubinage and violation."—*A Refutation of Deism,* 1814

"Christianity indeed has equaled Judaism in the atrocities, and exceeded it in the extent of its desolation. Eleven millions of men, women, and children have been killed in battle, butchered in their sleep, burned to death at public festivals of sacrifice, poisoned, tortured, assassinated, and pillaged in the spirit of the Religion of Peace, and for the glory of the most merciful God."—ibid.

"Intensity of belief, like that of every other passion, is precisely proportioned to the degrees of excitement."—ibid.

"It seems less credible that the God whose immensity is uncircumscribed by space, should have committed adultery with a carpenter's wife, than that some bold knaves or insane dupes had deceived the credulous multitude. We have perpetual and mournful experience of the latter. . . . Every superstition can produce its dupes, its miracles, and its mysteries; each is prepared to justify its peculiar tenets by an equal assemblage of portents, prophecies and martyrdoms."—ibid.

"It is among men of genius and science that atheism alone is found."—ibid.

"That miserable tale of the Devil and Eve, and an Intercessor with the childish mummeries of the God of the Jews, is irreconcilable with the knowledge of the stars. The plurality of worlds—the indefinite immensity of the universe—is a most awful subject of contemplation. He who rightly feels its mystery and grandeur is in no danger of seduction from the falsehoods of religious systems. . . ."—(Seldes)

"O Love . . . Justice, or Truth, or Joy! those only can / From slavery and religion's labyrinth caves / Guide us, as one clear star the seaman saves."—(Cardiff)

"That which is incapable of proof itself is no proof of anything else."—ibid.

"The blood shed by the votaries of the God of mercy and peace since the establishment of His religion, would probably suffice to drown all other sectaries in the habitable globe."—ibid.

"Think not the tyrants will rule forever, or the priests of the bloody faith."—ibid.

"Every reflecting mind must acknowledge that there is no proof of the existence of a Deity."—ibid.

"The educated man ceases to be religious."—ibid.

"The name of God has fenced about all crime with holiness."—(Noyes)

"Christianity peoples earth with demons, hell with men, and heaven with slaves."—ibid.

27

Ralph Waldo Emerson (1803–1882)

Dover

A dynamo of ideas, Ralph Waldo Emerson was one of nineteenth-century America's best-known writers and lecturers.

Born in Boston the son of a Unitarian minister, Emerson entered Harvard at fourteen and eventually became a Unitarian minister himself. But he rebelled against the traditional Christianity pervading the denomination in those days, and resigned.

After traveling to Europe and meeting major writers, Emerson returned to America to spend the rest of his life writing essays and speaking on the Lyceum circuit. He attacked most of the entrenched beliefs of his time.

Instead of Christianity, Emerson espoused a vague mystical concept called Transcendentalism, which claimed to perceive divinity in all matter of the universe, and which believed that human psyches are linked to a great Over-Soul. Emerson's colleagues in the movement included feminist Margaret Fuller, naturalist Henry David Thoreau, and several Unitarian leaders.

Transcendentalism was so abstruse that a sarcastic poet lauded the Emerson group, saying: "Many converts they've got / To I don't, nor they either, exactly know what."

When Emerson spoke of God, he seemed to mean the loving instincts within people, not an external, supernatural creator. "That which shows God in me, fortifies me," he wrote. "That which shows God out of me, makes me a wart and a wen."

Such declarations caused him to be branded an infidel and atheist. Near the end of his life, as often happens with renowned skeptics, church leaders spread rumors that Emerson had recanted and embraced Christianity. To refute the tales, his son Edward issued a statement in 1880 stating that his father "has not joined any church, nor has he retracted any views expressed in his writings after his withdrawal from the ministry."

Emerson's wife added: "Mr. Emerson left his pulpit as a matter of honor."

Emerson's Comments on Religion

"As men's prayers are a disease of the will, so are their creeds a disease of the intellect."—*Self-Reliance,* 1841

"The dull pray; the geniuses are light mockers."—*Representative Men,* 1850

"Who shall forbid a wise skepticism, seeing that there is no practical question on which anything more than an approximate solution can be had?"—ibid.

". . . In churches, every healthy and thoughtful mind finds itself . . . checked, cribbed, confined."—quoted by Edwin S. Gaustad in *Faith of our Fathers* (New York: Harper & Row, 1987), p. 135

"Really, it is beyond my comprehension."—Emerson's response when asked by a seminary professor whether he believed in God

"The god of the cannibals will be a cannibal, of the crusaders a crusader, and of the merchants a merchant."—*The Conduct of Life,* 1860

"By the irresistible maturing of the general mind, the Christian traditions have lost their hold."—ibid., "Worship"

"The word miracle, as pronounced by Christian churches, gives a false impression; it is a monster. It is not one with the blowing clover and the falling rain."—address to Harvard Divinity College, July 15, 1838

"Other world? There is no other world! Here or nowhere is the whole fact." —(Seldes)

"We need not assist the administration of the universe."—(Cardiff)

"The new church will be founded on moral science. Poets, artists, musicians, philosophers will be its prophet teachers. The noblest literature of the world will be its Bible—love and labor its holy sacraments—and instead of worshiping one savior, we will gladly build an altar in the heart for everyone who has suffered for humanity."—ibid.

"Our popular theology has gained in decorum, but not in principle, over the superstitions it has replaced."—ibid.

"What ministers had assumed as the distinctive revelations of Christianity, theologic criticism has matched by exact parallelisms from the stories and poems of Greece and Rome."—ibid.

"The vice of our theology is seen in the claim that the Bible is a closed book and that the age of inspiration is past."—ibid.

"It is the old story again: once we had wooden chalices and golden priests, now we have golden chalices and wooden priests."—*The Preacher,* 1867

"A sect or a party is an elegant incognito devised to save man from the vexation of thinking."—journal, 1831

"The most tedious of all discourses are on the subject of the Supreme Being." —journal, 1836

"Don't set out to teach theism from your natural history. . . . You'll spoil both." —journal, 1857

"If I should go out of church whenever I hear a false sentiment, I could never stay there five minutes. But why come out? The street is as false as the church."—*Essays,* second series, 1844

"The religions of the world are the ejaculations of a few imaginative men."—ibid., "The Poet"

"I knew a witty physician who . . . used to affirm that if there was disease in the liver, the man became a Calvinist, and if that organ was sound, he became a Unitarian."—ibid.

"An actually existent fly is more important than a possibly existent angel." —(Noyes)

"The cure for theology is mother-wit."—ibid.

"What is called religion effeminates and demoralizes. The scientific mind must have a faith, which is science. Let us have nothing now which is not its own evidence."—ibid.

"If I go into the churches in these days, I usually find the preacher, in proportion to his intelligence, to be cunning, so that the whole institution sounds hollow." —ibid.

"To aim to convert a man by miracles is a profanation of the soul."—ibid.

"We should not forgive the clergy for taking, on every issue, the immoral side." —ibid.

"Whoso would be a man must be a non-conformist."—ibid.

28

John Stuart Mill (1806–1873)

The gradual rise of humanism and liberalism—slowly bringing democracy, personal liberty, human rights, and social progress—had another champion in John Mill, a British philosopher, economist, and moralist.

His 1859 essay, *On Liberty,* was a landmark statement of the right of free speech. Like Locke before him, Mill contended that people should be allowed to hold unpopular opinions, including religious ones, without risking punishment.

Mill was the son of a historian, who subjected him to an intense classical education. By age ten, Mill was reading Greek and Latin works at the level of university students. While still in his teens, Mill began writing for British newspapers. Among his first efforts was a defense of Richard Carlile, a religious doubter who had been jailed six years for "blasphemous libel."

Mill participated in the London Debating Society and produced an outpouring of writings on logic, economics, philosophy, and politics. He was employed by the British East India Company and rose to be its chief examiner. In his forties, he married a strong-willed widow, Harriet Hardy, and was inspired by her to advocate women's rights.

In 1865, Mill was elected to Parliament, where he backed several reforms. But his popularity was damaged by his defense of Charles Bradlaugh, an agnostic who was denied a seat in Parliament because he refused to take a religious oath. Mill lost the subsequent election.

Mill was a religious skeptic, and so was his keen-minded wife, Harriet. Biographer Eugene August recounts: "Watching her first husband die of cancer prompted her to fierce outbursts against nature's senselessness, and she and Mill sometimes talked vehemently about 'our atheism.' "[1]

---

1. Eugene August, *John Stuart Mill: A Mind at Large* (New York: Charles Scribner's Sons, 1975), p. 245.

After Mill's death, his stepdaughter found three essays on religion among his papers, and published them as a single book. Their scorn for supernatural dogmas, miracles, and divine punishments outraged orthodox Christians. At the same time, Mill's agnostic friends fretted because the final essay wavered, partly embracing "supernatural hopes" and postulating the possibility of some sort of deity. As a liberal willing to look at all sides of an issue, Mill also did so with the ultimate question, the existence of God.

Mill's Views on Religion

"I will call no being good who is not what I mean when I apply that epithet to my fellow creatures; and if such a creature can sentence me to hell for not so calling him, to hell I will go."—*An Examination of Sir William Hamilton's Philosophy,* 1865

"A being who can create a race of men devoid of real freedom and inevitably foredoomed to be sinners, and then punish them for being what he has made them, may be omnipotent and various other things, but he is not what the English language has always intended by the adjective holy."—ibid.

"In the morality of private life, whatever exists of magnanimity, high-mindedness, personal dignity, even the sense of honor, is derived from the purely human, not the religious part of our education, and never could have grown out of a standard of ethics in which the only worth, professedly recognized, is that of obedience." —*On Liberty,* 1859

"A large proportion of the noblest and most valuable teaching has been the work, not only of men who did not know, but of men who knew and rejected the Christian faith."—ibid.

"So natural to mankind is intolerance in whatever they really care about, that religious freedom has hardly anywhere been practically realized."—ibid.

"Whatever crushes individuality is despotism . . . whether it professes to be enforcing the will of God or the injunctions of men."—ibid.

"Christian morality (so called) has all the characters of a reaction. . . . In its horror of sensuality, it made an idol of asceticism, which has been gradually compromised away into one of legality. It holds out the hope of heaven and the threat of hell, as the appointed and appropriate motives to a virtuous life—in this falling far below the best of the ancients, and doing what lies in it to give to human morality an essentially selfish character. . . . It is essentially a doctrine of passive obedience; it inculcates submission to all authorities found established."—ibid.

"The most intolerant of churches, the Roman Catholic Church. . . ."—ibid.

"Belief, thus, in the supernatural, great as are the services which it rendered in the early stages of human development, cannot be considered to be any longer required, either for enabling us to know what is right and wrong in social morality, or for supplying us with motives to do right and to abstain from wrong."—*Utility of Religion,* 1874

"Is there any moral enormity which might not be justified by imitation of such a Deity?"—remarking upon John Calvin's concept that God created hell and predetermined who will be tortured there

"Every established fact which is too bad to admit of any other defense is always presented to us as an injunction of religion."—*The Subjugation of Women,* 1869

"The world would be astonished if it knew how great a proportion of its brightest ornaments, of those most distinguished even in popular estimation for wisdom and virtue, are complete skeptics in religion."—(Cardiff)

"God is a word to express, not our ideas, but the want of them."—ibid.

"It is conceivable that religion may be morally useful without being intellectually sustainable."—ibid.

"My father taught me that the question 'Who made me?' cannot be answered, since it immediately suggests the further question, 'Who made God?' "—ibid.

"Modern morality is derived from Greek and Roman sources, not from Christianity."—ibid.

"The *ne plus ultra* of wickedness is embodied in what is commonly presented to mankind as the creed of Christianity."—ibid.

"Miracles have no claim whatever to the character of historical facts and are wholly invalid as evidence of any revelation."—*Theism,* 1874

"The principle itself of dogmatic religion, dogmatic morality, dogmatic philosophy, is what requires to be rooted out."—*The Spirit of the Age*

"It is historically true that a large proportion of infidels in all ages have been persons of distinguished integrity and honor."—(Noyes)

"On religion in particular, the time appears to me to have come, when it is a duty of all who, being qualified in point of knowledge, have, on mature consideration, satisfied themselves that the current opinions are not only false, but hurtful, to make their dissent known."—ibid.

29

Abraham Lincoln (1809–1865)

Dover

In the heart of nearly every American, a tender spot is held by Abraham Lincoln, the eloquent, tragic hero who suffered the torment of the nation's worst cataclysm.

Each schoolchild is taught about Lincoln's birth in a log cabin, his setbacks in rural politics, his agony in the Civil War, his emancipation of the slaves, and his martyrdom by an assassin. But none is taught that Lincoln rejected Christianity, never joined a church, and even wrote a treatise against religion. Such matters remain taboo in America.

After Lincoln's death, many clergymen declared that he had been a pious Christian. A photograph of Lincoln and his son Tad examining a book of Matthew Brady photos was widely distributed in churches with the misleading caption: "Lincoln Reading the Bible to his Son."

Actually, Lincoln was an enigma, sometimes superstitious, sometimes brooding over tragic forebodings, often inconsistent. After two of his sons died, the grieving president attended church a few times with his wife and invited spiritualists to the White House to seek the boys' departed souls. But he scoffed at the mediums during their séances.

At the behest of White House confidants, religious words were written into some of Lincoln's public pronouncements, inasmuch as the public expected it of their leader. But Lincoln's lifelong intimates knew him differently.

Allegations of disbelief had haunted him over the years. In 1843, after he lost a campaign for Congress, Lincoln said in a letter to his political supporters: ". . . It was everywhere contended that no Christian ought to vote for me because I belonged to no church and was suspected of being a Deist."

In 1846, his congressional campaign opponent publicly accused him of infidelity. Lincoln responded in a cautious circular: "That I am not a member of any Christian Church, is true; but I have never denied the truth of the scriptures; and

I have never spoken with intentional disrespect of religion in general, or of any denomination of Christians in particular."

When Lincoln first was considered presidential timber, a fellow Illinois
lawyer, Logan Hay, wrote to his nephew, future Secretary of State John Hay:
"Candor compels me to say that at this period, Mr. Lincoln could hardly be termed
a devout believer in the authenticity of the Bible (but this is for your ear only)."

Interviewer Opie Read once asked Lincoln his conception of God, to which
he replied: "The same as my conception of nature." Asked what he meant, Lincoln
said: "That it is impossible for either to be personal."

In the years following Lincoln's assassination, his former law partner, William
H. Herndon, made public statements such as: "Mr. Lincoln was an infidel, sometimes bordering on atheism." "He never mentioned the name of Jesus, except to
scorn and detest the idea of a miraculous conception." "He did write a little work
on infidelity in 1835–6, and never recanted. He was an out-and-out infidel, and
about that there is no mistake."

Herndon's remarks caused a storm among the clergy. In response, Herndon
discussed Lincoln's religious views extensively in a biography titled *The True
Story of a Great Life*. Here is an excerpt:

> In 1834, while still living in New Salem and before he became a lawyer, he was sur-
> rounded by a class of people exceedingly liberal in matters of religion. Volney's
> *Ruins* and Paine's *Age of Reason* passed from hand to hand, and furnished food for
> the evening's discussion in the tavern and village store. Lincoln read both these
> books and thus assimilated them into his own being. He prepared an extended
> essay—called by many a book—in which he made an argument against Christian-
> ity, striving to prove that the Bible was not inspired, and therefore not God's reve-
> lation, and that Jesus Christ was not the Son of God. The manuscript containing
> these audacious and comprehensive propositions he intended to have published or
> given a wide circulation in some other way. He carried it to the store, where it was
> read and freely discussed. His friend and employer, Samuel Hill, was among the lis-
> teners and, seriously questioning the propriety of a promising young man like Lin-
> coln fathering such unpopular notions, he snatched the manuscript from his hands
> and thrust it into the stove. The book went up in flames, and Lincoln's political fu-
> ture was secure. But his infidelity and his skeptical views were not diminished.

Herndon quoted statements by others to document the late president's disbelief. Some examples follow:

John T. Stuart, Lincoln's first law partner: "He was an avowed and open infidel, and sometimes bordered on atheism. . . . He went further against Christian
beliefs and doctrines and principles than any man I ever heard."

Supreme Court Justice David Davis, who administered Lincoln's estate: "He
had no faith, in the Christian sense of the term—had faith in laws, principles,
causes and effects."

Jesse W. Fell, to whom Lincoln had entrusted some of his writing: "He did not
believe in what are regarded as the orthodox or evangelical views of Christianity."

Mary Todd Lincoln: "Mr. Lincoln had no faith and no hope in the usual acceptation of those words. He never joined a church; but still, as I believe, he was a religious man by nature. He first seemed to think about the subject when our boy Willie died, and then more than ever about the time he went to Gettysburg; but it was a kind of poetry in his nature, and he was never a technical Christian."

Lincoln's Views on Religion

"My earlier views of the unsoundness of the Christian scheme of salvation and the human origin of the scriptures have become clearer and stronger with advancing years, and I see no reason for thinking I shall ever change them."—1862 letter to Judge J. S. Wakefield, after the death of Willie Lincoln

"The Bible is not my book nor Christianity my profession."—quoted by Joseph Lewis in a 1924 New York speech

"I am approached . . . by religious men who are certain they represent the Divine Will. . . . I hope it will not be irreverent in me to say, that if it be probable that God would reveal his will to others, on a point so connected with my duty, it might be supposed he would reveal it directly to me."—(Cardiff)

"It will not do to investigate the subject of religion too closely, as it is apt to lead to infidelity."—in *Manford's Magazine*

"In great contests, each party claims to act in accordance with the will of God. Both may be, and one must be wrong. God cannot be for and against the same thing at the same time."—memorandum, September 30, 1862

"We, on our side, are praying Him to give us victory, because we believe we are right; but those on the other side pray Him, too, for victory, believing they are right. What must He think of us?"—to the Rev. Byron Sunderland, Senate chaplain, 1862

"Both read the same Bible, and pray to the same God; and each invokes His aid against the other."—inaugural address, March 4, 1865

"I am not a Christian."—(Noyes)

"What is to be, will be, and no prayers of ours can arrest the decree."—ibid.

"I have never united myself to any church because I found difficulty in giving my assent without mental reservation to the long, complicated statements of Christian doctrine which characterize the articles of belief and the usual confession of faith."—ibid.

30

Charles Darwin (1809–1882)

Dover

Copernicus and Galileo dealt a jolt to religion in the sixteenth and early seventeenth centuries by proving that the earth isn't the center of the heavens, as the church maintained.

But their religious impact was mild, compared to the earthquake unleashed by Darwin's proof that humans and other living things evolved from simpler creatures.

His scientific breakthrough was a great leap forward in the understanding of life—and a great trauma for believers in the Bible's declaration that God specially fashioned men and women "a little lower than the angels."

Publication of *The Origin of Species* in 1859 triggered a ferocious backlash among the orthodox. Denunciations and debates raged. The provincial council of Cologne decreed in 1860: "We declare it to be clearly opposed to the Holy Scriptures and the Faith to say that the human body was produced by successive and spontaneous transformations of less perfect forms into more perfect forms."

The man who caused the firestorm was a shy and sickly scholar interested in research, not polemics. Charles Darwin was born into a wealthy family of English intellectuals. His grandfather, physician Erasmus Darwin, a scientist and poet, had befriended Benjamin Franklin and formed a discussion club with Joseph Priestley, discoverer of oxygen, and James Watt, inventor of the steam engine. Erasmus once noted after observing a revival meeting:

> Many theatrical preachers . . . successfully inculcate the fear of death and hell, and live luxuriously on the folly of their hearers. The latter have so much intellectual cowardice that they dare not reason about those things which they are directed by their priests to believe.

His grandson, Charles Robert Darwin, trained in medicine at the University of Edinburgh, but was repelled by the primitive surgery of the time. He turned to the study of theology at Cambridge, but found science more fascinating. While still a student at Cambridge, Darwin accepted a job as naturalist on a government research ship, the *Beagle*. This happenstance changed history.

For five years, Darwin roved the South Seas, observing animals, plants, and fossils, especially the differences in species isolated from each other on remote islands. In 1837 Darwin began a notebook "on transmutation of species." Eventually, he hit upon the idea of natural selection: that in the endless struggle for survival, "favourable variations would tend to be preserved and unfavourable ones to be destroyed. The result of this would be the formation of new species."

Darwin's health failed after his years at sea. Nursed by his wife, he lived on family wealth and wrote biological treatises. In 1856 he painstakingly began writing his theory of evolution. Two years later, Darwin was stunned when his colleague Alfred Wallace sent him a treatise reaching the same conclusions. The work of both men was read to the Linnean Society in 1858, and Darwin hurried to spell out his long-hoarded evidence in a series of monumental books.

Sir Gavin de Beer, director of the British Museum, said the religious backlash occurred because the new understanding of species "provides no evidence of divine or providential guidance or purposive design, because natural selection of fortuitous variations gives a scientifically satisfactory explanation of evolution without any necessity for miraculous interposition or supernatural interference with the ordinary laws of nature."[1]

Further, the uproar stemmed partly from Darwin's depiction of nature as a ruthless system of hunting, killing, devouring, fleeing, starving, freezing—an unlikely design for a loving creator. Through the storm, the frail researcher remained mostly silent, while his scientific friends defended him in debates and writings.

". . . As he grew older, Darwin abandoned the views of an orthodox member of the Church of England and became an agnostic," de Beer noted.[2] Darwin died at age seventy-three.

Today, more than a century later, the storm still hasn't abated. Some fundamentalist groups still try to prevent evolution from being taught in public school science classes.

Darwin's Views on Religion

"The assumed instinctive belief in God has been used by many persons as an argument for his existence. But this is a rash argument, as we should thus be compelled to believe in the existence of many cruel and malignant spirits, only a little more powerful than man; for the belief in them is far more general than in a beneficent deity."—*The Descent of Man,* 1871

1. *Encyclopaedia Britannica,* 1973, vol. 7, p. 84.
2. Ibid.

"For my part, I would as soon be descended from [a] baboon . . . as from a savage who delights to torture his enemies . . . treats his wives like slaves . . . and is haunted by the grossest superstitions."—ibid.

"My theology is a simple muddle. I cannot look at the universe as the result of blind chance, yet I can see no evidence of beneficent design, or indeed of design of any kind."—writing in 1870, quoted in the 1973 *Encyclopaedia Britannica*

"I have never been an atheist in the sense of denying the existence of a God. I think that generally (& more & more so as I grow older), but not always, that an agnostic would be the most correct description of my state of mind."—letter to the Rev. J. Fordyce, July 7, 1879, quoted in *The Collector,* No. 1, 1958

"The mystery of the beginning of all things is insoluble by us; and I for one must be content to remain an agnostic."—(Seldes)

"I cannot see so plainly as others do, and as I should wish to do, evidence of design and beneficence on all sides of us. There seems to me too much misery in the world. I cannot persuade myself that a beneficent and omnipotent God would have designedly created the ichneumonidae with the express intention of their feeding within the living bodies of caterpillars, or that a cat should play with a mouse."—(Cardiff)

"Science and Christ have nothing to do with each other. I do not believe that any revelation has ever been made."—ibid.

"I do not believe in any revelation."—(Noyes)

31

Charles Dickens (1812–1870)

Charles Dickens, widely deemed the greatest English novelist, was not quite a religious skeptic, nor was he quite a believer. Perhaps he typifies the uncertainty and contradictions in millions of people. Dickens cared deeply for religion's message of compassion, and he prayed regularly; yet he attacked church dogmas and rituals, scorned nearly every faith, and temporarily joined the Unitarians, who reject the divinity of Jesus.

Biographer Edgar Johnson wrote of Dickens:

> Inclining toward Unitarianism, he had little respect for mystical religious dogma. He hated the Roman Catholic Church, "that curse upon the world," as the tool and coadjutor of oppression throughout Europe. . . . He thought the influence of the Roman Church almost altogether evil. . . . He had rejected the Church of England and detested the influence of its bishops in English politics. . . .[1]

Sparing no group, Dickens also ridiculed fundamentalist evangelicals who whooped and danced in Victorian England. He lampooned them repeatedly in his works. For example, in chapter 15 of *Dombey and Son,* the Rev. Melchisedech Howler, Minister of the Ranting Persuasion, unleashes an arm-flailing sermon in the front parlor of a private home, driving his followers into the "rapturous performance of a sacred jig," which causes the floor to collapse "through into a kitchen below, and disabling a mangle belonging to one of the fold."

Dickens has been called a "human hurricane" of literature, theater, journalism, and the lyceum. Born into a lower-middle-class religious family, he hated the two-hour worship services he was forced to attend as a child. At age twelve Dickens was removed from school and put to work in a factory, because his father had been

---

1. Edgar Johnson, *Charles Dickens: His Tragedy and Triumph* (Boston: Little, Brown, 1952), pp. 1133 and 562.

imprisoned for debts. Both experiences marked him, and later provided inspiration for his novels.

Quick-minded, Dickens became an office clerk at fifteen, then a shorthand stenographer in law courts, and finally a reporter for a liberal newspaper. He was asked to write a serial narrative to accompany comic engravings—thus *Pickwick Papers* was born. It became a sensation and propelled Dickens instantly to fame as a writer.

Dickens churned out stories, plays, novels, and essays at a frenzied pace. He also performed on the stage, and edited reform-minded magazines which attacked the privileged classes for their abandonment of England's poor. Later in life, he made Lyceum tours, enchanting crowds with theatrical readings of scenes from his fiction.

When a pious member of Parliament introduced a bill to ban all recreation and public activity on the Sabbath, Dickens exploded with a ferocious pamphlet titled *Sunday under Three Heads.* He said the "saintly law-givers lift up their hands to heaven," championing a law for piety, but "the whole of the saintly venom" would fall upon the poor, whose only enjoyment was a Sunday outing after six days of drudgery. The pamphlet sneered at the stupid bigotry in a fundamentalist church: "There is something in the sonorous quavering of the harsh voices, in the lank and hollow faces of the men and the sour solemnity of the women, which bespeaks this a stronghold of intolerant zeal and ignorant enthusiasm."

During a trip to Rome, Dickens wrote to his friend John Forster that the elaborate Catholic worship rituals of Holy Week were "a great farce" in which the pious fell to their knees in "senseless and unmeaning degradation."

Dickens quit the Anglican Church and joined a Unitarian congregation. After a few years, he resumed attending his former church, then quit again, saying: "I cannot sit under a clergyman who addresses his congregation as though he had taken a return ticket to heaven and back."

But Dickens was a living contradiction. Amid all his scorn, he cared profoundly about religion, especially Christ's advocacy of kindness. He wrote a detheologized *Life of Our Lord* for his own nine children. He also prayed daily, and urged his offspring to do likewise. A year before his death, as his youngest son, Edward, was leaving for Australia, Dickens gave him a New Testament and a letter urging him to follow Jesus. In his will, he wrote a declaration of Christian belief.

Perhaps the riddle of Dickens was best summed up by biographer Hesketh Pearson:

> His attitude to the religious beliefs of his time was as independent as his attitude to the political faiths. He accepted the teachings of Christ, not the doctrines of the Christian churches; and he would have agreed with the view that, while the congregation is more important than any individual in it, the meanest worshiper is more important than the Church.[2]

---

2. Hesketh Pearson, *Dickens: His Character, Comedy, and Career* (New York: Harper & Brothers, 1949), p. 198.

Dickens's Views on Religion

"As to the church, my friend, I am sick of it. The spectacle presented by the indecent squabbles of priests of most denominations, and by the exemplary unfairness and rancor with which they conduct their differences . . . utterly repel me."—letter to William de Cerjat, 1864

"The preacher is a coarse, hard-faced man of forbidding aspect. . . . He stretches his body half out of the pulpit, thrusts forth his arms with frantic gestures, and blasphemously calls upon the Deity to visit with eternal torments those who turn aside from the word, as interpreted and preached by—himself. A low moaning is heard, the women rock their bodies to and fro, and wring their hands."—*Sunday under Three Heads*, 1836

"The congregation fall upon their knees and are hushed into profound stillness as he delivers an extempore prayer, in which he calls upon the sacred founder of the Christian faith to bless his ministry, in terms of disgusting and impious familiarity."—(Noyes)

"And now they sit down to a cold and cheerless dinner; the pious guardians of man's salvation having, in their regard for the welfare of his precious soul, shut up the bakers' shops."—ibid.

"I believe the dissemination of Catholicity to be the most horrible means of political and social degradation left in the world."—ibid.

"It is a good example of the superstitions of the monks that this missal was placed upon a tub, which . . . was uncovered and shown to be full of dead men's bones—bones, as the monks pretended, of saints."—ibid.

"Missionaries (Livingstone always excepted) are perfect nuisances, and leave every place worse than they found it."—quoted by Jack Lindsay in *Charles Dickens: A Biographical and Critical Study* (New York: Philosophical Library, 1950), p. 39

"I have a sad misgiving that the religion of Ireland lies as deep at the root of all its sorrows, even as English misgovernment and Tory villainy."—letter to John Forster, August 1846

"For his labors in the cause of that religion which has sympathy for men of every creed and ventures to pass judgment on none."—inscription on a silver cup which Dickens gave to Unitarian minister Edward Tagart

"I now most solemnly impress upon you the truth and beauty of the Christian religion, as it came from Christ Himself."—letter to Edward Dickens, who was leaving for Australia, 1869

32

Elizabeth Cady Stanton (1815–1902)

Dover

The struggle for women's rights in America was launched largely by one brilliant, determined activist who waged the battle for a half century.

Elizabeth Cady Stanton was born in Johnstown, New York, and raised in a climate of religious severity. She was gifted, but few schools of the early 1800s admitted females; so Elizabeth's father, a judge, arranged for her to attend male-only Johnstown Academy, where she won second prize in Greek. Since no degree-granting colleges were then open to women, she attended Emma Willard's academy at Troy, New York. Studying law with her father, Elizabeth was outraged by the many laws denying women the right to own property or control their lives. Her study could not lead to a career, because women were forbidden to practice law.

Denied access to other fields, Stanton became active in the abolition and temperance movements. She married an abolitionist lawyer in 1840 and accompanied him to London to a world conference against slavery. Women delegates were refused recognition, however: renowned clergymen contended that the will of God forbade their participation. But the convention allowed the two American women attending, Stanton and Lucretia Mott, to sit behind a curtain and hear the proceedings, without speaking. This experience bonded them in a determination to fight for equality for women.

Back in America, they called an 1848 conference that marked the start of the modern women's movement. Stanton sought the right to vote, as the key to other rights. Mott felt this demand was too drastic, but Frederick Douglass exhorted both delegates to pass a suffrage resolution.

Three years later, Stanton met Susan B. Anthony, a Unitarian social activist, and they became a team crusading tirelessly for women's rights through the last half of the nineteenth century. They were joined by fellow Unitarians Lucy Stone and Ralph Waldo Emerson, and other reformers. The advocates met scorn, ridicule, threats, and even violence, but never ceased their speeches, writings, meetings, and court challenges.

As she struggled for equal rights, Stanton often scoffed at supernaturalism and called religion a millstone around the necks of women.

Stanton had seven children and a happy home life. She died eighteen years before America finally ratified the Nineteenth Amendment to the Constitution, allowing women to vote.

Stanton's Views on Religion

"The memory of my own suffering has prevented me from ever shadowing one young soul with the superstitions of the Christian religion."—*Eighty Years and More,* 1898, p. 26

"I found nothing grand in the history of the Jews nor in the morals inculcated in the Pentateuch. I know of no other books that so fully teach the subjection and degradation of women."—ibid., p. 395

"How anyone, in view of the protracted sufferings of the race, can invest the laws of the universe with a tender loving fatherly intelligence, watching, guiding and protecting humanity, is to me amazing."—letter to Henry Stanton, August 2, 1880

"The religious superstitions of women perpetuate their bondage more than all other adverse influences."—(Wilcox/George)

"The Bible and Church have been the greatest stumbling blocks in the way of women's emancipation."—*Free Thought* magazine, September 1896

"The whole tone of church teaching in regard to women is, to the last degree, contemptuous and degrading."—ibid., November 1896

"To no form of religion is woman indebted for one impulse of freedom, as all alike have taught her inferiority and subjection."—(Gray)

"I have been into many of the ancient cathedrals—grand, wonderful, mysterious. But I always leave them with a feeling of indignation because of the generations of human beings who have struggled in poverty to build these altars to an unknown god."—from her diary

"When women understand that governments and religions are human inventions; that bibles, prayer-books, catechisms, and encyclical letters are all emanations from the brain of man, they will no longer be oppressed by the injunctions that come to them with the divine authority of 'thus saith the Lord.' "—(Vernon)

"All through the centuries, scholars and scientists have been imprisoned, tortured and burned alive for some discovery which seemed to conflict with a petty text of Scripture. Surely the immutable laws of the universe can teach more impressive and exalted lessons than the holy books of all the religions on earth."—ibid.

"I can truly say that all the cares and anxieties, the trials and disappointments of my whole life, are light, when balanced with my sufferings in childhood and youth from the theological dogmas which I sincerely believed, and the gloom connected with everything associated with the name of religion."—ibid.

"Out of the doctrine of original sin grew the crimes and miseries of asceticism, celibacy and witchcraft; woman becoming the helpless victim of all these delusions."—(Bufe)

"Throughout this protracted and disgraceful assault on American womanhood, the clergy baptized each new insult and act of injustice in the name of the Christian religion, and uniformly asked God's blessing on proceedings that would have put to shame an assembly of Hottentots."—a statement "for the betterment of woman" signed by Stanton, Susan B. Anthony, and Matilda Gage

"How can any woman believe that a loving and merciful God would, in one breath, command Eve to multiply and replenish the earth, and in the next, pronounce a curse upon her maternity? I do not believe that God inspired the Mosaic code, or gave out the laws about women which he is accused of doing."—(Cardiff)

"The Bible contains some of the most sublime passages in English literature, but is also full of contradictions, inconsistencies and absurdities."—ibid.

"The Christian church has throughout the ages used its influence in opposition to the freedom of woman."—ibid.

"All the men of the Old Testament were polygamists, and Christ and Paul, the central figures of the New Testament, were celibates, and condemned marriage by both precept and example."—ibid.

"Every form of religion which has breathed upon this earth has degraded woman. Man himself could not do this; but when he declares, 'Thus saith the Lord,' of course he can do it."—quoted by Madalyn Murray O'Hair in *Women and Atheism*

"Only those who have lived all their lives under the dark clouds of vague, undefined fears can appreciate the joy of a doubting soul suddenly born into the kingdom of reason and free thought. Is the bondage of the priest-ridden less galling than that of the slave, because we do not see the chains, the indelible scars, the festering wounds, the deep degradation of all the powers of the God-like mind?" —1860

"The real difficulty in woman's case is that the whole foundation of the Christian religion rests on her temptation and man's fall."—(Noyes)

"Through theological superstitions, woman finds her most grievous bondage."
—ibid.

"Among the clergy we find our most violent enemies, those most opposed to any change in woman's position."—ibid.

"I decline to accept Hebrew mythology as a guide to twentieth-century science."
—ibid.

33

Henry David Thoreau (1817–1862)

Library of Congress collection

Theologically, Henry David Thoreau was a thorough muddle. He penned scornful jabs at churches and preachers. He withdrew from one church and never joined another. He was labeled a pantheist, a transcendentalist, and even an atheist. Yet he contradicted himself frequently. He was worshipful toward nature. He spoke often of God—but sometimes he seemed to be speaking poetically of the teeming energy of life and stars. Like many people, Thoreau was erratic in religious thought.

Thoreau was born in Concord, Massachusetts, and spent most of his life there. His father was a bumbling pencil-maker, yet the family found enough money to send Henry to Harvard. He graduated in 1837 and tried teaching, but that post lasted only two weeks. He joined his father in pencil-making, then operated a school with his brother.

During the early 1800s, New England had been swept by a wave of Unitarianism. About 125 historic Congregational churches adopted the new faith. Although the early Unitarians were only slightly less orthodox than their predecessors, conservatives in the flocks quit to rejoin traditional churches.

Thoreau's parents remained in Unitarian First Parish in Concord. Henry also attended services there, especially to be near a young woman he was courting. But in 1841 Thoreau signed a formal statement ending his membership. Part of the reason may have been his annoyance that the church failed to take a strong stand against slavery. Thereafter, Thoreau associated with "come-outers," i.e., church dropouts.

Enchanted by nature, Thoreau decided to be a poet and writer. He had scant success, until he became friends with Ralph Waldo Emerson, a former Unitarian minister who had renounced the church a decade earlier. Emerson invited Thoreau to live in his Concord home while Thoreau pursued his writing.

Emerson was the hub of an intellectual clique of transcendentalists, thinkers who felt that intuition and emotions, as well as reason, are a reliable source of knowledge. (Biographer Henry Canby said the group consisted of "a great man at the center and amiable lunatics on the fringe."[1]) The group published a magazine, *The Dial,* which printed many of Thoreau's works. Other journals also began printing him. And he kept many diaries and notebooks.

Writing about missionaries to Canadian Indians, Thoreau said he saw no point in trying "to convert the Algonquins from their own superstitions to new ones." In another passage, he said it is appropriate for a church to be the ugliest building in a village, "because it is the one in which human nature stoops to the lowest and is the most disgraced."[2] Elsewhere, Thoreau stated that orthodox Christians think they love God, but actually love only his old clothes, "of which they make scarecrows for the children." He also spoke of "the Christian fable."

Horace Greeley published Thoreau's pieces in the *New York Tribune* and helped place his articles in magazines. But some were rebuffed because of what Greeley, addressing Thoreau, called "your defiant pantheism."

Some biographers think Thoreau was infatuated with Emerson's wife, Lidian, who had a devout streak. In 1843, while living briefly in New York, Thoreau wrote to Emerson that Lidian "almost persuades me to be a Christian, but I fear I as often lapse into heathenism."

In 1845, Thoreau built a hut on Emerson's property beside Walden Pond and lived in it for two years, communing with nature and producing his best writing. While there, he refused to pay his poll tax, in defiance of the government's militarism and tolerance of slavery. For this Thoreau was jailed overnight, thus becoming a pioneer of civil disobedience. He helped runaway slaves fleeing northward via the Underground Railroad.

In failing health, Thoreau lived with relatives. As he neared death, an aunt asked if he had made his peace with God. "I did not know that we had ever quarreled," he replied. When a friend asked about his hope for the hereafter, he said only, "One world at a time."

Thoreau's Comments on Religion

"Your church is a baby-house made of blocks."—*On the Duty of Civil Disobedience,* 1849

"I did not see why the schoolmaster should be taxed to support the priest, and not the priest the schoolmaster."—ibid.

---

1. Henry Canby, *Thoreau* (Boston: Houghton-Mifflin Co., 1939), p. 85.
2. Quoted in Edward Wagenknecht, *Henry David Thoreau: What Manner of Man?* (Amherst: University of Massachusetts Press, 1981), pp. 156–57.

"Trade curses everything it handles; and though you trade in messages from heaven, the whole curse of trade attaches to the business."—*Walden,* 1854

"Heaven might be defined as the place which men avoid."—*Excursions,* 1863

"There may be gods, but they care not what men do. I say—one world at a time."—(Cardiff)

"It is a sad mistake to acknowledge the personality of God."—(Noyes)

"There is more religion in man's science than there is science in his religion." —ibid.

"It must be submitted to the D.D.s [Doctors of Divinity]. I would it were the chickadees."—ibid.

"And I swear by the rood, I will be slave to no God."—ibid.

"The preachers deal with men of straw, as they are men of straw themselves." —ibid.

"What is it you tolerate, you church today? Not truth but a lifelong hypocrisy." —ibid.

"I have known many a man who pretended to be a Christian, in whom it was ridiculous."—quoted by Wagenknecht in *Henry David Thoreau: What Manner of Man?* p. 159

"The love of Nature and fullest perception of the revelation which she is to man is not compatible with the belief in the peculiar revelation of the Bible."—ibid., p. 161

"Jesus Christ . . . taught mankind but imperfectly how to live; his thoughts were all directed to another world. There is another kind of success than his."—ibid., p. 161

"My profession is to be always on the alert to find God in nature, to know his lurking-places, to attend all the oratorios, the operas, in nature."—ibid., p. 155

34

George Eliot (1819–1880)

In the Victorian era, when few public roles were open to women, a powerful "male" novelist was actually a woman writing under a pseudonym.

George Eliot now ranks among the immortals of literature. Today's schoolchildren are taught how she published under a man's name—but they do not learn that she scorned religion and lived much of her life "in sin" with a man she was not married to.

Born Mary Anne Evans in Warwickshire, England, she later compressed her name to Marian. The daughter of an ardently pious family, Marian attended a Baptist school where she developed fervent faith as a child. But reading the works of Sir Walter Scott shattered her simplistic orthodoxy. Her keen mind was drawn to rationalist books, and she befriended a freethinking couple, Charles and Caroline Bray.

Marian refused to accompany her family to church, and wrote her father a letter saying that it would be "vile hypocrisy" for her to "pretend to worship." The resulting family storm forced her to leave home briefly, but a compromise was reached: she returned home free to think as she wished, as long as she maintained a facade of respectability through church attendance. She did so, until her father died in 1849.

Meanwhile, at the home of the Brays, Marian met leading intellectuals such as Ralph Waldo Emerson, reformer Robert Owen, and publisher John Chapman. She translated German freethought books that were published by Chapman. When he bought the *Westminster Review,* he made Marian an editor; thereafter the journal flourished due to her brilliant writing. She had a brief romance with philosopher Herbert Spencer, one of the *Review*'s contributors.

Radical journalist George Henry Lewes and his wife practiced free love, but after she bore two children by another man, the marital bond evaporated. Lewes moved out, although English law prevented him from obtaining a divorce, since he had condoned her adultery. He and Marian Evans fell passionately in love, and lived openly as common-law husband and wife.

Encouraged by Lewes, she began writing fiction, which he submitted to publishers under the pseudonym George Eliot. Her stories were popular, and she turned to novels. The first, *Adam Bede,* was a brilliant success that went through eight printings in a year and was translated into five languages. She followed with *Silas Marner, The Mill on the Floss, Middlemarch,* and other renowned works. Fame attached to the novels caused inquiry about the author, and her identity soon leaked out.

Lewes and Eliot were a devoted couple. After he died in 1878, she collapsed in grief. A young friend, John Cross, aided her during the crisis. They eventually were married, but she died a few months later.

Herbert Spencer sought to have Eliot buried in the Poet's Corner of Westminster Abbey, but her agnosticism made it impossible. Her friends buried her in an unconsecrated cemetery beside Lewes. One of them, Thomas Henry Huxley, wrote: "George Eliot is known not only as a great writer, but as a person whose life and opinions were in notorious antagonism to Christian practice in regard to marriage, and Christian theory in regard to dogmas."

Eliot's Comments on Religion

"I could not without vile hypocrisy and a miserable truckling to the smile of the world . . . profess to join in worship which I wholly disapprove."—letter to her father, February 1842, explaining her refusal to attend church

"Given, a man with moderate intellect, a moral standard not higher than the average, some rhetorical affluence and a great glibness of speech, what is the career in which, without the aid of birth or money, he may most easily attain power and reputation in English society? Where is that Goshen of mediocrity in which a smattering of science and learning will pass for profound instruction, where platitudes will be accepted as wisdom, bigoted narrowness as holy zeal, unctuous egoism as God-given piety?"—"Evangelical Teaching: Dr. Cumming," an essay ridiculing the career of evangelism, printed in *Westminster Review,* 1850s

"Minds fettered by this doctrine no longer inquire concerning a proposition whether it is attested by sufficient evidence, but whether it accords with Scripture; they do not search for facts as such, but for facts that will bear out their doctrine. It is easy to see that this mental habit blunts not only the perception of truth, but the sense of truthfulness, and that the man whose faith drives him into fallacies treads close upon the precipice of falsehood. . . . So long as a belief in propositions is regarded as indispensable to salvation, the pursuit of truth *as such* is not possible."—ibid.

"Your dunce who can't do his sums always has a taste for the infinite."—*Felix Holt, the Radical,* 1860

"God, immortality, duty—how inconceivable the first, how unbelievable the second, how peremptory and absolute the third."—(Cardiff)

"It is time the clergy are told that thinking men, after a close examination of that doctrine [Christianity], pronounce it to be subversive of true moral development and, therefore, positively noxious."—ibid.

"A perverted moral judgment belongs to the dogmatic system."—ibid.

"Subtract from the New Testament the miraculous and highly impossible, and what will be the remainder?"—ibid.

"When the soul is just liberated from the wretched giant's bed of dogmas on which it has been racked and stretched ever since it began to think, there is a feeling of exultation and strong hope."—ibid.

"Fatally powerful as religious systems have been, human nature is stronger and wider, and though dogmas may hamper they cannot absolutely repress its growth."—ibid.

" 'Heaven help us,' said the old religion; the new one, from its very lack of that faith, will teach us all the more to help one another."—ibid.

"I am influenced at the present time by far higher considerations and by a nobler idea of duty than I ever was when I held the Evangelical belief."—ibid.

"My childhood was full of deep sorrows—colic, whooping-cough, dread of ghosts, hell, Satan, and a Deity in the sky who was angry when I ate too much plum-cake."—(Noyes)

35

Matthew Arnold (1822–1888)

During the exquisite era of Victorian poetry—one largely forgotten by today's video-crazed society—Matthew Arnold stood as a towering figure. He was eloquent in fathoming the human psyche, and in lamenting his loss of religious faith.

The son of the schoolmaster of the famed Rugby academy for boys, Arnold won writing prizes at Oxford, was appointed a national inspector of schools, and also taught poetry at Oxford. His career as a poet, and later an essayist, was pursued during off-hours.

Arnold's writing covered a myriad of topics. Religious doubt was a recurring theme, usually tinged with regret. In the poem "Dover Beach," he ponders the timeless ocean and reflects upon the vanishing "sea of faith." Without the solace of religion, Arnold concludes that the only comfort is for lovers to cling together, forming a shared sanctuary in the chaotic world "where ignorant armies clash by night."

In "Stanzas From the Grande Chartreuse," he ponders the Greek gods and "some fallen Runic stone—For both were faiths, and both are gone." As for himself, bereft of deities, he is "Wandering between two worlds, one dead, / The other powerless to be born."

With belief in the supernatural no longer possible, Arnold sought to substitute the kindness of Jesus as a purely human morality. But this outraged orthodox believers. Poet T. S. Eliot, a Catholic, later protested that Arnold wanted "to get all the emotional kick out of Christianity one can, without the bother of believing it. . . . The total effect of Arnold's philosophy is to set up Culture in the place of Religion."

Regardless, Arnold saw a world in which religion was losing its power to dominate societies and control people's minds. He said in "Dover Beach":

> The Sea of Faith
> Was once, too, at the full, and round earth's shore
> Lay like the folds of a bright girdle furl'd

But now I only hear
Its melancholy, long, withdrawing roar
Retreating. . . .

Arnold's Comments on Religion

"It is almost impossible to exaggerate the proneness of the human mind to take miracles as evidence, and to seek for miracles as evidence."—*Literature and Dogma,* 1873

"Miracles do not happen."—ibid., preface to the edition of 1883

"The personages of the Christian heaven and their conversations are no more matter of fact than the personages of the Greek Olympus and their conversations."—preface to *God and the Bible*

"Rigorous teachers seized my youth / And purged its faith, and trimm'd its fire / Show'd me the high, white star of Truth."—*Stanzas From the Grande Chartreuse*

". . . Your faith is now / But a dead time's exploded dream."—ibid.

" 'Christ,' some one says, 'was human as we are / No judge eyes us from Heaven, our sin to scan / We live no more, when we have done our span.' "—"The Better Part," 1867

"Pious fiction is still fiction."—"Amiel," an essay on Henri-Frédéric Amiel

"Be neither saint nor sophist led, but be a man."—(Cardiff)

"All the biblical miracles will at last disappear with the progress of science."—ibid.

"The theological faculty of the University of Paris, the leading medieval university, discussed seriously whether Jesus at his ascension had his clothes on or not. If he had not, did he appear before his apostles naked? If he had, what became of the clothes?"—(Noyes)

"All things seem to have what we call a law of their beings; whether we call this God or not is a matter of choice."—ibid.

"Protestant ministers cried out against Galileo's assertion of the earth's movement just as loudly as Catholic priests."—ibid.

"The church, as it now stands, no power can save."—ibid.

"So deeply unsound is the mass of traditions and imaginations of which popular religion consists, that future times will hardly comprehend its audacity in calling those who abjure it atheists."—ibid.

36

Thomas Henry
Huxley
(1825–1895)

After Charles Darwin's theory of evolution jarred religion in 1859, the clergy fought back with angry denunciations. The shy, ailing Darwin declined to defend himself, so a fellow English scientist took his place in debates against theologians. Thus was Thomas Henry Huxley thrust to the fore as a champion of science against religion—a role that earned him a niche in history.

Earlier in life, Huxley had been a self-taught medical student who signed aboard the H.M.S. *Rattlesnake* as assistant surgeon for a four-year trip around the world. He studied animal life during the journey and began publishing scientific articles. He also studied philosophers opposed to supernatural religion. After returning to England, Huxley became a teacher, lecturer, and a friend of scientists, including Darwin.

Huxley endorsed Darwin's principle of natural selection and gladly defended him in an 1860 debate against Bishop Samuel Wilberforce. The bishop scornfully asked whether Huxley was descended from an ape on his mother's or father's side. Huxley replied that he would prefer a guileless ape to a clever human who used his intellect "for the mere purpose of introducing ridicule into grave scientific discussion."

Thereafter, Huxley wrote and spoke constantly in defense of scientific inquiry, as opposed to biblical accounts of the world's origins. In an 1889 magazine article, he said he coined the word *agnostic* by adding the negative prefix "a-" to the name of the ancient Gnostics (meaning "those who know") who sought salvation through occultism. The new word fit people who felt it was impossible to know whether invisible gods, devils, heavens, and hells exist. (English freethinker George Jacob Holyoake also claimed to have coined the term.)

After his death, Huxley's legacy continued in a remarkable way through three famous grandsons. One, Aldous Huxley, became a renowned novelist. Another, Sir Julian Huxley, was a biologist who sought to demystify religion, and who became the first director-general of UNESCO. The third, physiologist Henry Fielding Huxley, shared a 1963 Nobel Prize for discoveries of nerve cell functions. Aldous and Julian likewise became critics of supernatural religion. Their skeptical remarks are printed later in this chapter.

Thomas Henry Huxley's Comments on Religion

"The dogma of the infallibility of the Bible is no more self-evident than is that of the infallibility of the popes."—*Controverted Questions,* 1892

"[Regarding Protestantism:] From Wyclif to Socinus, or even to Muntzer, Rothmann and John of Leyden, I fail to find a trace of any desire to set reason free. The most that can be discovered is a proposal to change masters. From being a slave of the papacy, the intellect was to become the serf of the Bible."—ibid.

"When I reached intellectual maturity and began to ask myself whether I was an atheist, a theist, or a pantheist; a materialist or an idealist; a Christian or a freethinker, I found that the more I learned and reflected, the less ready was the answer; until, at last, I came to the conclusion that I had neither art nor part with any of these denominations, except the last. . . . So I took thought, and invented what I conceived to be the appropriate title of 'agnostic.' It came into my head as suggestively antithetic to the 'gnostic' of church history, who professed to know so much about the very things of which I was ignorant."—"Agnosticism," reprinted in *An Anthology of Atheism and Rationalism,* edited by Gordon Stein (Amherst, N.Y.: Prometheus Books, 1980)

"Agnosticism, in fact, is not a creed, but a method, the essence of which lies in the rigorous application of a single principle . . . the axiom that every man should be able to give a reason for the faith that is in him."—ibid.

"In matters of the intellect, follow your reason as far as it will take you, without any other consideration. And negatively, in matters of the intellect do not pretend that conclusions are certain which are not demonstrated or demonstrable. That I take to be the agnostic faith, which if a man keep whole and undefiled, he shall not be ashamed to look the universe in the face, whatever the future may have in store for him."—ibid.

"It is wrong for a man to say that he is certain of the objective truth of any proposition unless he can produce evidence which logically justifies that certainty. This is what agnosticism asserts; and, in my opinion, it is all that is essential to agnosticism."—*Agnosticism and Christianity,* 1889

"Rome is the one great spiritual organization which is able to resist—and must, as a matter of life and death—the progress of science and modern civilization."— speech at Liverpool, 1869

"The clergy are at present divisible into three sections: an immense body who are ignorant and speak out; a small proportion who know and are silent; and a minute minority who know and speak according to their knowledge."—ibid.

"I neither deny nor affirm the immortality of man. I see no reason for believing in it, but, on the other hand, I have no means of disproving it."—letter to Charles Kingsley, 1860

"It would be well if ecclesiastical persons would reflect that ordination, whatever deep-seated graces it may confer, has never been observed to be followed by any visible increase in the learning or the logic of its subject."—*On the Hypothesis That Animals Are Automata,* 1874

"Every great advance in natural knowledge has involved the absolute rejection of authority."—(Wilcox/George)

"What are among the moral convictions most fondly held by barbarous and semi-barbarous people? They are the convictions that authority is the soundest basis of belief; that merit attaches to readiness to believe; that the doubting disposition is a bad one, and skepticism is a sin."—ibid.

"The deepest sin against the human mind is to believe things without evidence." —(Seldes)

"I have no faith, very little hope, and as much charity as I can afford."—(Cardiff)

"Agnosticism simply means that a man shall not say he knows or believes that for which he has no grounds for professing to believe."—ibid.

The man of science has learned to believe in justification, not by faith, but by verification."—ibid.

" 'Infidel' is a term of reproach which Christians and Mohammedans, in their modesty, agree to apply to those who differ from them."—ibid.

"The Bible account of the creation of Eve is a preposterous fable."—ibid.

"The ecclesiastical system is the deadly enemy of science."—ibid.

"The most remarkable achievement of the Jew was to impose on Europe for eighteen centuries his own superstitions."—ibid.

"The foundation of morality is to . . . give up pretending to believe that for which there is no evidence, and repeating unintelligible propositions about things beyond the possibilities of knowledge."—*Essays on Controversial Questions,* 1889

"Evolution excludes creation and all other kinds of supernatural interventions." —(Noyes)

"Extinguished theologians lie about the cradle of every science as the strangled snakes beside that of Hercules."—ibid.

"I know that I am, in spite of myself, exactly what the Christian would call, and, so far as I can see, is justified in calling, atheist and infidel."—ibid.

"I cannot see one shadow or tittle of evidence that the great unknown underlying the phenomena of the universe stands to us in the relation of a father, who loves us and cares for us as Christianity asserts."—ibid.

"In Japan, in China, in Hindustan, in Greece or in Rome, we find underlying all other theological notions the belief in ghosts."—ibid.

"Skepticism is the highest duty and blind faith the one unpardonable sin."—ibid.

"The geologist . . . wisely keeps both eyes on facts and ignores the Pentateuchal mythology altogether."—ibid.

"The physical world is made up of atoms and ether. There is no room in it for ghosts."—ibid.

Julian Huxley (1887–1975)

"A personal god, be he Jehovah, or Allah, or Apollo, or Amen-Ra, or without name but simply God, I know nothing of. What is more, I am not merely agnostic on the subject. It seems to me quite clear that the idea of personality in God or in any supernatural being or beings has been put there by man. . . . Therefore I disbelieve in a personal God in any sense in which that phrase is ordinarily used. For similar reasons, I disbelieve in the existence of Heaven or Hell in any conventional Christian sense. As for any pretended knowledge about the Last Judgment, or the conditions of existence in Purgatory, it could be disregarded as what it is, mythology from racial childhood, and left to die a natural death, if it did not require to be attacked as the too-frequent cause of unfortunate practical effects, such as causing believers to pay money to priests for the supposed benefit of souls in another world. As to the existence of another world or another life at all, there I am simply agnostic. I do not know. I find extreme difficulties, in the light of physiological and psychological knowledge, in understanding how a soul could exist apart from a body. . . ."—*Religion without Revelation,* 1927, rev. 1956 (New York: Mentor, 1958), p. 18

"God is one among several hypotheses to account for the phenomena of human destiny, and it is now proving to be an inadequate hypothesis. To a great many people, including myself, this realization is a great relief, both intellectually and morally. It frees us to explore the real phenomena for which the God hypothesis seeks to account, to define them more accurately, and to work for a more satisfying set of concepts. . . ."—ibid., preface

"... Religion of the highest and fullest character can co-exist with a complete absence of belief in revelation in any straightforward sense of the word, and of belief in that kernel of revealed religion, a personal god."—ibid., p. 13

"The closing months of the year A.D. 999 were accompanied by the most improbable scenes of orgy, terror, and prayer, owing to the belief that the world would end at the millennium; and even in our time the members of an American sect sold all their possessions very cheap and went to await the end of the world and a translation to heaven on a convenient hilltop. Experience has quite definitely shown (if only humanity could be persuaded to profit by her!) that some reasons for holding a belief are much more likely to be justified by the event than others."—ibid., p. 15

"Newton showed that gods did not control the movements of the planets; Laplace in a famous aphorism affirmed that astronomy had no need of the god hypothesis; Darwin and Pasteur between them did the same for biology; and in our own century, the rise of scientific psychology and the extension of historical knowledge have removed gods to a position where they are no longer of value in interpreting human behavior and cannot be supposed to control human history or interfere with human affairs. . . . Operationally, God is beginning to resemble not a ruler, but the last fading smile of a cosmic Cheshire Cat."—ibid., p. 58

"The supernatural is being swept out of the universe in the flood of new knowledge of what is natural. It will soon be as impossible for an intelligent, educated man or woman to believe in a god as it is now to believe that the earth is flat, that flies can be spontaneously generated, that disease is a divine punishment, or that death is always due to witchcraft."—ibid., p. 62

"We are used to discounting the river-gods and dryads of the Greeks as poetical fancies, and even the chief figures in the classical Pantheon—Venus, Minerva, Mars, and the rest—as allegories. But, forgetting that they once carried as much sanctity as our saints and divinities, we refrain from applying the same reasoning to our own objects of worship."—ibid., p. 90

"... Have nothing to do with Absolutes, including absolute truth, absolute morality, absolute perfection and absolute authority."—*The Humanist Frame,* 1961

"The solution . . . would seem to lie in dismantling the theistic edifice, which will no longer bear the weight of the universe as enlarged by recent science, and attempting to find new outlets for the religious spirit. God, in any but a purely philosophical—and one is almost tempted to say Pickwickian—sense, turns out to be a product of the human mind. As an independent or unitary being active in the affairs of the universe, he does not exist."—*Science, Religion and Human Nature,* Conway Memorial Lecture, 1930

"Prayers for rain are still offered in church, but very few people (and no Humanists) believe that God has any influence on the weather. We know that there is no hell full of devils inside the earth, and nothing like the traditional orthodox Christian idea of heaven up in the sky."—(Greeley)

"Another conflict is that between the passion for getting at the truth that characterizes some great minds, including the highest type of scientific mind, and the tendency to assert and believe what we desire, which is found in so many human beings and so many religious beliefs."—ibid.

"The Mississippi floods are terrible; but they are not divine vengeance which ruins the innocent with the guilty. Bubonic plague or influenza will not be stayed with prayers. . . ."—ibid.

Aldous Huxley (1894–1963)

"If we must play the theological game, let us never forget that it is a game. Religion, it seems to me, can survive only as a consciously accepted system of make-believe."—*Texts and Pretexts,* 1932

"You never see animals going through the absurd and often horrible fooleries of magic and religion. . . . Dogs do not ritually urinate in the hope of persuading heaven to do the same and send down rain. Asses do not bray a liturgy to cloudless skies. Nor do cats attempt, by abstinence from cat's meat, to wheedle the feline spirits into benevolence. Only man behaves with such gratuitous folly. It is the price he has to pay for being intelligent but not, as yet, quite intelligent enough."—"Amor Fati," in *Texts and Pretexts*

"History reveals the Church and the State as a pair of indispensable Molochs. They protect their worshiping subjects, only to enslave and destroy them."—"Variations on a Philosopher," in *Themes and Variations,* 1950

"Jerusalem is . . . the slaughterhouse of the religions. . . . [One is touched by] the hopelessness of the inhabitants of Jerusalem, for whom the holiest of cities is a prison of chronic despair punctuated by occasional panic when the hand grenades start flying. . . ."—in *Encounter* magazine, London, December 1955

"I'm all for sticking pins into episcopal behinds."—quoted by Peter McWilliams in *Ain't Nobody's Business If You Do,* p. 326

"Mr. Mercaptan went on to preach a brilliant sermon on that melancholy sexual perversion known as continence."—ibid., p. 442

37

Leo Tolstoy (1828–1910)

Many people who reject supernatural Christianity nonetheless embrace Christ's message of compassion. Tolstoy carried this pattern to an extreme. He renounced organized religion and was excommunicated by the Russian Orthodox Church—yet he became almost a monk, living in service to others.

Regarded by some as the greatest novelist of all time, Tolstoy was born to wealth as a landed count who enjoyed the privileges of Russia's aristocracy under the czars. He served as a military officer in the Crimean War, married a loving young wife, and fathered many children. His profoundly moving novels and short stories brought him fame and even greater wealth.

Yet Tolstoy was wracked by growing moral pangs, mostly over the cruel inequality of Russian life. It distressed him to live in well-fed comfort while peasants half-starved. When aristocratic women in low-cut gowns partied while their coachmen shivered outside in the snow, he felt a deep sense of wrong. It troubled him that peasants were cannon fodder in wars and that priests in ermine, gold, and jewels were as parasitic as the nobles.

When in his forties, Tolstoy went through what biographer Nathan Dole called a "soul-storm," a religious rebellion as sweeping as his fictional epics.[1] Increasingly, he doubted Orthodox Christianity and despised its lofty power in Russia. He temporarily ceased writing fiction and produced nonconformist books such as *Critique of Dogmatic Theology* and *My Confession*. He declared that Christ was only human, that miracles are not real, and that humanity does not survive death. He accused priests of perverting the humane message of Jesus into a ruthless vehicle of power. Tolstoy called the Church an "impenetrable forest of stupidity" and a "conscious deception that serves as a means for one part of the people to govern the other."[2]

---

1. Nathan Haskell Dole, *The Life of Lyof N. Tolstoy* (New York: Charles Scribner's Sons, 1923), p. 300.

2. Tikhon Polner, *Tolstoy and His Wife* (New York: W. W. Norton, 1945), p. 126.

Ecclesiastical censors banned the publication of these books and ordered the manuscripts burned. But copies were smuggled out of Russia, printed abroad, and returned to Russia, where they circulated clandestinely. Priests duly began denouncing Tolstoy as an "impious infidel" and demanded his imprisonment. But his immense popularity made him untouchable.

Tolstoy became obsessed with helping others. He dropped his noble title, wore peasant clothes, refused to let servants tend him, made his own boots, and worked in fields alongside laborers. He wanted to give away all his possessions, but his wife and children protested, so he signed over everything in their names. He ceased accepting money for his writing. When famine swept rural provinces, the czar and the Church denied that it was occurring; but Tolstoy organized mass feeding kitchens, for which he was rebuked from the nation's pulpits.

Tolstoy helped free "old believer" bishops who had been imprisoned for their religion. ("Old believers" were dissident Christians who refused to accept changes that the Russian Orthodox Church had imposed in the seventeenth century.) He also defended the persecuted Dukhobors, religious oddballs who removed their clothes and set fire to their homes as protests. He resumed accepting money for his books, but used the funds to help eight thousand Dukhobors move to Canada. Tolstoy's ideal of simple, compassionate living attracted followers, who created their own communes. Some were jailed as dangerous radicals by priests and czarist police for criticizing the church and refusing military service.

In 1901, patriarchs of the Holy Synod ordered priests to deny church rituals to the aging writer. They officially excommunicated him in a decree of anathema which stated:

> . . . He [Tolstoy] denies the living and personal God glorified in the Holy Trinity, Creator and Providence of the universe; he refutes Our Lord Jesus Christ, God made Man, Redeemer and Savior of the world, who suffered for us and for our salvation, and who has been raised from the dead; he refutes the Immaculate Conception of the human manifestation of Christ the Lord, and the virginity, before and after the Nativity, of Mary, Mother of God, most pure and eternally virgin; he does not believe in the life hereafter or in judgment after death; he refutes all the Mysteries of the Church and their beneficial effect; and, flaunting the most sacred articles of faith of the Orthodox community, he has not feared to mock the greatest of all mysteries: the Holy Eucharist. . . .

The excommunication had little effect on Tolstoy, who continued writing. He was more severely affected by conflict with his wife over his desire for monkish poverty. Finally, at age eighty-two, he left home to find a hermit-like refuge, but soon caught pneumonia and died.

Tolstoy's Comments on Religion

". . . To regard Christ as God, and to pray to him, are to my mind the greatest possible sacrilege."—letter to the Holy Synod, April 4, 1901, in response to his excommunication

"A peasant dies calmly because he is not a Christian. He performs the rituals as a matter of course, but his true religion is different. His religion is nature, with which he has lived."—quoted by Polner, *Tolstoy and His Wife,* p. 114

"Why must children die? I have reached the conclusion that the only purpose in the life of every man is to strengthen love within himself, and by strengthening it within himself, to infect other people with it."—after the death of his seven-year-old son, ibid., p. 170

"I am convinced that the teaching of the church is in theory a crafty and evil lie, and in practice a concoction of gross superstition and witchcraft."—(Cardiff)

"We have become so accustomed to the religious lie that surrounds us that we do not notice the atrocity, stupidity and cruelty with which the teaching of the Christian church is permeated."—ibid.

"It is true, I deny an incomprehensible Trinity, and the fable regarding the fall of man, which is absurd in our day. It is true, I deny the sacrilegious story of a God born of a virgin to redeem the race."—ibid.

"If there is no higher reason—and there is none—then my own reason must be the supreme judge of my life."—*My Confession,* 1882

"Religious superstition consists in the belief that the sacrifices, often of human lives, made to the imaginary being are essential, and that men may and should be brought to that state of mind by all methods, not excluding violence."—*The Slavery of Our Times,* 1900

"Freethinkers are those who are willing to use their minds without prejudice and without fearing to understand things that clash with their own customs, privileges, or beliefs. This state of mind is not common, but it is essential for right thinking; where it is absent, discussion is apt to become worse than useless."—*War and Peace,* 1862

"The Christian churches and Christianity have nothing in common save in name: they are utterly hostile opposites. The churches are arrogance, violence, usurpation, rigidity, death; Christianity is humility, penitence, submissiveness, progress, life."—*The Kingdom of God Is within You,* 1893

"The religious superstition is encouraged by means of the institution of churches, processions, monuments, festivities. . . . The so-called clergy stupefy the masses.

. . . They befog the people and keep them in an eternal condition of stupefaction."—ibid.

"One may say with one's lips: 'I believe that God is one, and also three'—but no one can believe it, because the words have no sense."—*What Is Religion?* 1902)

"I was taught the soldier's trade, that is, to resist evil by homicide; the army to which I belonged . . . was sent forth with a Christian benediction."—quoted by Carol Z. Rothkopf in *Immortals of Literature: Leo Tolstoy* (New York: Franklin Watts Inc., 1968), p. 102

"The teaching of the church, theoretically astute, is a lie in practice and a compound of vulgar superstitions and sorcery."—(Noyes)

"Church teachings are but fiction. I have knowledge of their inanity."—ibid.

"The educated minority, although no longer believing in the existing religious teaching, still pretend to believe."—ibid.

38

Robert Green Ingersoll (1833–1899)

Dover

No other American had a career like that of the amazing Robert Ingersoll, the premier lecturer in an era when public speeches were a major form of mass entertainment and education. Called "the American Demosthenes" and "the Shakespeare of oratory," he drew audiences as great as fifty thousand in a quarter century of touring the nation.

Ingersoll was a self-educated dynamo who might have become a national political figure, had he not felt compelled to declare, over and over, in city after city, that religion is childish superstition which impedes human progress.

He was born in Dresden, New York, the son of an abolitionist Congregationalist minister who moved from state to state. Although he had had little formal education, Ingersoll read voraciously and was admitted to the Illinois bar in 1854. He and his brother, Ebon Clark, opened a lucrative law practice in Peoria, where Robert met and married an avowed atheist's strong-spirited daughter, who influenced him greatly.

In the 1850s, Ingersoll opposed slavery and became a champion of women's rights. He addressed a suffrage meeting led by Susan B. Anthony. He also quit the Democratic party because it embraced slavery, and joined the Republicans, largely because of his admiration for Abraham Lincoln.

During the Civil War, Ingersoll rose to the rank of colonel and headed the 11th Illinois cavalry, but he was captured with his troop and sent home as a parolee. After the war, he was selected as attorney general of Illinois and became a vivid speaker for Republican candidates in elections around America. He moved his law practice to Washington and then to New York City.

Meanwhile, Ingersoll had been giving public lectures in the cause that stirred him most: the struggle against supernaturalism. He began denouncing religion in lecture halls; soon he was crisscrossing the nation as a controversial but popular speaker. As a supporter of the evolutionary theory, he was called a "bulldog for Darwin."

Ingersoll perfected more than thirty skeptical lectures with titles such as "Why I Am an Agnostic" and "The Liberty of Man, Woman and Child." Paid as much as $3,500 for a single talk, he earned the equivalent of one million dollars a year in today's dollars. He became friends with many scientists, writers, and human rights leaders of his day. He might even have been elected governor of Illinois or gained a cabinet appointment in Washington, had he not claimed his agnosticism. Such a public declaration of disbelief was tantamount to political suicide, then as now.

Although fundamentalist clergymen deemed Ingersoll a devil, none could point to any blemish in his personal morals. Since his untimely death in 1899, he has been somewhat of a saint of rationalist humanism in America.

Ingersoll's Views on Religion

"It has always seemed absurd to suppose that a god would choose for his companions, during all eternity, the dear souls whose highest and only ambition is to obey."—"Individuality"

"Who at the present day can imagine the courage, the devotion to principle, the intellectual and moral grandeur it once required to be an infidel, to brave the Church, her racks, her fagots, her dungeons, her tongues of fire—to defy and scorn her heaven and her hell—her devil and her God?"—ibid.

"The Church hates a thinker precisely for the same reason a robber dislikes a sheriff, or a thief despises the prosecuting witness."—ibid.

"Heresy is what the minority believe; it is the name given by the powerful to the doctrines of the weak."—"Heretics and Heresies"

"Who can estimate the misery that has been caused by this infamous doctrine of eternal punishment? Think of the lives it has blighted—of the tears it has caused—of the agony it has produced. Think of the millions who have been driven to insanity by this most terrible of dogmas. This doctrine renders God the basest and most cruel being in the universe. . . . There is nothing more degrading than to worship such a god."—ibid.

". . . I would have the pope throw away his tiara, take off his sacred vestments, and admit that he is not acting for God—is not infallible—but is just an ordinary Italian. I would have all the cardinals, archbishops, bishops, priests and clergymen admit that they know nothing about theology, nothing about hell or heaven, nothing about the destiny of the human race, nothing about devils or ghosts, gods or angels. I would like to see the whole world free—free from injustice—free from superstition."—"What I Want for Christmas"

"Eternal punishment is eternal revenge, and can be inflicted only by an eternal monster. . . . Infinite punishment is infinite cruelty, endless injustice, immortal meanness. To worship an eternal jailer hardens, debases, and pollutes even the vilest soul."—"Origin of God and the Devil"

"The idea of hell was born of ignorance, brutality, fear, cowardice, and revenge. This idea testifies that our remote ancestors were the lowest beasts."—ibid.

"The doctrine of eternal punishment is in perfect harmony with the savagery of the men who made the orthodox creeds. It is in harmony with torture, with flaying alive and with burnings. The men who burned their fellow-men for a moment, believed that God would burn his enemies forever."—"Crumbling Creeds"

"Did it ever occur to you that if God wrote the Old Testament and told the Jews to crucify or kill anybody who disagreed with them in religion, and that this God afterward took upon himself flesh and came to Jerusalem, and taught a different religion, and the Jews killed him—did it ever occur to you that he reaped exactly what he had sown?"—"Orthodoxy"

"Give me the storm and tempest of thought and action, rather than the dead calm of ignorance and faith!"—"The Gods," 1872

"Man, gathering courage from a succession of victories over the obstructions of nature, will attain a serene grandeur unknown to the disciples of any superstition."—ibid.

"An honest God is the noblest work of man."—ibid.

"To hate man and worship God seems to be the sum of all creeds."—"Some Mistakes of Moses"

"The 'Sabbath' was born of asceticism, hatred of human joy, fanaticism, ignorance, egotism of priests and the cowardice of people."—ibid.

"A false friend, an unjust judge, a braggart, hypocrite, and tyrant, sincere in hatred, jealous, vain and revengeful, false in promise, honest in curse, suspicious, ignorant, infamous and hideous—such is the God of the Pentateuch."—ibid.

"In all ages, hypocrites, called priests, have put crowns on the heads of thieves, called kings."—*Prose Poems and Selections,* 1884

"No man of any humor ever founded a religion."— "What Must Be Done to Be Saved?"

"There can be but little liberty on earth while men worship a tyrant in heaven." —ibid.

"I have had some trouble in regarding evil as having been intended by infinite Goodness."—letter to Mrs. J. C. Euwer, November 23, 1886

"The country that has got the least religion is the most prosperous, and the country that has got the most religion is in the worst condition."—speech in Boston, April 23, 1880

"Our hope of immortality does not come from any religion, but nearly all religions come from that hope."—quoted in the *Chicago Times,* November 14, 1879

"The church has always been willing to swap off treasures in heaven for cash down."—speech in Chicago, September 20, 1880

"Miracles are the children of mendacity."—speech in New York, April 25, 1881

"Strange, but true, that those who have loved God most have loved men least."—ibid.

"The inspiration of the Bible depends upon the ignorance of the gentleman who reads it."—ibid.

"One good schoolmaster is worth a thousand priests."—speech in New York, May 1, 1881

"The history of intellectual progress is written in the lives of infidels."—ibid.

"A believer is a bird in a cage; a freethinker is an eagle parting the clouds with tireless wing."—(Seldes)

"For many centuries, the sword and cross were allies. Together they attacked the rights of man. They defended each other."—ibid.

"I believe it was Magellan who said, 'The Church says the earth is flat; but I have seen its shadow on the moon, and I have more confidence even in a shadow than in the Church.' On the prow of his ship were disobedience, defiance, scorn, and success."—ibid.

"Is it possible that an infinite God created this world simply to be the dwelling-place of slaves and serfs? Simply for the purpose of raising orthodox Christians? That he did a few miracles to astonish them? That all the evils of life are simply his punishments, and that he is finally going to turn heaven into a kind of religious museum filled with Baptist barnacles, petrified Presbyterians and Methodist mummies?"—ibid.

"Surely there is grandeur in knowing that in the realm of thought, at least, you are without a chain. . . . Surely it is worth something to feel that there are no priests, no popes, no parties, no governments, no kings, no gods, to whom your intellect can be compelled to pay a reluctant homage."—ibid.

"It seems almost impossible for religious people to really grasp the idea of intellectual freedom. They seem to think that a man is responsible for his honest thoughts; that unbelief is a crime, that investigation is sinful; that credulity is a virtue, and that reason is a dangerous guide."—*Atheist Truth versus Religion's Ghosts,* preface

"If any man wishes to have God recognized in the constitution of our country, let him read the history of the Inquisition, and let him remember that hundreds of millions of men, women and children have been sacrificed to placate the wrath, or win the approbation of this God."—"God in the Constitution," an article in the *Arena,* January 1890

"The church in all ages and among all peoples has been the consistent enemy of the human race. Everywhere and at all times, it has opposed the liberty of thought and expression. It has been the sworn enemy of investigation and intellectual development. It has denied the existence of facts, the tendency of which was to undermine its power. It has always been carrying fagots to the feet of Philosophy. It has erected the gallows for Genius. It has built the dungeon for Thinkers. And today the orthodox church is as much opposed as it ever was to the mental freedom of the human race."—ibid.

"Happiness is the only good, reason the only torch, justice the only worship, humanity the only religion, and love the only priest."—eulogy at the grave of his brother, Ebon

"Supernatural religion will fade from this world, and in its place we shall have reason. In the place of the worship of something we know not of, will be the religion of mutual love and assistance—the great religion of reciprocity. Superstition must go. Science will remain."—(Cardiff)

"For ages, a deadly conflict has been waged between a few brave men and women of thought and genius upon the one side, and the great ignorant religious mass on the other. This is the war between science and faith."—ibid.

"The inventor of the plow did more good than the maker of the first rosary; because, say what you will, plowing is better than praying."—ibid.

"An intelligent man cannot believe that a miracle ever was, or ever will be performed. Ignorance is the soil in which belief in miracles grows."—ibid.

"Christianity has always opposed every forward movement of the human race. Across the highway of progress it has always been building breastworks of bibles, tracts, commentaries, prayerbooks, creeds and dogmas."—ibid.

"Nothing has the same prospect of longevity as a good religious lie."—ibid.

"I know absolutely nothing about God. I have always lived, you see, in one of the rural districts of the universe."—ibid.

39

Mark Twain (1835–1910)

Dover

Wonderfully funny, sad, exuberant, sardonic, and human, Mark Twain is perhaps America's most beloved writer. He is a familiar national fixture, like the Grand Canyon or the White House.

Less known, however, is the scorn Twain felt for religion. His contempt for supernaturalism was kept secret for half a century after his death, lest it ruin his stature in Christian America. Even now, his agnosticism is never mentioned in public schools, and rarely in the public media.

Born Samuel Langhorne Clemens, Mark Twain grew up in Hannibal, Missouri, on the bank of the mighty Mississippi, where he soaked up the boisterous, bawdy, colorful life of a river town. He quit school at thirteen to become an apprentice printer, and soon was writing sketches for a newspaper published by his older brother. When Twain was seventeen, one of his humorous pieces was printed in a Boston journal.

At eighteen he became a roving printer, working in St. Louis, New York, Philadelphia and Washington before rejoining his brother in Iowa. At twenty-two, Twain headed for South America—but on the steamboat down the Mississippi, he decided to become a river pilot. He plied the trade for four years, until the Civil War halted river traffic. Then he headed West, prospected for gold, and wrote for a Nevada paper.

In 1863 he adopted the pseudonym Mark Twain, from a shout uttered by rivermen when they measure two fathoms of water depth. Two years later, the rowdy tale "The Celebrated Jumping Frog of Calaveras County," published in the New York *Evening Press,* launched Twain to national fame. Twain's journalistic travels took him to South America, Europe, and the Middle East, from where he sent back humorous accounts. His writings gained ever greater acclaim, and he became a popular lecturer.

In 1870 Twain married an upstate New York woman; was briefly part owner of a Buffalo newspaper; and then, on the strength of his earnings, built a huge home in Hartford, Connecticut, where both his family life and his writing career flowered. *The Adventures of Tom Sawyer, The Prince and the Pauper, Adventures of Huckleberry Finn,* and *A Connecticut Yankee in King Arthur's Court* immortalized him in American literature. His depth was especially revealed in *Huckleberry Finn,* as the white urchin grows to respect a runaway slave.

Amid his success, Twain encountered tragedy. A son died in infancy. Unlucky investments put Twain into bankruptcy. As he wrote and toured to earn money to repay creditors, his oldest daughter died, then his wife, then his youngest daughter.

Late in life, deeply bitter, Twain unleashed the religious disbelief he had revealed only in hints before. He wrote stark fantasies such as *The War Prayer,* in which fervent patriots beg God for a massacre of the enemy. He scoffed at religion in *Letters From the Earth,* a spoof in which Satan visits the planet, examines its people, and writes accounts to fellow angels in heaven.

After Twain's death in 1910, his only survivor, his daughter Clara, and his publishers suppressed *Letters From the Earth* and several other anticlerical stories. *The Mysterious Stranger,* which denies the existence of a beneficent Providence, was first published only in 1916. And it was not until 1962 that Clara allowed the *Letters* to be released.

Twain's Views on Religion

"I cannot see how a man of any large degree of humorous perception can ever be religious—except he purposely shut the eyes of his mind & keep them shut by force."—*Mark Twain's Notebooks and Journals,* edited by Frederick Anderson, 1979, notebook 27, August 1887–July 1888

". . . No church property is taxed, and so the infidel and the atheist and the man without religion are taxed to make up the deficit in the public income thus caused."—ibid., notebook 21

"Faith is believing what you know ain't so."—"Pudd'nhead Wilson's New Calendar," in *Following the Equator,* 1897

"In religion and politics, people's beliefs and convictions are in almost every case gotten at second-hand, and without examination, from authorities who have not themselves examined the questions at issue but have taken them at second-hand from other nonexaminers, whose opinions about them were not worth a brass farthing."—*Mark Twain's Autobiography*

"In prayer we call ourselves 'worms of the dust,' but it is only on a sort of tacit understanding that the remark shall not be taken at par."—"Does the Race of Man Love a Lord?" in *North American Review,* April 1902

"It ain't those parts of the Bible that I can't understand that bother me, it is the parts that I do understand."—(Peter)

"One of the proofs of the immortality of the soul is that myriads have believed it. They also believed the world was flat."—ibid.

"Man . . . is kind enough when he is not excited by religion."—comment by a horse (Cardiff)

"The prophets wrote book after book and epistle after epistle, yet never once hinted at the existence of a great continent on our side of the water; yet they must have known it was there, I should think."—ibid.

"Christianity does not convert the Hindus, because our Bible miracles are not so large as theirs."—ibid.

"If you know a man's nationality, you can come within a split hair of guessing the complexion of his religion. . . . And when you know a man's religious complexion, you know what sort of religious books he reads when he wants some more light, and what sort of books he avoids, lest by accident he get more light than he wants."—ibid.

"If he was seeking after the Only True Religion, he found it in one or another of the three thousand that are on the market."—ibid.

"Missionarying—that least excusable of all human trades."—ibid.

"After a long time and many questions, Satan said, 'The spider kills the fly, and eats it; the bird kills the spider and eats it; the wildcat kills the goose; the—well they all kill each other. It is murder all along the line. Here are countless multitudes of creatures, and they all kill, kill, kill, they are all murderers. And they are not to blame, Divine One?' 'They are not to blame. It is the law of their nature. And always the law of nature is the Law of God.' "—*Letters From the Earth* (Perennial Library, 1974), p. 13

"The human being . . . naturally places sexual intercourse far and away above all other joys—yet he has left it out of his heaven."—ibid., p. 17

"Man is a marvelous curiosity. . . . He thinks he is the Creator's pet. . . . He prays to Him, and thinks He listens. Isn't it a quaint idea? Fills his prayers with crude and bald and florid flatteries of Him, and thinks He sits and purrs over these extravagancies and enjoys them. He prays for help, and favor, and protection, every day; and does it with hopefulness and confidence, too, although no prayer of his has ever been answered. The daily affront, the daily defeat, do not discourage him, he goes on praying just the same. There is something almost fine about his perseverance. I must put one more strain upon you: he thinks he is going to heaven! He has salaried teachers who tell him that. They also tell him there is a hell, of everlasting fire, and that he will go to it if he doesn't keep the Commandments. . . ." —ibid., "Satan's Letter," pp. 14–15

"You have noticed that the human being is a curiosity. In times past he has had (and worn out and flung away) hundreds and hundreds of religions; today he has hundreds and hundreds of religions, and launches not fewer than three new ones every year. . . ."—ibid., "Letter 3," p. 20

"Many of these people have the reasoning facility, but no one uses it in religious matters."—ibid., p. 24

"Even the Church, which is credited with having spilt more innocent blood, since the beginning of its supremacy, than all the political wars put together have spilt, has observed a limit. A sort of limit. But you notice that when the Lord God of Heaven and Earth, adored Father of Man, goes to war, there is no limit. He is totally without mercy—he, who is called the Fountain of Mercy. He slays, slays, slays! All the men, all the beasts, all the boys, all the babies; also all the women and all the girls, except those that have not been deflowered."—ibid., "Letter 11," p. 52

"Man is the religious animal. He is the only religious animal. He is the only animal that has the True Religion—several of them. He is the only animal that loves his neighbor as himself and cuts his throat, if his theology isn't straight. He has made a graveyard of the globe in trying his honest best to smooth his brother's path to happiness and heaven."—ibid., "The Damned Human Race," subsection: "The Lowest Animal," pp. 179–80

"In August 1572 . . . in Paris and elsewhere in France . . . it was Christian against Christian. The Roman Catholics, by previous concert, sprang a surprise upon the unprepared and unsuspecting Protestants, and butchered them by the thousands—both sexes and all ages. This was the memorable St. Bartholomew's Day. At Rome the Pope and the Church gave public thanks to God when the happy news came. During several centuries, hundreds of heretics were burned at the stake every year because their religious opinions were not satisfactory to the Roman Church. . . ."—ibid., pp. 175–76

"No other creature's religion has wrought such marvels of murderous atrocity as the meek and lowly religion of the Frenchman. . . . The Frenchman is nothing if not pious. He is not content to be pious all by himself; he requires his neighbor to be pious also—otherwise he will kill him and make him so. Yes, if that neighbor declines to lead a holy life, he will take an ax and convert him. . . ."—ibid., "The French and the Commanches," pp. 146–48

"During many ages there were witches. The Bible said so. The Bible commanded that they should not be allowed to live. Therefore the Church, after doing its duty in but a lazy and indolent way for eight hundred years, gathered up its halters, thumbscrews, and firebrands, and set about its holy work in earnest. She worked hard at it night and day during nine centuries and imprisoned, tortured, hanged, and burned whole hordes and armies of witches, and washed the Christian world clean with their foul blood. Then it was discovered that there was no such thing as witches, and never had been. One doesn't know whether to laugh or to cry. Who discovered that there was no such thing as a witch—the priest, the parson? No, these never discover anything. . . ."—*Europe and Elsewhere*

". . . If man continues in the direction of enlightenment, his religious practice may, in the end, attain some semblance of human decency."—ibid.

40

Algernon Charles Swinburne (1837–1909)

In prudish Victorian England, the libertine poet Algernon Charles Swinburne was both a sensation and an outrage.

Born in London the son of an admiral, Swinburne was raised an Anglican, educated at Eton, and showered with upper-class privileges. But when he entered Oxford, he turned rebel.

In the 1850s, Swinburne biographer John Cassidy writes, "the religious roads ran out of Oxford in three directions." The high road led to Anglicanism, and a side road to Catholicism. "The third road—growing in importance—belonged to those who repudiated the Bible, Christianity, and all formalized religion, adopting in their stead a vague agnosticism which accepted the idea of a great creative force or principle, but ridiculed as childish the concept of an anthropomorphic deity."[1] Swinburne himself was befriended by a liberal student who "had rejected religious orthodoxy as puerile nonsense." Soon, the young poet was "a scorner of Christianity generally and of Roman Catholicism in particular." He galloped down the third road of repudiation at breakneck speed. Cassidy says Swinburne joined "countless other Victorian intellectuals who, shying away from the term 'atheist,' disdained any form of religious belief. . . . To Swinburne, all religions, and Christianity especially, were but gigantic hoaxes promulgated by tyrants like Napoleon III and the pope to enslave the masses politically through religious superstition. Accordingly, he hated both the exploiters and their tools, the clergy."[2]

Swinburne was expelled from Oxford, presumably for drunkenness, and entered on a career of brilliant versifying and self-destructive dissipation. His vivid, wanton poems both enchanted and horrified Victorians with their eroticism and irreligion.

---

1. John A. Cassidy, *Algernon Charles Swinburne* (New York: Twayne Publishers, 1964), p. 35.
2. Ibid., pp. 36–37.

When Swinburne wrote of "the supreme evil, God," poet Christina Rossetti was so shocked that she pasted a strip of paper over the line. In "Before a Crucifix," he professed that humanity, not Jesus, is the crucified victim.

Perhaps homosexual, Swinburne had miserable love affairs and lapsed often into alcoholism. But a friend helped the poet to sobriety and took him into his home, enabling him to survive into his seventies.

Swinburne's Comments on Religion

"But the Gods of your fashion, that take and that give / In their pity and passion, that scourge and forgive / They are worms that are bred in the bark that falls off; they shall die and not live."—"Hertha"

". . . the supreme evil, God."—"Atalanta in Calydon"

"The beast faith lives on its own dung."—"Dirae," 1875

"Sleep, shall we sleep after all? for the world is not sweet in the end / For the old faiths loosen and fall, the new years ruin and rend. . . . There is no God found stronger than death; and death is a sleep."—"Hymn to Proserpine"

"Thou hast conquered, O pale Galilean; the world has grown grey from thy breath."—ibid.

"God, if a God there be, is the substance of men which is man."—"The Hymn of Man"

". . . Man, with a child's pride . . . Made God in his likeness, and bowed / Him to worship the Maker he made."—(Cardiff)

"O blood poured forth in pledge to fate / Of nameless lives in divers lands, / O slain and spent and sacrificed / People, the grey-grown speechless Christ."—"Before a Crucifix"

41

John Burroughs (1837–1921)

Dover

John Burroughs, one of America's great naturalists, grew up in an unlettered farm family in the Catskill Mountains of New York state. He was gifted with a keen mind, a curiosity about nature, a zest for science and philosophy, and a poetic sense of wonder.

After a scant education, Burroughs became a schoolteacher at seventeen and used his first earnings to buy the books of John Locke. At nineteen, he married and began trying to sell his poetry and writings about nature.

Burroughs and his new wife moved to Washington, where he became a government clerk. They rented a house where the Senate Office Building now stands, which was at that time part of a farm. His writing began to sell—first nature stories for magazines, then exquisite books about the outdoors.

In the 1870s, Burroughs moved his family back to the Catskills, where he spent the rest of his life writing vivid accounts of nature, with poetic or philosophical commentary.

Burroughs's writing revealed his spiritual feeling for all the universe—a feeling that biographer William Sloane Kennedy has called his "scientific pantheism."[1] Burroughs scorned supernatural Christianity as well as any theology that would "damn infants or endorse murderers."

In 1863 Burroughs befriended Walt Whitman, and later wrote the first biography of the great poet. He also became friends with renowned figures such as Theodore Roosevelt, Thomas Edison, and Henry Ford. At age seventy-six, he learned to drive in a car given to him by Ford.

At age eighty-four, Burroughs died aboard a train in Ohio. Inscribed on his tombstone were two lines from his poetry:

---

1. William Sloane Kennedy, *The Real John Burroughs* (New York: Funk & Wagnalls Co., 1924).

I stand amid the eternal ways,
And what is mine shall know my face.

Burroughs's Comments on Religion

"If we take science as our sole guide, if we accept and hold fast that alone which is verifiable, the old theology must go."—*The Light of Day,* 1900

"Science has done more for the development of Western civilization in 100 years than Christianity did in 1,800 years."—ibid.

"For my part, the longer I live the less I feel the need of any sort of theological belief, and the more I am content to let unseen powers go on their way with me and mine without question or distrust."—ibid.

"The deeper our insight into the methods of nature . . . the more incredible the popular Christianity seems to us."—ibid.

"In the light of modern astronomy, one finds himself looking in vain for the God of his fathers, the magnified man who ruled the ancient world."—ibid.

"Can we ascribe form to infinite space? No more can we ascribe personality to God."—ibid.

"When I look up at the starry heavens at night and reflect upon what is it that I really see there, I am constrained to say, 'There is no God.' . . . It is not the works of some God that I see there. . . . I see no lineaments of personality, no human traits, but an energy upon whose currents, solar systems are bubbles."—ibid.

"Joy in the universe, and keen curiosity about it all—that has been my religion."
—journal entry, February 18, 1910

"The Christianity you believe in is a whining, simpering, sentimental religion."
—(Cardiff)

"We cannot keep the old beliefs, the old creeds, if we would. They belong to a condition of mind that is fast being outgrown."—ibid.

"We must get rid of the great moral governor, or head director. He is a fiction of our brains."—ibid.

"Of the hereafter I have no conception. This life is enough for me."—ibid.

"Our civilization is not founded upon Christianity; it is founded upon reason and science."—ibid.

"Science makes no claim to infallibility; it leaves that claim to be made by theology."—(Vernon)

"We cannot love God as our fathers did, but we can love our neighbors much more. . . . Skeptics and disbelievers could never slaughter each other as the Christians have."—ibid.

"The atmosphere of our time is fast becoming cleared of the fumes and deadly gases that arose during the carboniferous age of theology."—ibid.

"The God of the Puritans, of Calvinism, was a monster too horrible to contemplate."—ibid.

"What remains, then, for those who cannot pray? This alone: to love virtue, to love truth."—(Noyes)

42

William James
(1842–1910)

Dover

A rtist, psychologist, scientist, physician, writer, philosopher, theologian—Harvard professor William James was a man of many dimensions.

Technically, James was a Christian who attended church faithfully. Yet he wasn't a believer in the ordinary sense. He craved a relationship with "the divine," but felt none. The notion of an all-loving God who is also omnipotent—thus responsible for the diseases, earthquakes, famines, and other horrors that inflict human misery—was unthinkable to him. So he postulated the possibility of a limited God. At bottom, James seemed to think that belief in a God cannot be justified logically, but such a belief may be based on emotions and desires.

Son of an eccentric New York writer and brother of the novelist Henry James, William James at first studied to be an artist. Then he earned a medical degree from Harvard and joined the faculty as a physiology professor. Later he switched to psychology and wrote major texts on the subject. Still later he switched to philosophy and focused on his agonized search for faith. He studied all types of belief and wrote *The Varieties of Religious Experience,* a classic in the field.

There is something sad and touching about James's yearning for religion, and his inability to attain it in any standard manner. Biographer Bernard Brennan notes: "James declared that, far from ever having had a mystical experience, he actually found it impossible to pray; but he envied those gifted to do so."[1]

---

1. Bernard P. Brennan, *William James* (New York: Twayne's U.S. Author Series, 1968), p. 99.

James's Views on Religion

"My personal position is simple. I have no living sense of commerce with a God. I envy those who have, for I know the addition of such a sense would help me immensely. The Divine, for my active life, is limited to abstract concepts which, as ideals, interest and determine me, but do so but faintly, in comparison with what a feeling of God might effect, if I had one."—1904 letter quoted by Brennan, *William James*, p. 99

". . . I have grown so out of Christianity that entanglements therewith on the part of a mystical utterance has to be abstracted from and overcome, before I can listen. Call this, if you like, my mystical germ. It is a very common germ. It creates the rank and file of believers."—ibid, p. 100

"It is so human a book [the Bible] that I don't see how belief in its divine authority can survive the reading of it."—ibid.

"If we have to give up all hope of seeing into the purposes of God, or to give up theoretically the idea of final causes, and of God anyhow as vain and leading to nothing for us, we can, by our will, make the enjoyment of our brothers stand us in stead of a final cause."—letter to Thomas W. Ward, January 1868

"Religion, in short, is a monumental chapter in the history of human egotism." —*The Varieties of Religious Experience*, 1902

"A new sort of religion of nature . . . has entirely displaced Christianity from the thought of a large part of our generation."—ibid.

"Religious experience, in other words, spontaneously and inevitably engenders myths, superstitions, dogmas, creeds, and metaphysical theologies, and criticisms of one set of these by the adherents of another."—ibid.

"I have to confess that my own personal feeling about immortality has never been of the keenest order."—(Cardiff)

"The vast literature of proofs for God's existence drawn from the order of nature, which a century ago seemed so overwhelmingly convincing, today does little more than gather dust in our libraries, for the simple reason our generation has ceased to believe in the kind of God it argued for."—ibid.

"An external Creator and His institutions may still be verbally confessed in church in formulas that linger by their mere inertia, but the life is out of them, we avoid dwelling on them, the sincere heart in us is elsewhere."—ibid.

"Modern man . . . has not ceased to be credulous. . . . The need to believe haunts him."—(Peter)

43

Ambrose Bierce (1842–1914)

Dover

Ambrose Bierce was unique as an American writer. Like Edgar Allan Poe, he relished horror and the supernatural—yet he was wickedly funny in lampooning religion.

After serving as a Union officer in the Civil War, Bierce went to San Francisco, where he began writing for newspapers and magazines. He married and moved to London, where he wrote for English journals. After his return to the United States, he went once more to California, and then went to Washington, D.C., all the while crafting columns full of hilarious jabs at religiosity and pomposity.

In 1906, Bierce's irreverent one-liners were collected into *The Devil's Dictionary,* which became a classic that has been reprinted repeatedly. Bierce also wrote fiction, especially eerie tales from the Civil War.

He studied philosophy and logic, but rebelled at the abstruse technicalities of the field. Noting that logic has major premises and minor premises, Bierce wrote in his *Collected Works* (1912) that "Religions are conclusions for which the facts of nature supply no major premises." In the same volume, he noted: "Nothing is more logical than persecution. Religious tolerance is a kind of infidelity." Further: "Theology is a thing of unreason altogether, an edifice of assumption and dreams, a superstructure without a substructure."

His wry whimsy crafted many epigrams, such as: "Camels and Christians receive their burdens kneeling."

In 1913, Bierce went to Mexico and followed Pancho Villa's rebel army. He was never heard from again, and presumably was killed during a battle.

From The Devil's Dictionary

Adore, v. To venerate expectantly.

Altar, n. The place whereon the priest formerly raveled out the small intestine of the sacrificial victim for purposes of divination and cooked its flesh for the gods. The word is now seldom used, except with reference to the sacrifice of their liberty and peace by a male and a female fool.

Brahma, n. He who created the Hindoos, who are preserved by Vishnu and destroyed by Siva—a rather neater division of labor than is found among the deities of some other nations. The Abracadabranese, for example, are created by Sin, maintained by Theft and destroyed by Folly. The priests of Brahma, like those of the Abracadabranese, are holy and learned men who are never naughty.

Caaba, n. A large stone presented by the archangel Gabriel to the patriarch Abraham, and preserved at Mecca. The patriarch had perhaps asked the archangel for bread.

Christian, n. One who believes that the New Testament is a divinely inspired book admirably suited to the spiritual needs of his neighbor. One who follows the teachings of Christ insofar as they are not inconsistent with a life of sin.

Clairvoyant, n. A person, commonly a woman, who has the power of seeing that which is invisible to her patron—namely, that he is a blockhead.

Clergyman, n. A man who undertakes the management of our spiritual affairs as a method of bettering his temporal ones.

Deluge, n. A notable first experiment in baptism which washed away the sins (and sinners) of the world.

Evangelist, n. A bearer of good tidings, particularly (in a religious sense) such as assure us of our own salvation and the damnation of our neighbors.

Excommunication, n. . . . Damning, with bell, book and candle / Some sinner whose opinions are a scandal. / A rite permitting Satan to enslave him / Forever, and forbidding Christ to save him.

Faith, n. Belief without evidence in what is told by one who speaks without knowledge, of things without parallel.

Heathen, n. A benighted creature who has the folly to worship something he can see and feel.

Houri, n. A comely female inhabiting the Mohammedan Paradise to make things cheery for the good Mussulman, whose belief in her existence marks a noble discontent with his earthly spouse, whom he denies a soul.

Infidel, n. In New York, one who does not believe in the Christian religion; in Constantinople, one who does. A kind of scoundrel imperfectly reverent of, and niggardly contributory to, divines, ecclesiastics, popes, parsons, canons, monks, mollahs, voodoos, presbyters, . . . abbés, nuns, missionaries, exhorters, deacons, friars, hadjis, high-priests, muezzins, brahmins, medicine-men, confessors, . . . archbishops, bishops, abbots, priors, preachers, padres, abbotesses, . . . vicars, pastors, rabbis, ulemas, lamas, sacristans, vergers, dervishes, lectors, church wardens, cardinals, prioresses, suffragans, acolytes, rectors, curés, sophis, muftis and pumpums.

Koran, n. A book which the Mohammedans foolishly believe to have been written by divine inspiration, but which Christians know to be a wicked imposture, contradictory to the Holy Scriptures.

Piety, n. Reverence for the Supreme Being, based upon His supposed resemblance to man. The pig is taught by sermons and epistles / To think the God of Swine has snout and bristles.

Pray, v. To ask that the laws of the universe be annulled in behalf of a single petitioner, confessedly unworthy.

Rack, n. An argumentative implement formerly much used in persuading devotees of a false faith to embrace the living truth.

Redemption, n. Deliverance of sinners from the penalty of their sin, through their murder of the deity against whom they sinned. The doctrine of Redemption is the fundamental mystery of our holy religion, and whoso believeth in it shall not perish, but have everlasting life in which to try to understand it.

Religion, n. A daughter of Hope and Fear, explaining to Ignorance the nature of the Unknowable.

Reliquary, n. A receptacle for such sacred objects as pieces of the true cross, short-ribs of saints, the ears of Balaam's ass, the lung of the cock that called Peter to repentance, and so forth. Reliquaries are commonly of metal, and provided with a lock to prevent the contents from coming out and performing miracles at unseasonable times.

Reprobation, n. In theology, the state of a luckless mortal prenatally damned. The doctrine of reprobation was taught by Calvin, whose joy in it was somewhat marred by the sad sincerity of his conviction that although some are foredoomed to perdition, others are predestined to salvation.

Revelation, n. A famous book in which St. John the Divine concealed all that he knew. The revealing is done by the commentators, who know nothing.

Reverence, n. The spiritual attitude of a man to a god and a dog to a man.

Saint, n. A dead sinner revised and edited.

Scriptures, n. The sacred books of our holy religion, as distinguished from the false and profane writings on which all other faiths are based.

Trinity, n. In the multiplex theism of certain Christian churches, three entirely distinct deities consistent with only one. Subordinate deities of the polytheistic faith, such as devils and angels, are not dowered with the power of combination. . . . In religion we believe only what we do not understand, except in the instance of an intelligible doctrine that contradicts an incomprehensible one. In that case we believe the former as part of the latter.

44

Friedrich Nietzsche (1844–1900)

AP/Wide World Photos

A mental giant of the nineteenth century, Nietzsche taught that the dynamic person—the *Übermensch,* the "higher man"—perceives frauds in the prevailing culture, renounces them, and proceeds to build alternate personal values.

Nationalism and militarism were among the cultural doctrines that Nietzsche scorned, but none so vehemently as belief in invisible gods and devils. He saw religion as degrading superstition, bending people to docile obedience. The higher man, he said, must struggle to find truth through reason, and expunge from himself all vestiges of the supernatural explanations inculcated by society. As Walter Kaufmann puts it: "Nietzsche is one of the first thinkers with a comprehensive philosophy to complete the break with religion."[1]

Most of Nietzsche's life was lonely and painful. His father, a Lutheran preacher, died when his son was only five, deeply affecting the child. The young Nietzsche was raised by women, which may have been a factor in his inability to find love and marriage.

At age twenty, Nietzsche shocked his mother by refusing to participate in Easter worship. He wrote to his sister that her religion lacked "objective truth," and that he would forgo the consolations of faith to pursue truth, even if it proved to be "abhorrent or ugly."

During a brief stint of military service, Nietzsche suffered injury and illness, which left him frail for the rest of his life. His vision was also poor.

At the University of Leipzig, Nietzsche was so brilliant that he was awarded a doctorate without examination. At the age of twenty-four, he became a professor at the University of Basel, where he began his major writings. But he was mostly ignored by both academia and society. A decade later, Nietzsche resigned

---

1. Walter Kaufmann, *The Portable Nietzsche* (New York: Viking Press, 1954).

in poor health and lived on a small university pension. He continued writing books that went more or less unnoticed.

Apparently, during a rare visit to a brothel, Nietzsche contracted syphilis, which caused him to go insane at the end of his life. After his death, his genius finally was recognized. However, the Nazi claim that his *Übermensch* meant the "master race" of Aryans was another societal fraud which Nietzsche would have renounced. He despised anti-Semitism, militarism, and nationalism, the pillars upon which Nazism stood.

Nietzsche's Comments on Religion

"I call Christianity the one great curse, the one great intrinsic depravity, and the one great instinct of revenge, for which no means are venomous enough, or secret, subterranean and small enough—I call it the one immortal blemish on the human race."—*The Antichrist,* 1888

"I condemn Christianity, and I bring against the Christian Church the most terrible of all accusations. . . . The Christian Church has left nothing untouched with its depravity, it has made a worthlessness of every value, a lie out of every truth. . . ."—ibid.

"Out of terror, the type has been willed, cultivated and attained: the domestic animal, the herd animal, the sick bruteman—the Christian."—ibid.

"So long as the priest, that professional negator, slanderer and poisoner of life, is regarded as a superior type of human being, there can be no answer to the question, What is truth?"—ibid.

"Priests . . . these turkey-cocks of God."—ibid.

" 'Sins' are indispensable to every society organized on an ecclesiastical basis; they are the only reliable weapons of power; the priest lives upon sins; it is necessary to him that there be 'sinning.' . . . Sin is man's self-desecration *par excellence.* It was invented in order to make science, culture, and every elevation and ennobling of man impossible."—ibid.

"It is at an end with priests and gods, if man becomes scientific. Moral: science is the thing forbidden in itself—it alone is forbidden. Science is the first sin, the germ of all sin, original sin. This alone is morality: Thou shalt not know."—ibid.

"Definition of Protestantism: hemiplegic paralysis of Christianity—and of reason. . . . The uncleanest variety of Christianity that exists, and the most incurable and indestructible."—ibid.

"Whoever has theological blood in his veins is shifty and dishonorable in all things. The pathetic thing that grows out of this condition is called faith."—ibid.

"Great intellects are skeptical."—ibid.

"It is so little true that martyrs offer any support to the truth of a cause that I am inclined to deny that any martyr has ever had anything to do with the truth at all."—ibid.

"The concepts, 'the other world,' 'last judgment,' 'immortality of soul,' 'soul' itself: they are torture instruments, they are systems of cruelty through which the priest became master."—ibid.

"One should not go to church if one wants to breathe pure air."—*Beyond Good and Evil,* 1886

"All gods hitherto have been sanctified, rebaptized devils."—ibid.

"Christianity gave Eros poison to drink. He did not die of it, certainly, but degenerated to vice."—ibid.

"Wherever on earth the religious neurosis has appeared, we find it tied to three dangerous dietary demands: solitude, fasting and sexual abstinence."—*The Genealogy of Morals,* 1887

"After coming into contact with a religious man, I always feel I must wash my hands."—*Why I Am a Destiny,* 1888

"There is not sufficient love and goodness in the world to permit us to give some of it away to imaginary beings."—*Human, All-Too-Human,* 1878

"People whose daily life appears too empty and monotonous easily grow religious; this is comprehensible and excusable, but they have no right to demand religious sentiments from those whose daily life is not empty and monotonous."—ibid.

"Jesus died too soon. He would have repudiated his doctrine if he had lived to my age."—*Thus Spake Zarathustra,* 1885

"God is a thought that makes crooked all that is straight."—ibid.

"Convictions are more dangerous enemies of truth than lies."—ibid.

". . . Two great European narcotics, alcohol and Christianity."—*The Twilight of the Gods,* 1888

"The biblical account of Jesus is a gross thaumaturgist fable."—(Cardiff)

"Simple truths ascertained by scientific methods can only be perceived when men have lost all faith in inspiration and in the miraculous revelation of truth."—ibid.

"The only excuse for God is that he doesn't exist."—ibid.

45

Other Figures of the Nineteenth Century

Walt Whitman: Dover

Skepticism escalated in the nineteenth century, reaching what might be termed a golden age of disbelief. In the aftermath of the Enlightenment, an upsurge in science—especially the revolutionary breakthrough by Charles Darwin—spurred many intellectuals to renounce supernaturalism.

For example, the French novelist George Sand (Lucile Dupin, Baroness Dudevant, 1804–1876) wrote that she had rejected Christianity's anthropomorphic God, "made in our image, silly and malicious, vain and puerile, irritable or tender, after our fashion." Just before her death, she asked that no religious rites be allowed at her burial. Victor Hugo gave her funeral oration.

Other great figures of the nineteenth century made no public declarations, but simply shunned religion. The immortal composer Ludwig van Beethoven, for instance, ignored the church and lived a purely secular life. Biographer George Marek says Beethoven was born Catholic but "never became a practicing one. There is no record of his ever attending church service or observing the orthodoxy of his religion. He never went to confession. . . . Generally he viewed priests with mistrust."[1]

Fellow composer Joseph Haydn called Beethoven an atheist. As Beethoven lay dying in 1827, religious friends summoned a priest to perform the last rites. The mighty musician endured it, then remarked sardonically: "Applaud, friends, the comedy is over."

As the century progressed, freethought societies and publications blossomed. Agnosticism reached its heyday. A torrent of skeptical statements appeared. Following are various expressions of doubt by other renowned people which span the period from the Romantic age to the first years of the twentieth century.

---

1. George Marek, *Beethoven: Biography of a Genius* (New York: Funk & Wagnalls, 1969).

Scientists

"There is no limit to understanding the world in natural rather than supernatural terms."—John William Draper (1811–1882), American chemist

"The history of science is not a mere record of isolated discoveries; it is a narrative of the conflict of two contending powers, the expansive force of the human intellect on one side, and the compression arising from traditionary faith and human interest on the other."—Draper, *History of the Conflict between Religion and Science,* 1874

"Man has conceived a God in his own likeness. It is in the name of this pretended God that monarchs and pontiffs have in all the ages, and under cover of all religions, bound humanity in a slavery from which it has not yet freed itself. . . . It is in the names of the gods of Olympus that the Greeks condemned Socrates to drink the hemlock; it is in the name of Jehovah that the high-priests and Pharisees crucified Jesus. It is in the name of Jesus, himself become God, that fanaticism ignominiously condemned to the stake men like Giordano Bruno, Vanini, Étienne Dolet, John Huss, Savanarola, and numerous other heroic victims; that the Inquisition ordered Galileo to belie his conscience; that thousands and thousands of unfortunates accused of witchcraft were burnt alive in popular ceremonies; it was with the express benediction of Pope Gregory XIII that the butchery of St. Bartholomew drenched Paris in blood."—Camille Flammarion (1842–1925), French astronomer, *Dreams of an Astronomer*

"The supernatural does not exist."—Flammarion (Cardiff)

"Men have had the vanity to pretend that the whole creation was made for them, while in reality the whole creation does not suspect their existence."—Flammarion (Noyes)

"Sire, I have no need of that hypothesis."—Pierre Laplace (1749–1827), French astronomer and mathematician, after Napoleon asked why he did not mention God in his *Celestial Mechanics*

"The telescope sweeps the skies without finding God."—Laplace (Noyes)

"I know of no book which has been a source of brutality and sadistic conduct, both public and private, that can compare with the Bible."—Sir James Paget (1814–1899), surgeon, pathologist, and friend of Darwin, Huxley, Pasteur, Prime Minister Gladstone, and writers Tennyson, Browning, and Eliot

"Man's special creation is entirely unsupported by facts, as well as in the highest degree improbable."—Alfred R. Wallace (1823–1913), evolutionist colleague of Charles Darwin (Noyes)

Writers

"My parents never bound us to any church."—Louisa May Alcott (1832–1888), American novelist (Noyes)

"We are always making God our accomplice so that we may legalize our own inequities. Every successful massacre is consecrated by a *Te Deum,* and the clergy have never been wanting in benedictions for any victorious enormity."—Henri Frédéric Amiel (1821–1881), Swiss poet and philosopher, *Journal intime,* 1866

"After a woman gets too old to be attractive to men, she turns to God."—Honoré de Balzac (1799–1850), French novelist (Cardiff)

"Today the writer has replaced the priest."—Balzac, ibid.

"Thanks to the toleration preached by the encyclopedists of the eighteenth century, the sorcerer is exempt from torture."—Balzac (Noyes)

"Who knows most, doubts most."—Robert Browning (1812–1889), English poet

"The candid incline to surmise of late that the Christian faith proves false." —Browning, "Gold Hair," 1864

". . . The pig-of-lead-like pressure of the preaching man's immense stupidity." —Browning, "Christmas Eve," 1850

"Mothers, wives, and maids / These are the tools wherewith priests manage men."—Browning, *The Ring and the Book,* 1869

"I am no Christian."—Browning (Noyes)

"An honest God's the noblest work of man."—Samuel Butler (1835–1902), English novelist, spoofing Alexander Pope's remark that "An honest man's the noblest work of God" (cf. the quote from Robert Ingersoll, p. 158)

"Prayers are to men as dolls are to children. They are not without use and comfort, but it is not easy to take them very seriously."—Butler, "Unprofessional Sermons," *Note-Books*

"A clergyman can hardly ever allow himself to look facts fairly in the face. It is his profession to support one side; it is impossible, therefore, for him to make an unbiased examination of the other."—Butler, *The Way of All Flesh* (1903)

"Christians have burnt each other, quite persuaded / That all the Apostles would have done as they did."—George Gordon, Lord Byron (1788–1824), *Don Juan,* 1819

"I do not believe in any revealed religion. I will have nothing to do with your immortality; we are miserable enough in this life, without the absurdity of speculating upon another."—Byron, letter to the Rev. Francis Hodgson, 1811

"I hope to merit Heaven by making earth a Hell."—Byron, quoting a zealot in *Childe Harold,* 1812

"We have fools in all sects, and impostors in most; why should I believe mysteries no one can understand, because written by men who chose to mistake madness for inspiration and style themselves Evangelicals?"—Byron (Noyes)

"I am surrounded here by parsons and Methodists, but as you will see, not infested with the mania."—Byron, ibid.

"Of religion I know nothing—at least, in its favor."—Byron, ibid.

"The fable of a god or gods visiting the earth did not originate with Christianity."—Richard Carlile (1790–1843), English writer (Cardiff)

"Just in the ratio that knowledge increases, faith diminishes."—Thomas Carlyle (1795–1881), English writer (Cardiff)

"God does nothing."—Carlyle (Noyes)

"It is not possible that educated, honest men can even profess much longer to belief in historical Christianity."—Carlyle, ibid.

"Not one man in ten thousand has goodness of heart or strength of mind to be an atheist."—Samuel Taylor Coleridge (1772–1834), to Thomas Allsop, ca. 1820

"Whenever philosophy has taken into its plan religion, it has ended in skepticism; and whenever religion excludes philosophy, or the spirit of free inquiry, it leads to willful blindness and superstition."—Coleridge, *Alsop's Letters, Conversations and Recollections of Samuel Taylor Coleridge,* 1836

"Clergymen who publish pious frauds in the interest of the church are the orthodox liars of God."—Coleridge (Cardiff)

"He that dies a martyr proves that he was not a knave, but by no means that he was not a fool."—Charles Caleb Colton (1780–1832), *Lacon,* 1820

"Some reputed saints that have been canonized ought to have been cannonaded."—Colton, ibid.

"Religion has treated knowledge sometimes as an enemy, sometimes as a hostage; often as a captive and more often as a child."—Colton, ibid.

"We owe almost all our knowledge not to those who have agreed, but to those who have differed."—Colton, ibid.

"Precisely in proportion to our own intellectual weakness will be our credulity as to those mysterious powers assumed by others."—Colton, ibid.

"See yonder preacher to his people pass / Borne up and swelled by tabernacle-gas."—George Crabbe (1754–1832), English poet, *The Borough,* 1810

" 'Faith' is a fine invention, when gentlemen can *see* / But microscopes are prudent, in an emergency."—Emily Dickinson (1830–1886), American poet, ca. 1860

"So long as man remains free, he strives for nothing so incessantly and so painfully as to find someone to worship. But man seeks to worship what is established beyond dispute, so that all men would agree at once to worship it. For these pitiful creatures are concerned not only to find what one or the other can worship, but to find something that all would believe in and worship; what is essential is that all may be *together* in it. This craving for *community* of worship is the chief misery of every man individually and of all humanity from the beginning of time. For the sake of common worship, they've slain each other with the sword. They have set up gods and challenged one another, 'Put away your gods and come and worship ours, or we will kill you and your gods!' And so it will be to the end of the world, even when gods disappear from the earth; they will fall down before idols just the same."—Fyodor Dostoyevski (1821–1881), Russian novelist, *The Brothers Karamazov,* 1880

". . . Beyond the grave they will find nothing but death. But we shall keep the secret, and for their happiness we shall allure them with the reward of heaven and eternity."—Dostoyevski, ibid., remark of the Grand Inquisitor

"Catholics and Protestants, while engaged in burning and murdering each other, could cooperate in enslaving their black brethren."—Alexandre Dumas (1802–1870), French novelist (Noyes)

"It is necessary to sleep upon the pillow of doubt."—Gustave Flaubert (1821–1880), French novelist (Cardiff)

"The absurdity of a religious practice may be clearly demonstrated without lessening the number of persons who indulge in it."—Anatole France (1844–1924)

"It is almost impossible systematically to constitute a natural moral law. Nature has no principles. She furnishes us with no reason to believe that human life is to be respected. Nature, in her indifference, makes no distinction between good and evil."—France (Peter)

"You see how wide the gulf that separates me from the Christian church."—Margaret Fuller (1810–1850), American writer (Cardiff)

"Christianity, above all, consoles; but there are naturally happy souls who do not need consolation. Consequently, Christianity begins by making such souls unhappy, for otherwise it would have no power over them."—André Gide (1869–1951), Nobel Prize-winning French author, journal, October 10, 1893

"Religions revolve madly around sexual questions."—Rémy de Gourmont (1858–1915), French writer

"There is no doctrine of Christianity but what has been anticipated by the Vedas [religious writings of India]."—Horace Greeley (1811–1872), American newspaper editor (Cardiff)

"The creator who could put a cancer in a believer's stomach is above being interfered with by prayers."—Bret Harte (1836–1902), American short-story writer (Noyes)

"The garb of religion is the best cloak for power."—William Hazlitt (1778–1830), English essayist, "On the Clerical Character," *Political Essays,* 1819

"If your right eye offends you, pluck it out / If your right arm offends you, cut it off / And if your reason offends you, become a Catholic."—Heinrich Heine (1797–1856), German poet (Cardiff)

"He who fights with priests may make up his mind to have his poor good name torn and befouled by the most infamous lies and the most cutting slanders."—Heine, ibid.

"I consider it a degradation and a stain on my honor to submit to baptism in order to qualify myself for state employment in Prussia."—Heine (Noyes)

"All religions have based morality on obedience, that is to say, on voluntary slavery. That is why they have always been more pernicious than any political organization. For the latter makes use of violence, the former—of the corruption of the will."—Alexander Herzen (1812–1870), Russian political writer, *From the Other Shore,* 1855

"It is a matter of surprise that men whose Christian honesty, purity, and self-devotedness are conceded on every hand, are often men with whom we do not like to associate."—J. G. Holland (1819–1881), American editor and writer, *Everyday Topics,* 1876

"The man who is always worrying about whether or not his soul would be damned generally has a soul that isn't worth a damn."—Oliver Wendell Holmes, Sr. (1809–1894), American man of letters

"We are all tattooed in our cradles with the beliefs of our tribe; the record may seem superficial, but it is indelible. You cannot educate a man wholly out of the superstitious fears which were implanted in his imagination, no matter how utterly his reason may reject them."—Holmes (Wilcox/George)

"Men are idolaters, and want something to look at and kiss, or throw themselves down before; they always did, they always will; and if you don't make it of wood, you must make it of words."—Holmes, *The Poet at the Breakfast Table,* 1872

"The truth is that the whole system of beliefs which comes in with the story of the fall of man . . . is gently falling out of enlightened human intelligence."—Holmes (Noyes)

"I lie, I cheat, do anything for pelf / But who on earth can say I am not pious?"—Thomas Hood (1799–1845), English poet, *Blanca's Dream,* 1827

"When you tell me that your Deity made you in his own image, I reply that he must have been very ugly."—Victor Hugo (1802–1885), French novelist (Cardiff)

"Every step which the intelligence of Europe has taken has been in spite of the clerical party."—Hugo, ibid.

"There is in every village a torch: the schoolmaster—and an extinguisher: the parson."—Hugo (Noyes)

"Sacrificing the earth for paradise is giving up the substance for the shadow." —Hugo, ibid.

"The good Count never set forth on a ravage without observing the rites of confession, absolution and communion."—Washington Irving (1783–1859) (Noyes)

"Even the weakest disputant is made so conceited by what he calls religion, as to think himself wiser than the wisest who thinks differently from him."—Walter Savage Landor (1775–1864), English poet and writer, "Melanchthon and Calvin," *Imaginary Conversations* (1824–29)

"It seems to me that the bane of our country is a profession of faith either with no basis of real belief, or with no proper examination of the grounds on which the creed is supposed to rest."—James Russell Lowell (1819–1891), American poet and editor (Noyes)

"Whatever may be God's future, we cannot forget His past."—W. H. Mallock, *Is Life Worth Living?* 1879

"Already we have been the nothing we dread to be."—Herman Melville (1819–1891), American novelist (Noyes)

"When I was quite a boy I had a spasm of religion which lasted six weeks. . . . But I never since have swallowed the Christian fable."—George Meredith (1828–1909), English novelist (Cardiff)

"Could Britain accept the fables of her priests . . . she would find comfort in their opiates."—Meredith, ibid.

"The man or the country that fights priestcraft and priests is to my mind striking deeper for freedom than can be struck anywhere."—Meredith (Gray)

"Women have never invented a religion; they are untainted with that madness, and they are not moralists."—George Moore (1852–1933), Irish novelist, *Confessions of a Young Man,* 1888

"Faith, fanatic faith, once wedded fast / To some dear falsehood, hugs it to the last."—Thomas Moore (1779–1852), Irish poet, *Lalla Rookh,* 1817

"The heaven of each is but what each desires."—Moore, ibid.

"It does not seem to me that the evidence concerning the being of a God, and concerning immortality, is such as to enable us to assert anything in regard to either of these topics."—Charles Eliot Norton (1827–1908), a founder of the *Nation* magazine, letter to John Ruskin, 1869

"So far as the most intelligent portion of society at the present day is concerned, the church in its actual constitution is an anachronism."—Norton, *Church*, 1868

"The loss of religious faith among the most civilized portion of the race is a step from childishness toward maturity."—Norton, letter to Goldwin Smith, June 14, 1897

"Christianity has ever been the enemy of human love. . . . Christianity has made of death a terror which was unknown to the gay calmness of the pagan."—Ouida (Maria Louise Ramée) (1839–1908), English novelist, *The Failure of Christianity*

"Of all the powerless things on earth, Christianity is the most powerless."—Ouida (Cardiff)

"The radical defect in Christianity is that it tried to win the world by a bribe, and it has become a nullity."—Ouida, ibid.

"Some who do not consider that Christianity has proved a failure, do, nevertheless, hold that it is open to question whether the race, as a race, has been much affected by it, and whether the external and visible evil and good which have come of it do not pretty nearly balance one another."—Coventry Patmore (1823–1896), English poet, *Christianity and Progress*

"After reading all that has been written, and after thinking all that can be thought, on the topics of God and the soul, the man who has a right to say that he thinks at all will find himself face to face with the conclusion that, on these topics, the most profound thought is that which can be the least easily distinguished from the most superficial sentiment."—Edgar Allan Poe (1809–1849), American writer, *Marginalia*, 1844–49

"The idea of God, infinity, or spirit stands for the possible attempt at an impossible conception."—Poe (Cardiff)

"The pioneers and missionaries of religion have been the real cause of more trouble and war than all other classes of mankind."—Poe, ibid.

"No man who ever lived knows any more about the hereafter . . . than you and I; and all religion . . . is simply evolved out of chicanery, fear, greed, imagination and poetry."—Poe (Noyes)

" 'The Heavenly Father feedeth the fowls of the air'—and in winter He letteth them starve to death."—Jules Renard (1864–1910), French writer

"I profess no religious faith and practice no religious observances."—Dante Gabriel Rossetti (1828–1882), Italian-English poet and painter (Cardiff)

"I appreciate and respect your faith, but cannot share it with you."—George Sand (1804–1876), French novelist, letter to a friend (Gray)

"There never was on this earth a body of educated and cultured men so thoroughly agnostic and atheistic as the mass of Confucian scholars."—Arthur H. Smith, *Chinese Characteristics,* 1892

"All religions are founded on the fear of the many and the cleverness of the few." —Stendhal (Marie-Henri Beyle) (1783–1842), French novelist (Wilcox/George)

"Christian love among the churches look'd the twin of heathen hate."—Alfred, Lord Tennyson (1809–1892), English poet laureate, "Locksley Hall Sixty Years After"

"There lives more faith in honest doubt, believe me, than in half the creeds." —Tennyson, *In Memoriam*

"In our windy world, what's up is faith, what's down is heresy."—Tennyson, *Harold,* 1876

"The churches have killed their Christ."—Tennyson, *Maud,* 1855

"We are self-uncertain creatures, and we may, Yea, even when we know not, mix our spites and private hates with our defense of Heaven."—Tennyson, *Becket,* 1884

"We have but faith; we cannot know."—Tennyson (Noyes)

"Whatever a man prays for, he prays for a miracle. Every prayer reduces itself to this: 'Great God, grant that twice two be not four.' "—Ivan Turgenev (1818–1883), Russian novelist

"The feeling which prompts prayer . . . I should like to see guided, not extinguished—devoted to practicable objects instead of wasted upon air."—John Tyndall (1820–1893), Irish physicist, *Fragments of Science for Unscientific People,* 1871

"Science, testing absolutely all thoughts, all works, has already burst well upon the world—a sun, mounting, most illuminating, most glorious, surely never again to set. But against it, deeply entrench'd, holding possession, yet remains (not only through the churches and schools, but by imaginative literature, and unregenerate poetry) the fossil theology of the mythic-materialistic, superstitious, untaught and credulous fable-loving, primitive ages of humanity."—Walt Whitman (1819–1892), American poet, *Democratic Vistas,* 1870

"I think I could turn and live with animals / They are so placid and self-contain'd . . . / They do not lie awake in the dark and weep for their sins / They do not make me sick discussing their duty to God."—Whitman (Cardiff)

"Pointing to another world will never stop vice among us; shedding light over this world can alone help us."—Whitman, ibid.

"Why, who makes much of a miracle? As to me, I know of nothing else but miracles. . . . Seeing, hearing, feeling are miracles, and each part and tag of me is a miracle; this head, more than churches, Bibles, and all the creeds."—Whitman (Noyes)

"There is no god more divine than yourself."—Whitman, ibid.

"Truth, in matters of religion, is simply the opinion that has survived."—Oscar Wilde (1854–1900), Irish playwright and novelist, *The Critic as Artist,* 1891

"Medievalism, with its saints and martyrs, its love of self-torture, its wild passion for wounding itself, its gashing with knives, and its whipping with rods—Medievalism is real Christianity, and the medieval Christ is the real Christ."—Wilde, "The Soul of Man under Socialism," in the *Fortnightly Review,* 1891

"The worst vice of the fanatic is his sincerity."—Wilde (Wilcox/George)

"A thing is not necessarily true because a man dies for it."—Wilde, ibid.

"I cannot conceive anything better for the culture of a country than the presence in it of a body of men [the clergy] whose duty it is to believe in the supernatural, to perform daily miracles, and to keep alive that mythopoeic faculty which is so essential for the imagination."—Wilde, "The Decay of Lying," 1891

"Science is the record of dead religions."—Wilde, *Phrases and Philosophies for the Use of the Young,* 1891

"Religion consoles some women. Its mysteries have all the charm of a flirtation."—Wilde (Cardiff)

"Piety is sweet to infant minds."—William Wordsworth (1770–1850), English poet, *The Excursion,* 1814

"Civilization will not attain to its perfection until the last stone from the last church falls on the last priest!"—Émile Zola (1840–1902), French novelist and essayist (Cardiff)

"Has science ever retreated? No! It is Catholicism which has always retreated before her, and will always be forced to retreat."—Zola (Noyes)

Reformers, Scholars, and Revolutionaries

"The idea that any personal deity could find pleasure or profit in torturing a poor woman, by accident, with a fiendish cruelty known to man only in perverted and insane temperaments, could not be held for a moment. For pure blasphemy, it made pure atheism a comfort."—Henry Adams (1838–1918), American historian, grandson and great-grandson of presidents John Adams and John Quincy Adams, after the death of his sister in 1870

"The religious persecution of the ages has been done under what was claimed to be the command of God."—Susan B. Anthony (1820–1906), American reformer (Noyes)

"All religions, with their gods, demigods, prophets, messiahs and saints, are the product of the fancy and credulity of men who have not yet reached the full development and complete possession of their intellectual powers."—Mikhail A. Bakunin (1814–1876), Russian anarchist and writer, *God and the State* (1883)

"The first revolt is against the supreme tyranny of theology, of the phantom of God. As long as we have a master in heaven, we will be slaves on earth." —Bakunin, ibid.

"Christianity is the complete negation of common sense and sound reason." —Bakunin, ibid.

"God, or rather the fiction of God, is thus the sanction and the intellectual and moral cause of all the slavery on earth, and the liberty of men will not be complete, unless it will have completely annihilated the inauspicious fiction of a heavenly master."—Bakunin, *Oeuvres,* vol. 1, p. 143

"Theology is the science of the divine lie. . . ." Bakunin (Seldes)

"People go to church for the same reasons they go to a tavern: to stupefy themselves, to forget their misery, to imagine themselves, for a few minutes anyway, free and happy."—Bakunin, *Circular Letter to My Friends in Italy*

"The idea of god implies the abdication of human reason and justice; it is the most decisive negation of human liberty and necessarily ends in the enslavement of mankind both in theory and practice."—Bakunin (Gray)

"We are materialists and atheists, and we glory in the fact."—Bakunin (Noyes)

"Religion is a collective insanity."—Bakunin, ibid.

"There is no pestilence in a state like a zeal for religion, independent of morality."—Jeremy Bentham (1748–1832), English philosopher and jurist (Noyes)

"The spirit of dogmatic theology poisons anything it touches."—Bentham, ibid.

"The atheist does not say, 'There is no God,' but he says, 'I know not what you mean by God; the word God is to me a sound conveying no clear or distinct affirmation.' "—Charles Bradlaugh (1833–1891), English freethinker and reformer, *A Plea for Atheism,* 1864

"If special honor is claimed for any, then heresy should have it as the truest servitor of humankind."—Bradlaugh, from a speech in London, September 25, 1881

"Christianity demands entire subordination to its edicts. Until the majority of the people are emancipated from authority over their minds, we are not safe."—abolitionist Lucy Colman, American abolitionist, in her autobiography, *Reminiscences* (Buffalo, N.Y., 1891), p. 7

"The universe displays no proof of an all-directing mind."—Auguste Comte (1798–1857), French philosopher (Cardiff)

"The heavens declare the glory of Kepler and Newton."—Comte (Noyes)

"I particularly request that no Christian mummeries or tomfooleries be performed at my grave, but that I be buried as an agnostic."—John Sholto Douglas, 8th Marquis of Queensberry (1844–1900), English sportsman (Cardiff)

"Christianity has in fact long vanished, not only from the reason but also from the life of mankind, and it is nothing more than a fixed idea."—Ludwig Feuerbach (1804–1872), German philosopher, *On Philosophy and Christianity,* 1839

"Whenever morality is based on theology, whenever right is made dependent on divine authority, the most immoral, unjust, infamous things can be justified and established."—Feuerbach, *The Essence of Christianity,* 1841

"It is as clear as the sun and as evident as the day that there is no God and that there can be none."—Feuerbach (Cardiff)

"God has not created man, but man created God."—Feuerbach (Noyes)

"[Christianity's past is] the history of fraud, superstition, misery and bloodshed; until these last two centuries, when its power has dwindled almost to nothing." —John Fiske (1842–1901), American historian and philosopher

"Is it honest for me to go and sit there on communion day and drink the wine and eat the bread while feeling it all to be mummery?"—Fiske, letter to his mother, March 20, 1860

"One and all, the orthodox creeds are crumbling into ruins everywhere. We now witness the constructive work on a foundation that will endure through the ages. That foundation is the god of science—revealed to us in terms that will harmonize with our intelligence."—Fiske, quoted in Frederick W. Clampett, *Luther Burbank: Our Beloved Infidel* (New York: Macmillan, 1926)

"[Christianity entailed] a mass of metaphysical assumptions, wherein science was disowned, where reason was discredited, and where blind, unquestioning faith was regarded as the only passport to true Christian knowledge."—Fiske, quoted by John Spender Clark in *The Life and Letters of John Fiske* (Boston, 1917), vol. 1, p. 103

"Three-fourths of the body of the doctrine known as Christianity, unwarranted by scripture and never dreamed of by Christ or his Apostles, first took coherent shape in the writings of this mighty Roman [Augustine]."—Fiske (Cardiff)

"The Hindu sacred writings contain all the myths and fables found in the Christian Bible."—Fiske (Cardiff)

"The careful student of history will discover that Christianity has been of very little value in advancing civilization, but has done a great deal toward retarding it." —Matilda Joslyn Gage, suffragist colleague of Susan B. Anthony and Elizabeth Cady Stanton, *Woman, Church and State,* 1893

"The Christian theory of the sacredness of the Bible has been at the cost of the world's civilization."—Gage (Noyes)

"All Christendom professes to receive the Bible as the word of God, and what does it avail?"—William Lloyd Garrison (1805–1879), American editor and abolitionist (Noyes)

"The proofs of the existence of God are to such an extent fallen into discredit that they pass for something antiquated, belonging to days gone by."—Georg W. F. Hegel (1770–1831), German philosopher (Noyes)

"I do not believe there is such a thing as a God."—G. J. Holyoake (1817–1906), during a London lecture, 1868 (For a different speech, this English reformer was sentenced to six months in prison.)

"The truth is that no profession of faith or lack of faith has anything to do with a man's morals. . . . Away with the bugbear that to be good we must be pious." —from the *Iconoclast,* 1870, published by Lester F. Ward, founder of American sociology

"Until doubt began, progress was impossible."—motto of the *Iconoclast*

"The priests will always be too many for you."—Benjamin Jowett (1817–1893), English classicist

"When it began, Christianity was regarded as a system entirely beyond the range and scope of human reason; it was impious to question; it was impious to examine; it was impious to discriminate. On the other hand, it was visibly instinct with the supernatural. Miracles of every order and degree of magnitude were flashing forth incessantly from all its parts."—William E. H. Lecky (1838–1903), Irish historian, *History of the Rise and Influence of the Spirit of Rationalism in Europe,* 1866

"Almost all Europe, for many centuries, was inundated with blood, which was shed at the direct instigation or with the full approval of the ecclesiastical authorities."—ibid., vol. 2, p. 32

"The doctrine of a material hell in its effect was to chill and deaden the sympathies, predispose men to inflict suffering, and to retard the march of civilization."— Lecky, quoted in Clampett, *Luther Burbank: Our Beloved Infidel,* p. 102

"There is no wild beast so ferocious as Christians who differ concerning their faith."—Lecky (Cardiff)

"Whenever the clergy were at the elbow of the civil arm, no matter whether they were Catholic or Protestant, persecution was the result."—Lecky, ibid.

"The church fathers laid it down as a distinct proposition, that pious frauds are justifiable and even laudable."—Lecky, ibid.

"Fierce invectives against women form a conspicuous and grotesque portion of the writings of the Church fathers."—Lecky, ibid.

"Religion is the sigh of the oppressed creature, the feelings of a heartless world, just as it is the spirit of unspiritual conditions. It is the opium of the people."—Karl Marx (1818–1883), German political philosopher, *A Criticism of the Hegelian Philosophy of Right,* 1844

"The first requisite for the happiness of the people is the abolition of religion." —Marx, ibid.

"Men of generous culture or of great learning, and women of eminent piety and virtue, from the humble cottage to the throne, have been led out for matters of conscience and butchered before a mad rabble lusting after God. The limbs of men and women have been torn from their bodies, their eyes gouged out, their flesh mangled and slowly roasted, their children barbarously tortured before their eyes, because of religious opinion."—Joel Moody, *Science of Evil,* 1871

"Where it is a duty to worship the sun, it is pretty sure to be a crime to examine the laws of heat."—John Morley (1838–1923), English politician and writer, "Voltaire," *Critical Miscellanies,* 1872

"All religions die of one disease—that of being found out."—Morley (Cardiff)

"You [Christianity] have so debilitated the minds of men and women that generations must come and go before Europe can throw off the yoke of your superstition."—Morley, ibid.

"The church is now more like the Scribes and Pharisees than like Christ. What are now called 'essential doctrines' of the Christian religion, he [Christ] does not even mention."—Florence Nightingale (1820–1910), English humanitarian and nurse (Cardiff)

"Religion is a functional weakness."—Max Nordau (1849–1923), German physician and author, *Conventional Lies of Our Civilization,* 1884

"The last superstition of the human mind is the superstition that religion in itself is a good thing, though it might be free from dogma. I believe, however, that the religious feeling, as feeling, is wrong, and the civilized man will have nothing to do with it. . . . [When the] shadow of religion disappeared forever . . . I felt that I was free from a disease."—Samuel Putnam, former Congregationalist minister, *My Religious Experience,* 1891

"The moment that one loses confidence in God, or immortality in the universe, [one becomes] more self-reliant, more courageous, and the more solicitous of aid where only human aid is possible."—Putnam, ibid.

"No miracle has ever taken place under conditions which science can accept. Experience shows, without exception, that miracles occur only in times and in countries in which miracles are believed in, and in the presence of persons who are disposed to believe them."—Ernest Renan (1823–1892), French historian, *The Life of Jesus,* 1863

"I know few Christians so convinced of the splendor of the rooms in their Father's house, as to be happier when their friends are called to those mansions. . . . Nor has the Church's ardent 'desire to depart, and be with Christ,' ever cured it of the singular habit of putting on mourning for every person summoned to such departure."—John Ruskin (1819–1900), English philosopher and artist (Cardiff)

"Surely our clergy need not be surprised at the daily increasing distrust in the public mind of the efficacy of prayer."—Ruskin, ibid.

"Morality does not depend on religion."—Ruskin, ibid.

"I never yet met with a Christian whose heart was thoroughly set upon the world to come, and, so far as human judgment could pronounce, perfect and right before God, who cared about art at all."—Ruskin, *The Stones of Venice,* 1853

"Incidents from the *Iliad* and the Exodus come within the same degrees of credibility."—Ruskin (Noyes)

"Religion is . . . the most pernicious single influence in human society, without one redeeming feature."—Theodore Schroeder, American lawyer and founder of the Free Speech League, forerunner of the American Civil Liberties Union, 1864 (Gray)

"[Agnostics are] people who, like myself, confess themselves to be hopelessly ignorant concerning a variety of matters, about which metaphysicians and theologians, both orthodox and heterodox, dogmatize with the utmost confidence."—Herbert Spencer (1820–1903), English philosopher, 1863 (Wilcox/George)

"The 'Creed of Christendom' is alien to my nature, both emotional and intellectual."—Spencer (Cardiff)

"There is no origin for the idea of an afterlife, save the conclusion which the savage draws from the notion suggested by dreams."—Spencer, ibid.

"Religion has been compelled by science to give up one after another of its dogmas, of those assumed cognitions which it could not substantiate."—Spencer, *First Principles,* 1862

"We hear with surprise of the savage who, falling down a precipice, ascribes the failure of his foothold to a malicious demon; and we smile at the kindred notion of the ancient Greek, that his death was prevented by a goddess who unfastened for him the thong of the helmet by which his enemy was dragging him. But daily, without surprise, we hear men who describe themselves as saved from shipwreck by 'divine interposition' . . . and the Christian priest who says prayers over a sick man in the expectation that the course of the disease will be stayed, differ only in respect of the agent from whom they expect supernatural aid."—Spencer, ibid.

"The idea of disembodied spirits is wholly unsupported by evidence, and I cannot accept it."—Spencer (Noyes)

"The cruelty of a Fijian god, who, represented as devouring the souls of the dead, may be supposed to inflict torture during the process, is small compared with the cruelty of a God who condemns men to tortures which are eternal."—Spencer, ibid.

"I now believe in nothing, to put it shortly; but I do not the less believe in morality."—Leslie Stephen (1832–1904), English critic and biographer, in his journal, January 26, 1865

"Christianity . . . that musty old theology, which already has its grave clothes on, and is about to be buried. . . . A wall of Bible, brimstone, church and corruption has hitherto hemmed women into nothingness."—Lucy Stone (1818–1893), American suffragist, quoted by Andrea Moore Kerr in *Lucy Stone: Speaking Out for Equality*

World Leaders

"Christianity is the enemy of liberty and of civilization. It has kept mankind in chains."—August Bebel (1840–1913), German socialist, Reichstag speech, March 31, 1881

"When socialism comes into power, the Roman Church will advocate socialism with the same vigor [with which] it is now favoring feudalism and slavery."—Bebel, address to the Social Democratic Party Congress, Jena, 1906

"We aim in the domain of politics at republicanism; in the domain of economics at socialism; in the domain of what is today called religion, at atheism."—Bebel, summarizing his party's agenda

"The Catholic priest, from the moment he becomes a priest, is a sworn officer of the pope."—Otto von Bismarck (1815–1898), Prussian statesman, speech in the Prussian upper house, April 12, 1886

"I have wished to crush Rome that I might crush Christianity."—Bismarck (Noyes)

"I have seldom met an intelligent person whose views were not narrowed and distorted by religion."—U.S. President James Buchanan (1791–1868) (Noyes)

"I know that human prejudice—especially that growing out of race and religion— is cruelly inveterate and lasting."—U.S. President Grover Cleveland (1837–1908) (Noyes)

"I took the repeal of the Corn Laws as light amusement compared with the difficult task of inducing the priests of all denominations to agree to suffer the people to be educated."—Richard Cobden (1804–1865), British champion of free trade and universal education, in letter to a friend, 1846

"Man is made to adore and obey: but if you will not command him, if you give him nothing to worship, he will fashion his own divinities. . . ."—Benjamin Disraeli (1804–1881), English politician and author, *Coningsby,* 1844, book 4, chapter 13

"The Vatican is a dagger in the heart of Italy."—Giuseppe Garibaldi (1807–1882), Italian military and nationalist leader, letter to Charles Darwin about evolution

"Man has created God, not God, man."—Garibaldi (Cardiff)

"The priest is the personification of falsehood."—Garibaldi (Noyes)

"In 1850, I believe, the church property in the United States, which paid no tax, amounted to $87 million. In 1900, without a check, it is safe to say, this property will reach a sum exceeding $3 billion. I would suggest the taxation of all property equally."—U.S. President Ulysses S. Grant (1822–1885) (Noyes)

"When I remember thee in days to come, O Jerusalem, it will not be with pleasure. The musty deposits of 2,000 years of inhumanity, intolerance, and uncleanliness lie in the foul-smelling alleys. . . . The amiable dreamer of Nazareth has only contributed to increasing the hatred. . . . What superstition and fanaticism on every side!"—Theodor Herzl (1860–1904), founder of modern Zionism, after a visit to Jerusalem in 1898

"I regard religion itself as quite unnecessary for a nation's life; science is far above superstition; and what is religion, Buddhism or Christianity, but superstition, and therefore a possible source of weakness to a nation?"—Hirobumi Ito (1841– 1909), Japanese prime minister in the 1890s, quoted in S. L. Gulick, *The Evolution of the Japanese*

"The Puritan hated bear-baiting, not because it gave pain to the bear, but because it gave pleasure to the spectators."—Thomas B. Macaulay (1800–1859), English writer and politician, *History of England,* 1848, vol. 1, chapter 2

"The Church is the handmaid of tyranny and the steady enemy of liberty." —Macaulay (Cardiff)

"With respect to the doctrine of a future life, a North American Indian knows just as much as any ancient or modern philosopher."—Macaulay (Noyes)

"Not two hundred men in London believe in the Bible."—Macaulay, ibid.

"If Sir Thomas More could have believed in the nonsense of transubstantiation, men may always believe in it."—Macaulay, ibid.

"The hostility of the people to the friars was beyond doubt one of the causes of the rebellion."—U.S. President William McKinley (1843–1901), reporting on the Philippine uprising (Noyes)

"I am without religious feeling."—Charles Sumner (1811–1874), American statesman (Cardiff)

"All creeds are fallible and uncertain evidences of evangelical piety."—Daniel Webster (1782–1852), American lawyer and statesman (Noyes)

Others

"The orthodox faith painted God as a revengeful being, and yet people talk about loving such a being."—P. T. Barnum (1810–1891), American showman (Noyes)

"Me pray? Never! I'm an atheist."—Sarah Bernhardt (1844–1923), French actress (Cardiff)

"The more I study religions, the more I am convinced that man never worshipped anything but himself."—Sir Richard Burton (1812–1890), English explorer (Gray)

"It is strange beyond anything I can think to be able to believe in *any* of the known religions."—Kate Greenaway (1846–1901), English painter and illustrator (Cardiff)

"There is no such source and cause of strife, quarrel, fights, malignant opposition, persecution, and war, and all evil in the state, as religion. Let it once enter into our civil affairs, our government soon would be destroyed. Let it once enter our common schools, they would be destroyed. Those who made our Constitution saw this, and used the most apt and comprehensive language in it to prevent such a catastrophe."—Supreme Court of Wisconsin, *Weiss* v. *District Board,* March 18, 1890

Part Six

The Early
Twentieth Century

46

Thomas Alva Edison (1847-1931)

Dover

America's supreme inventor—creator of the electric light, the phonograph, the movie projector, the carbon telephone transmitter, and a thousand other devices—was also a whimsical skeptic who laughed at supernatural beliefs.

Edison, "the wizard of Menlo Park," was a revered American celebrity in the early years of the twentieth century. But he stirred national wrath in 1910 by giving blunt answers in news interviews.

In one, a reporter asked: "What does God mean to you?" Edison replied: "Not a damn thing." The hypothesis of an invisible deity is merely "an abstraction," he said, adding that "billions of prayers" had been uttered with no discernible effect on disasters or wars.[1]

In another interview, Edison stated: "So far as religion of the day is concerned, it is a damned fake. . . . Religion is all bunk. . . . All bibles are man-made."[2]

A full-page article in the *New York Times* said of Edison: "A merciful and loving Creator he considers not to be believed in. Nature, the supreme power, he recognizes and respects, but does not worship."

The news reports caused a storm: Angry ministers protested from their pulpits. Thousands of irate letters arrived at Edison's New Jersey laboratory. A Catholic cardinal wrote in *Columbian Magazine* that Edison's views on profound questions carried no weight because he was, after all, "a mere mechanic." Edison's business investors begged him not to taint Edison Industries by further blasphemy.

Edison tried to explain away his earlier statements by saying he believed in "a supreme intelligence." But the controversy lingered for years.

Occasionally, the inventor played games with his detractors. In 1920, he announced that he was working on an electronic device to communicate with departed souls: "It will give them a better opportunity to express themselves than Ouija boards

---

1. Matthew Josephson, *Edison: A Biography* (New York: McGraw-Hill, 1959), p. 437
2. (Cardiff, Seldes, Gray)

or tilting tables." When a minister inquired about installing lightning rods on his church spire, Edison replied: "By all means, as Providence is apt to be absent-minded."

Edison had been an agnostic since boyhood, and he was unorthodox in other ways. He attended school only three months in his entire life. Teachers labeled Edison retarded, but his mother knew better and taught him at home, where his keen mind flowered. By age twelve, he had read Gibbon's *The Decline and Fall of the Roman Empire,* Burton's *Anatomy of Melancholy,* and other classics. He read Paine's famed attack on Christianity, *The Age of Reason,* and later recounted: "I can still remember the flash of enlightenment that shone from his pages."

According to biographer Matthew Josephson, "the skeptical writings of Darwin, Huxley and Tyndall were the favorite reading of Edison's youth." Biographer Wyn Wachhorst states, "Edison rejected three fundamental tenets of Christianity: the divinity of Christ, a personal God, and immortality."[3]

Science became Edison's obsession. Even while working as a newsboy on a passenger train, he conducted experiments in a private corner. At age twenty-one, he repaired a broken telegraph ticker in a New York gold market office and landed a job as an electrical technician. Later, he struck out on his own, creating the world's first industrial research laboratory. Success followed upon success. Fame and wealth came to him. Nor did growing deafness deter him.

After his first wife died, Edison courted Mina Miller, a devout Methodist, with whom he clashed over religion. In 1898, when President McKinley publicly thanked God for victory in the Spanish-American War, Edison wrote to her: "But the same God gave us yellow fever, and to be consistent McKinley ought to have thanked him for that also."

After they were married, Mina invited clergymen to dinner, to pressure her agnostic husband. Once she entertained six Methodist bishops, triggering a ferocious theological debate that ended when Edison said, "I'm not going to listen to any more of this nonsense!" and stormed out.[4]

Afterward, the Edisons agreed not to discuss religion, and so lived happily until his death at age eighty-four.

Edison's Views on Religion

"I cannot believe in the immortality of the soul. . . . No, all this talk of an existence for us, as individuals, beyond the grave is wrong. It is born of our tenacity of life— our desire to go on living—our dread of coming to an end as individuals. I do not dread it, though. Personally, I cannot see any use of a future life."—interview in the *New York Times,* October 2, 1910, sect. 5, p. 1

---

3. Wyn Wachhorst, *Thomas Alva Edison: An American Myth* (Cambridge, Mass.: MIT Press, 1982).

4. Josephson, *Edison: A Biography,* p. 438.

"We do not know the gods of the religions. . . . No, nature made us—nature did it all—not the gods of the religions."—ibid.

"I have never seen the slightest scientific proof of the religious theories of heaven and hell, of future life for individuals, or of a personal God. . . . I work on certain lines that might be called, perhaps, mechanical. . . . Proof! Proof! That is what I have always been after. I do not know the soul, I know the mind. If there is really any soul, I have found no evidence of it in my investigations. . . . I do not believe in the God of the theologians; but that there is a Supreme Intelligence, I do not doubt."—statement issued amid the public controversy generated in 1910, in Josephson, *Edison: A Biography,* p. 438

"When a man is dead, he is dead! My mind is incapable of conceiving such a thing as a soul. I may be in error, and man may have a soul; but I simply do not believe it."—*Do We Live Again?*

"I do not believe that any type of religion should ever be introduced into the public schools of the United States."—(Seldes)

"My conscience seems to be oblivious to Sundays. It must be encrusted with a sort of irreligious tartar."—entry in his diary

"I wish to thank you for Mr. Lewis' book on 'Lincoln the Freethinker.' This is another of the many publications brought out in late years which are dispelling the clouds of superstition and breaking our bondage to a mythical religion."—letter to Lincoln Publishing Co., November 19, 1924

"The great trouble is that the preachers get the children from six to seven years of age, and then it is almost impossible to do anything with them. Incurably religious—that is the best way to describe the mental condition of so many people. Incurably religious."—conversation with Joseph Lewis on December 3, 1929, reported in Joseph Lewis, *Atheism and Other Addresses* (reprint New York: Arno Press, 1972)

"Thomas Paine . . . has been called an atheist, but atheist he was not. Paine believed in a supreme intelligence, as representing the idea which other men often express by the name of deity. His Bible was the open face of nature, the broad skies, the green hills. He disbelieved the ancient myths and miracles taught by established creeds. But the attacks on those creeds—or on persons devoted to them—have served to darken his memory, casting a shadow across the closing years of his life. When Theodore Roosevelt termed Tom Paine a dirty little atheist, he surely spoke from lack of understanding."—from an introduction Edison wrote for a book on Paine in 1916

"The endeavor to change universal power by selfish supplication I do not believe in."—(Noyes)

"Why we come here, and where we are going, is beyond my ken."—ibid.

47

Luther Burbank (1849–1926)

Dover

One of America's most beloved scientists was Luther Burbank, who improved the world's food supply. In an era when agriculture still was the chief occupation, he was a brilliant botanist who bred high-yield fruit trees, vegetables, grains, and other crops.

As a schoolboy in Massachusetts, Burbank was intrigued by the scientific discoveries of Charles Darwin. He began gardening to support his widowed mother, and experimented with cross-pollination to produce better foods. Eventually he moved to California, where he established an experimental farm.

Like many scientists, Burbank rejected supernaturalism. He kept his skepticism to himself until the notorious 1925 "Scopes Monkey Trial" in Tennessee, in which William Jennings Bryan waged fundamentalism's battle against Darwin's theory of evolution.

In January 1926, while being interviewed by a young newspaper reporter, Burbank "went public" with his disbelief. He said religious dogmas are nonsense, and called himself "an infidel." The disclosure was telegraphed around the world, causing a shock wave. There followed a storm of letters and visits to the aging scientist. Burbank's close friend Episcopal minister Frederick Clampett wrote:

> Poor Luther Burbank, who never injured a fellow mortal in his more than seventy years, the gentlest, purest, kindliest of men, was made the object of a narrow, bitter, religious war of words. . . . This champion of the poor and the afflicted was pestered by women of the several evangelical churches, who had formed groups of praying circles to supplicate their God that he might grant the deluded and benighted Burbank light, repentance and forgiveness. His home was besieged by self-appointed representatives of the "faithful" who implored him to recant.[1]

---

1. Frederick W. Clampett, *Luther Burbank: Our Beloved Infidel* (New York: Macmillan, 1926; reprint Greenwood, Conn.: Greenwood Press, 1979), pp. 34–35.

The "angry tumult of incarnated fanaticism," as Clampett called it, only strengthened Burbank's resolve. In a followup interview, the elderly scientist reiterated: "I am an infidel. I know what an infidel is, and that's what I am."

Several churches asked him to speak, to clarify his views. He accepted one invitation, to San Francisco's First Congregational Church. In his talk to the parishioners, Burbank spoke gently, but insisted that religious concepts such as hell are "superstition gone to seed."

Many people supported Burbank. Ina Coolbrith, California's poet laureate, sent him a book of her poems inscribed "To our beloved infidel."

Burbank died soon afterward. Friends felt that the strain of the tempest hastened his death. His open-air funeral was attended by ten thousand mourners. His eulogy was given by Judge Ben Lindsey of Denver, a freethinker whom Burbank previously had asked to perform this duty. Judge Lindsey told the throng:

> Luther Burbank will rank with the great leaders who have driven heathenish gods back into darkness. . . . Burbank had a philosophy that actually works for human betterment, that dares to challenge the superstition, hypocrisy and sham, which so often have worked for cruelties, inquisitions, wars and massacres. . . .
>
> Thomas Edison, who believes very much as Luther Burbank, once discussed with me immortality. He pointed to the electric light, his invention, saying: "There lives Tom Edison." So Luther Burbank lives. He lives forever in the myriad fields of strengthened grain, in the new forms of fruits and flowers, and plants, and vines, and trees, and above all, the newly watered gardens of the human mind. . . .[2]

Burbank's Views on Religion

". . . As a scientist, I cannot help feeling that all religions are on a tottering foundation. . . . I am an infidel today. I do not believe what has been served to me to believe. I am a doubter, a questioner, a skeptic. When it can be proved to me that there is immortality, that there is resurrection beyond the gates of death, then will I believe. Until then, no."—*San Francisco Bulletin*, January 22, 1926, p. 1

"The idea that a good God would send people to a burning hell is utterly damnable to me—the ravings of insanity, superstition gone to seed! I don't want to have anything to do with such a God."—address to members of the First Congregational Church, San Francisco, January 31, 1926

"We must not be deceived by blind leaders of the blind, calmly expecting to be 'saved' by anyone except by the kingdom within ourselves."—ibid.

---

2. *Freethought Today*, August 1993, p. 8.

"For the little soul that cries aloud for continued personal existence for itself and its beloved, there is no hope."—ibid.

"Euripides long ago said, 'Who dares not speak his free thought is a slave.' I nominated myself as an 'infidel' as a challenge to thought for those who are asleep."—ibid.

"The devil has never concerned me, as I have always used my own conscience, not the dictum of any cult."—ibid.

"Let us have one world at a time, and let us make the journey one of joy to our fellow passengers and just as convenient and happy for them as we can, and trust the rest as we trust life. Let us read the Bible without the ill-fitting colored spectacles of theology, just as we read other books, using our judgment and reason, listening to the voice, not the noisy babble without. Most of us possess discriminating reasoning powers. Can we use them or must we be fed by others like babes?"—ibid.

"Mr. Bryan was an honored friend of mine, yet this need not prevent the observation that the skull with which nature endowed him visibly approached the Neanderthal type. . . . Those who would legislate against the teaching of evolution should also legislate against gravity, electricity and the unreasonable velocity of light, and also should introduce a clause to prevent the use of the telescope, the microscope and the spectroscope, or any other instrument of precision which may in the future be invented, constructed or used for the discovery of truth."—*Science and Civilization*

"Science, which is only another name for truth, now holds religious charlatans, self-deceivers and God-agents in a certain degree of check—agents and employees, I mean, of a mythical, medieval, man-made God, anthropomorphic in constitution."—from a summary of his beliefs prepared by Burbank for his friend, the Rev. Frederick Clampett, quoted in Clampett's *Luther Burbank: Our Beloved Infidel*, p. 137

"The word 'religion' has acquired a very bad name among those who really love truth, justice, charity. It also exhales the musty odor of sanctimony and falsehood."—ibid.

"Scientists gladly accept any new truth which can be demonstrated by experiment, that is, proved by the very law of the cosmos. Not so with any new conceptions of religion; these are fought by the use of persecution and venom. Many of the current religious beliefs literally carried into practice would stampede humanity into the old jungle ideas and habits."—ibid., p. 132

"Science has shown us all we know about what we call God. There is no other real knowledge besides—all else is theorizing without a shadow of proof for those who think."—ibid., p. 136

"The integrity of one's own mind is of infinitely more value than adherence to any creed or system. We must choose between a dead faith belonging to the past and a living, growing, ever-advancing science belonging to the future."—ibid., p. 133

"There is no personal salvation; there is no national salvation, except through science."—(Seldes)

"I am an infidel in the true sense of that word."—ibid.

"Those who take refuge behind theological barbed wire fences, quite often wish they could have more freedom of thought, but fear the change to the great ocean of scientific truth as they would a cold bath plunge."—*Why I Am an Infidel*

"Most people's religion is what they want to believe."—ibid.

"Do not feed children on maudlin sentimentalism or dogmatic religion; give them nature."—(Noyes)

48

Elbert Hubbard
(1856–1915)

Dover

Elbert Hubbard, one of America's most popular writers at the turn of the twentieth century, turned his verbal outpourings into a one-man industry.

An Illinois native, Hubbard settled in New York State and founded Roycroft Press in East Aurora, just outside of Buffalo. He published *The Philistine,* an avant-garde magazine, and wrote "Little Journey" booklets, biographies of famous people. Later he added a second magazine, *The Fra.* A persistent theme in Hubbard's writing was contempt for supernaturalism. Again and again, he attacked belief in a spirit world.

Hubbard's most famous essay, "A Message to Garcia," first printed in an 1899 issue of *The Philistine,* praised the perseverance of an American officer in the Spanish-American War who penetrated the jungles of Cuba to contact the leader of Cuban rebels against the Spanish. In his other writing, Hubbard sometimes seemed liberal, sometimes conservative; but he always upheld diligence, honesty, persistence, integrity, and effective work.

He enlarged his printing plant to include an art school and workshops for handmade furniture, wrought iron, leather goods, and other crafts.

In 1915, Hubbard was a passenger on the British liner *Lusitania,* which was torpedoed by a German submarine off the coast of Ireland. He died along with 1,200 other passengers. The sinking impelled America into World War I.

After Hubbard's death, Roycroft Press published several collections of his comments, including many scathing jabs at religion.

Hubbard's Views on Religion

"Who are those who will eventually be damned? Oh, the others, the others, the others!"—*The Roycroft Dictionary of Epigrams,* 1923

"Heaven: The Coney Island of the Christian imagination."—ibid.

"God: The John Doe of philosophy and religion."—ibid.

"Miracle: An event described by those to whom it was told by men who did not see it."—ibid.

"Christianity supplies a Hell for the people who disagree with you, and a Heaven for your friends."—*The Note Book,* 1927

"Martyrs and persecutors are the same type of man. As to which is the persecutor and which the martyr, this is only a question of transient power."—ibid.

"Dogma is a lie reiterated and authoritatively injected into the mind of one or more persons who believe that they believe what someone else believes."—ibid.

"Orthodoxy: That peculiar condition where the patient can neither eliminate an old idea nor absorb a new one."—ibid.

"No man should dogmatize except on the subject of theology. Here he can take his stand, and by throwing the burden of proof on the opposition, he is invincible. We have to die to find out whether he is right."—ibid.

"Formal religion was organized for slaves: it offered them consolation which earth did not provide."—*The Philistine*

"A good man in an exclusive heaven would be in hell."—ibid.

"Theology is an attempt to explain a subject by men who do not understand it. The intent is not to tell the truth but to satisfy the questioner."—ibid.

"Faith is the effort to believe what your common sense tells you is not true."—(Wilcox/George)

"A mystic is a person who is puzzled before the obvious, but who understands the nonexistent."—ibid.

"Theology is Classified Superstition."—(Cardiff)

"Gradually the consensus of intelligence has pushed theology off into the dustbin of oblivion, with alchemy and astrology."—ibid.

"Theology is voodooism; in matters of importance it is in the class with alchemy, astrology, palmistry, augury and allopath medicine."—ibid.

"Organized religion, being founded on superstition, is, perforce, not scientific. And all that which is not scientific—that is, truthful—must be bolstered up by force, fear and falsehood. Thus we always find slavery and organized religion going hand in hand."—ibid.

"Voltaire freed countless millions from theological superstition, that Bastille of the brain."—ibid.

"When certain unmarried men, who had lost their capacity to sin, sat indoors, breathing bad air, and passed resolutions about what was right and what wrong, making rules for the guidance of the people, instead of trusting to the natural, happy instincts of the individual, they ushered in the Dark Ages. These are the gentlemen who blocked human evolution absolutely for a thousand years."—ibid.

". . . All religions were made and formulated by men. . . . What we call God's justice is only man's idea of what he would do if he were God."—ibid.

"The bitterness of theology toward science arises from the fact that as we find things out, we dispense with the arbitrary god, and his business agent, the priest, who insists that no transaction is legal unless he ratifies it."—ibid.

"Poverty, ignorance, repression, superstition, coercion, disease, with nights of horror and days of fear, are slinking away into the past; and they have slunk further and further away, the more Christianity's clutch upon the throat of the race has been loosened."—ibid.

"Do you say that religion is still needed? Then I answer that Work, Study, Health and Love constitute religion. . . . Most formal religions have pronounced the love of man for woman and woman for man an evil thing. . . . They have said that sickness was sent from God. . . . Now we deny it all, and again proclaim that these will bring you all the good there is: Health, Work, Study—Love!"—ibid.

"Theology, by diverting the attention of men from this life to another, and by endeavoring to coerce all men into one religion, constantly preaching that this world is full of misery, but the next world would be beautiful—or not, as the case may be—has forced on men the thought of fear where otherwise there might have been the happy abandon of nature."—ibid.

"Men whose lives are doubtful want a strong government and a hot religion."—(Noyes)

"Great sinners are apt to be very religious; and conversely the best men who have ever lived have been at war with established religions."—ibid.

49

Sigmund Freud (1856–1939)

AP/Wide World Photos

Sigmund Freud, the great Viennese explorer of the mind, is recognized world-wide as the chief founder of modern psychiatry. His explanation of childhood sexual urges and the Oedipus complex, of the action of repressed thoughts in the subconscious, of wish-fulfillment in dreams, and of other hidden mental processes have become part of the world's scientific knowledge.

But the public is generally unaware that Freud was a fervent crusader against religion, which he deemed an obstacle to human intelligence.

Popular television host Phil Donahue wrote that Freud prodded the Western world to think scientifically and drop the "childish ways" of believing in spirit realms. Here is Donahue's summation of Freud's message:

> "Grow up," he seemed to be saying, as if giving a child a spoonful of castor oil. "Forget those silly old tales. There's no heaven, no hell, no angels, or devils or gods or saviors. Be brave and accept the natural world of science." Religion's eleventh commandment is "Thou shalt not question," and Freud saw in that pro-hibition a bar to scientific inquiry, which begins with questions.[1]

Similarly, biographer Philip Rieff remarked: "Religion may have been the original cure; Freud reminds us that it was also the original disease."[2] And British Jewish leader Jacob Meitlis recalled that Freud, his friend, felt that "all religions were matters created by human beings, and he could discern no trace of sanctity in any of them."[3]

Again and again in his writing, Freud contended that small children have awe-

1. Phil Donahue, *The Human Animal* (New York: Simon & Schuster, 1985), p. 382.
2. Philip Rieff, "The Religion of the Fathers," in *Freud: The Mind of the Moralist* (New York: Viking, 1959).
3. Ronald W. Clark, *Freud: The Man and the Cause* (New York: Random House, 1980), p. 523.

some images of their fathers as powerful protectors and punishers, and that, years later, this fantasy of the Great Father, still buried in the subconscious, attaches itself to the imaginary God of religion. Thus, unwittingly, believers worship the submerged infantile memory of their fathers. Repeatedly, Freud called religion a "universal obsessional neurosis."

Freud's scientific realism developed at an early age. A brilliant student, he entered medical school under physiologist Ernst Brücke, who taught that the human psyche is purely biological, not mystical or divine. Brücke had himself been influenced by physicist Hermann Helmholtz's contention that "no other forces than the common physical-chemical ones are active within the organism."

Throughout his career of analyzing human behavior, Freud attempted to apply scientific methods to understanding fears, feelings, and fantasies. Today, his methods have been partly abandoned, yet he is known as the principal pioneer in grasping the submerged elements of human nature.

Incidentally, the manner of Freud's death foreshadowed today's euthanasia controversy, as it has focused on Dr. Jack Kevorkian, who assists hopeless patients in painless expiration. A heavy cigar smoker, Freud developed mouth cancer that blighted the last twenty-two years of his life. While he strove to continue working and writing, he underwent thirty-three operations and eventually was forced to wear a grotesque prosthesis. Finally exhausted, he persuaded his physician to give him enough morphine to end his suffering forever.

Freud's Views on Religion

"Neither in my private life nor in my writings, have I ever made a secret of being an out-and-out unbeliever."—letter to Charles Singer

"Religion is an attempt to get control over the sensory world, in which we have been placed, by means of the wish-world which we have developed inside us as a result of biological and psychological necessities. But it cannot achieve its end. Its doctrines carry with them the stamp of the times in which they originated, the ignorant childhood days of the human race. Its consolations deserve no trust. . . . If one attempts to assign to religion its place in man's evolution, it seems not so much to be a lasting acquisition, as a parallel to the neurosis which the civilized individual must pass through on his way from childhood to maturity."—*Moses and Monotheism,* 1939

"Religion is an illusion and it derives its strength from the fact that it falls in with our instinctual desires."—*New Introductory Lectures in Psychoanalysis,* 1933

"The God-Creator is openly called Father. Psychoanalysis concludes that he really is the father, clothed in the grandeur in which he once appeared to the small child.

The religious man's picture of the creation of the universe is the same as his picture of his own creation. . . . He therefore looks back on the memory-image of the overrated father of his childhood, exalts it into a deity, and brings it into the present and into reality. The emotional strength of this memory-image and the lasting nature of his need for protection are the two supports for his belief in God." —ibid.

"Religion . . . comprises a system of wishful illusions together with a disavowal of reality, such as we find in an isolated form nowhere else but in amentia, in a state of blissful hallucinatory confusion."—*The Future of an Illusion,* 1927

"Religion is comparable to a childhood neurosis."—ibid.

"Our knowledge of the historical worth of certain religious doctrines increases our respect for them, but does not invalidate our proposal that they should cease to be put forward as the reasons for the precepts of civilization. On the contrary! Those historical residues have helped us to view religious teachings, as it were, as neurotic relics. . . ."—ibid.

"The different religions have never overlooked the part played by the sense of guilt in civilization. What is more, they come forward with a claim . . . to save mankind from this sense of guilt, which they call sin."—*Civilization and its Discontents,* 1930

"Religions originate in the child's and young mankind's fears and need for help. It cannot be otherwise."—to colleague Ludwig Binswanger in 1927, quoted in Clark, *Freud: The Man and the Cause,* p. 469

"The Nazis? I am not afraid of them. Help me rather to combat my true enemy . . . Religion, the Roman Catholic Church."—to colleague René Laforgue, ibid., p. 491

"The Catholic Church so far has been the implacable enemy of all freedom of thought."—(Cardiff)

"When a man is freed of religion, he has a better chance to live a normal and wholesome life."—(Gray)

"Monotheism . . . revealed the father nucleus which had always lain hidden behind every divine figure. . . . A return to the historical roots of the idea of God . . . the intimacy and intensity of the child's relation to the father."—quoted in *Webster's New World Dictionary of Quotable Definitions*

"Religion is a universal, obsessional neurosis of mankind."—quoted by Dr. John R. Everett, president of Hollins College, in *Encyclopedia Americana,* 1955

"A religion, even if it calls itself a religion of love, must be hard and unloving to those who do not belong to it."—*Group Psychology and the Analysis of the Ego,* 1921

"When once the Apostle Paul had posited universal love between men as the foundation of his Christian community, extreme intolerance on the part of Christendom toward those who remained outside it became the inevitable consequence."—(Peter)

"How strange this tragically mad land you have visited must have seemed to you. [The Holy Land] has never produced anything but religions, sacred frenzies, presumptuous attempts to overcome the outer world of appearances by means of the inner world of wishful thinking."—from a letter to novelist Arnold Zweig, who had just returned from a visit to Palestine

"I can muster no sympathy whatever for the misguided piety that makes a national religion from a piece of the wall of Herod, and for its sake challenges the feelings of the local natives."—discussing Zionism, the Wailing Wall, and the Palestinian problem in a letter to Albert Einstein, 1930

50

George Bernard Shaw (1856–1950)

AP/Wide World Photos

A whimsical maverick, the great playwright George Bernard Shaw scoffed at religion, lampooned Christianity, and once called himself an atheist; yet he had a tinge of mysticism and speculated that a "life force" impels all creatures.

Shaw was born in Dublin to impecunious Protestant parents who mostly ignored religion, but felt socially superior to Irish Catholics. Shaw's first published writing, when he was nineteen, was a letter to *Public Opinion* belittling a Dublin revival staged by the renowned American evangelist Dwight Moody. Shaw said crowds attend such services for free entertainment, and those who are converted become "highly objectionable members of society."

After his mother went to London to pursue a singing career, Shaw joined her. In those years of his youth, he declared that he was, "like Shelley, a socialist, an atheist, and a vegetarian." He became a leader of the Fabian Society of socialists; he also plunged into fiction writing, with scant financial success.

Shaw spoke vigorously in support of Charles Bradlaugh, an agnostic lecturer who had been elected to the House of Commons but refused admittance because he would not take a religious oath. Bradlaugh headed England's National Secular Society. After his death in 1891, society members invited Shaw to speak, eyeing him as a possible leader. But Shaw attacked the group as fundamentalist in its militancy.

After the turn of the century, Shaw's plays began to score successes in London and America. Most of them were laced with his socialistic scorn for ruling classes and exploiters. Several also tweaked religion. And some expressed his concept of the life force.

Shaw became a celebrated figure of the twentieth century, renowned for his iconoclastic wit. He was awarded the Nobel Prize for literature in 1925. He produced fifty-four plays and more than twenty volumes of other writings before his death at age ninety-four. He went to his grave a skeptic.

Warren Sylvester Smith, editor of *Shaw on Religion,* summed it up:

Shaw would never allow himself to be called a Christian. Yet he can be classed as an unbeliever only in the sense that there was, as he said at the end of his life, no church in the world that would receive him, or any in which he could consent to be received.[1]

Shaw's Views on Religion

"At present there is not a single credible established religion in the world." —*Major Barbara,* 1905, preface

"Popular Christianity has for its emblem a gibbet, for its chief sensation a sanguinary execution after torture, for its central mystery an insane vengeance bought off by a trumpery execution."—ibid.

"Learning learns but one lesson: doubt!"—*The Admirable Bashville,* 1901

"It is not disbelief that is dangerous to our society, it is belief."—*Androcles and the Lion,* 1912

"No sooner had Jesus knocked over the dragon of superstition than Paul boldly set it on its legs again in the name of Jesus."—ibid., preface

"There has really never been a more monstrous imposition perpetrated than the imposition of the limitations of Paul's soul upon the soul of Jesus."—ibid.

"The conversion of Paul was no conversion at all: it was Paul who converted the religion that has raised one man above sin and death into a religion that delivered millions of men so completely into their dominion that their own common nature became a horror to them, and the religious life became a denial of life."—ibid.

"The followers of Paul and Peter made Christendom, whilst the Nazarenes were wiped out."—ibid.

"Heaven, as conventionally described, is a place so inane, so dull, so useless, so miserable, that nobody has ever ventured to describe a whole day in heaven, though plenty of people have described a day at the seaside."—*Misalliance,* 1910

"The fact that a believer is happier than a skeptic is no more to the point than the fact that a drunken man is happier than a sober one. The happiness of credulity is a cheap and dangerous quality."—quoted by Julian Huxley in *Religion without Revelation* (New York: Mentor Books, 1958), p. 12

---

1. Warren Sylvester Smith, "George Bernard Shaw," in *The Encyclopedia of Unbelief* (Amherst, N.Y.: Prometheus Books, 1985), p. 620.

"Without their fictions, the truths of religion would for the multitude be neither intelligible nor even apprehensible. . . . There is nothing in religion but fiction."
—*Back to Methuselah*, 1924

"I loathe the mess of mean superstitions and misunderstood prophecies which is still rammed down the throats of children under the name of Christianity."
—(Cardiff)

"When religious and ethical formulae become so obsolete that no man of strong mind can believe them, they have also reached the point at which no man of high character will profess them."—ibid.

"For the Catholic, there are but two countries, heaven and hell; but two conditions of men, salvation and damnation."—ibid.

"The world scraps its old steam engines and dynamos but not its old prejudices, its old moralities, its old religions. . . ."—ibid.

"Bible fetishism, after standing up to all the rationalistic batteries of Hume, Voltaire, and the rest, collapsed before the onslaught of much less gifted evolutionists, solely because they discredited it as a biological document; so that from that moment it lost its hold, and left literate Christendom faithless."—ibid.

"If dwindling sects like the Church of England, the Church of Rome, the Greek Church, and the rest, persist in trying to cramp the human mind within the limits of these grotesque perversions of natural truths and poetic metaphors, then they must be ruthlessly banished from the schools."—ibid.

"Shakespeare had no conscious religion."—ibid.

"Martyrdom is the only way in which a man can become famous without ability."—(Wilcox/George)

"There are scores of thousands of sects who are ready at a moment's notice to reveal the will of God on every possible subject."—(Peter)

"We have not lost faith, but we have transferred it from God to the medical profession."—ibid.

"If a woman opens a consulting firm on Bond Street, and sits there in strange robes professing to tell the future by cards or crystals or revelations made to her by spirits, she is prosecuted as a criminal for imposture. But if a man puts on strange robes and opens a church in which he professes to absolve us from the guilt of our misdeeds, to hold the keys of heaven and hell . . . to alleviate the lot of souls in purgatory, to speak with the voice of God, and to dictate what is sin and what is not to all the world, the police treat him with great respect; and nobody dreams of prosecuting him as an outrageous impostor."—(Gray)

"Emotional excitement reaches men through tea, tobacco, opium, whisky and religion."—(Noyes)

"Every church is in a state of frightful pecuniary dependence on Pharisees who use it to whitewash the most sordid commercial scoundrelism by external observances."—ibid.

"There is not one single established religion that an intelligent, educated man can believe."—ibid.

51

Clarence Darrow
(1857–1938)

Dover

Amirus Darrow was a Unitarian minister who abandoned even that vague faith and lived as a total agnostic. He and his wife, Emily, fostered a love of books, mental independence, and social justice in their eight children. Their home in rural Kinsman, Ohio, was a secret refuge on the Underground Railroad for runaway slaves. Neighbors ostracized the Darrows and called them atheists.

One of their children, Clarence, went on to become an American symbol of fearless rebellion against injustice and oppression of the mind.

After studying law and gaining admission to the Ohio bar, young Darrow moved to Chicago in 1887, where he immediately joined the effort to free anarchists charged with murder in the Haymarket Riot.

Later, Darrow became counsel of the North Western Railway, and could have grown wealthy—but he quit in order to work without pay defending Eugene V. Debs and other unionists arrested in a strike.

Thereafter, he constantly took unpopular cases, defending people despised by most of society. In 1907, Darrow succeeded in clearing labor radical "Big Bill" Haywood, who had been charged in the assassination of a former Idaho governor. In 1924, through an impassioned attack on the death penalty, he gained life sentences instead of execution for Richard Loeb and Nathan Leopold, wealthy Chicago teenagers who had murdered a younger boy for thrills.

Darrow's most sensational case was the 1925 "Scopes Monkey Trial" in Dayton, Tennessee. After fundamentalist politician William Jennings Bryan announced he would go to Tennessee to help prosecute a teacher charged with teaching evolution, Darrow rushed there to aid the defense.

"My object, and my only object," Darrow wrote in his autobiography, "was to focus the attention of the country on the program of Mr. Bryan and the other fundamentalists in America. I knew that education was in danger from the source that has always hampered it—religious fanaticism."[1]

Darrow said the accused teacher, John Scopes, was on trial "for the crime of teaching the truth." In the famous courtroom showdown, the judge refused to let Darrow present scientific evidence about evolution. So Darrow called Bryan to the witness stand as an expert on the Bible and exposed him, as Irving Stone said, "as an ignoramus with a childlike mind." Technically, the accused teacher was convicted, but in the eyes of thinking America, the trial was a victory by science over superstition.

Darrow went on to other major cases, such as his defense of an African-American family arrested for fighting off a mob seeking to drive blacks from a white Detroit neighborhood.

Like his father, Darrow was a humanist and disbeliever in the supernatural. He wrote essays dismissing the notion of gods, devils, heavens, and hells. He felt that the fantasy of a life after death prevented people from feeling greater sympathy for each other on earth. One of Darrow's essays ends eloquently:

> When we fully understand the brevity of life, its fleeting joys and unavoidable pains; when we accept the fact that all men and women are approaching an inevitable doom; the consciousness of it should make us more kindly and considerate of each other. This feeling should make men and women use their best efforts to help their fellow travelers on the road, to make the path brighter and easier . . . for the wayfarers who must live a common life and die a common death.[2]

At Darrow's funeral in 1938, a judge eulogized: "In Clarence Darrow's heart was infinite pity and mercy for the poor, the oppressed, the weak, and the erring—all races, all colors, all creeds, all humankind. . . . His great abilities were given freely to the cause of human liberty and for the succor of the weak and the unfortunate."

Another speaker said: "Darrow was born in Kinsman, Ohio, and he has been a kinsman to all mankind."

Darrow's Comments on Religion

"I don't believe in God because I don't believe in Mother Goose."—from a speech given in Toronto, 1930

"In spite of all the yearnings of men, no one can produce a single fact or reason to support the belief in God and in personal immortality."—article in *The Sign* magazine, May 1938

---

1. Clarence Darrow, *The Story of My Life* (New York: Charles Scribner's Sons, 1932).
2. Clarence Darrow, "The Myth of the Soul," in *Why I Am an Agnostic, and Other Essays* (Amherst, N.Y.: Prometheus Books, 1995), p. 39.

"If there is any God in the universe, I don't know it. Some people say they know it instinctively. Well, the errors and foolish things that men have known instinctively are so many we can't talk about them."—*Why I Am an Agnostic, and Other Essays,* p. 50

"I am an agnostic because I trust my reason. It may not be the greatest that ever existed. I am inclined to admit that it isn't. But it is the best I have."—ibid, p. 50.

"I feel, with Herbert Spencer, that whether the universe had an origin—and if it had—what the origin is will never be known by man."—ibid., p. 12

"Preachers pray for rain, knowing full well that no such prayer was ever answered. When a politician is sick, they pray for God to cure him, and the politician almost invariably dies. The modern clergyman who prays for rain and the health of the politician is no more intelligent in this matter than the primitive man who saw a separate miracle in the rising and setting of the sun. . . ."—ibid., p. 15

"Can anyone with intelligence really believe that a child born today should be doomed because the snake tempted Eve and Eve tempted Adam? To believe that is not God-worship; it is devil-worship."—ibid., p. 16

"When Voltaire was born, there was really but one church, which, of course, was ignorant, tyrannical and barbarous in the extreme. All creeds are alike, and whenever there is but one, and the rulers honestly believe in that one, they are bound to be ignorant, barbarous and cruel. All sorts of heresies were punishable by death. If anyone dared to write a pamphlet or book that questioned any part of the accepted faith, the book was at once consigned to the flames, and the author was lucky if he did not meet the same fate. Religion was not maintained by the precepts of the priest, but by the prison, the torture chamber and the fagot. Everyone believed; no one questioned."—ibid., pp. 53–54

"Upon what evidence, then, are we asked to believe in immortality? There is no evidence. One is told to rely on faith, and no doubt this serves the purpose so long as one can believe blindly whatever he is told."—ibid., p. 24

"The origin of the absurd idea of immortal life is easy to discover; it is kept alive by hope and fear, by childish faith, and by cowardice."—(Seldes)

"[Religion is based on] the insistence that over and above all is a purpose and a guiding hand that is beneficent and kind, and would not leave a hair unnumbered or let a sparrow fall unnoticed to the ground. Those who cherish such hallucinations forget that the all-loving power is inflicting tuberculosis, cancer, famine and pestilence on the trusting, simple sons of men."—*The Story of My Life*

"Religion is the belief in future life and in God. I don't believe in either."—*New York Times* interview, April 19, 1936

"I do not consider it an insult, but rather a compliment to be called an agnostic. I do not pretend to know where many ignorant men are sure—that is all that agnosticism means."—Scopes trial, Dayton, Tennessee, July 13, 1925

"I have suffered from being misunderstood, but I would have suffered a hell of a lot more if I had been understood."—quoted by Peter McWilliams in *Ain't Nobody's Business If You Do*, p. 817

"Whether it was a fire kindled to burn a heretic in Geneva—a gibbet erected to kill a witch in Salem—or a scaffold made to put to death an ordinary 'criminal,' it has ever been the same: the punishment of the creature for the creator's fault." —(Cardiff)

"The constant cries and pleadings of the ages have brought back no answering sound to prove that death is anything but death."—ibid.

"Every man knows when his life began. . . . If I did not exist in the past, why should I, or could I, exist in the future?"—ibid.

"The purpose of man is like the purpose of the pollywog—to wiggle along as far as he can without dying; or, to hang to life until death takes him."—ibid.

52

Francisco Ferrer (1859–1909)

Modern School Collection Rutgers University

Francisco Ferrer—a Spanish crusader against illiteracy, monarchy, militarism, and religion—was, in one sense, the last major European figure executed for heresy.

As a young man, he became sympathetic to political reformers opposing the entrenched power of the church and the aristocracy. Agitation and uprisings were common. Employed as a railway inspector, Ferrer helped Spanish dissidents escape into France. After an 1886 upheaval, he, too, was forced to flee.

In Paris, Ferrer renounced violence and began to see secular education as the best instrument to lift the populace out of darkness. At that time, nearly half of Spain's people could not read or write. Ferrer taught Spanish in Paris; one of his pupils, a wealthy humanitarian, left him a million gold francs to create nonreligious schools in Spain.

Ferrer's first "modern school" opened in Barcelona in 1902: it was coeducational and admitted both rich and poor. Religion was excluded; the scientific outlook prevailed. Ferrer scoffed at faith in the supernatural as "ancient error." He championed the rights of women, in opposition to the male supremacy fostered by the church. The all-powerful Catholic hierarchy deemed Ferrer and his "godless schools" to be agents of Satan.

Soon, forty of Ferrer's schools were operating in Barcelona, and textbooks from his publishing house were adopted by eighty others. Both children and their parents were learning to read in Ferrer's schools.

In 1906, an anarchist who had been Ferrer's rival for a woman threw a bomb at King Alfonso XIII and his bride on their wedding day, then killed himself. Ferrer was jailed and his schools were closed.

The following year, Ferrer was acquitted, but was kept under police surveillance. He organized the International League of Rational Education, thus worsening his conflict with the church.

In 1909, women demonstrated against conscription of their husbands to fight a war in Morocco. The unrest escalated into strikes and a "Tragic Week" uprising in which many churches and convents were destroyed. A prominent clergyman declared: "The partisans of the godless schools must be suppressed if peace is to be reestablished and Spain returned to God."

A military tribunal accused Ferrer and three other men of fomenting the rioting. Their trial was a travesty of hearsay and innuendo, with defense witnesses excluded. Ferrer was shot in a military fortress on October 13, 1909. His execution caused shock and anger around Europe. When parliament reconvened, Liberal members denounced the Conservative administration so furiously that Premier Antonio Maura was forced to resign.

However, Pope Pius X sent a gold-handled sword engraved with his felicitations to the military prosecutor who had obtained Ferrer's death.

Ferrer's Views on Religion

"When their god and his exploiters cease to be adored and served, we shall live like comrades in mutual respect and affection."—written on his jail cell wall in 1906

"I desire that on no occasion . . . shall demonstrations of a political or religious character be made before my remains. . . ."—final will, written on Ferrer's Barcelona prison cell wall in 1909 on the eve of his execution

"Let no more gods or exploiters be served. Let us learn rather to love each other."—ibid.

"When the masses become better informed about science, they will feel less need for help from supernatural Higher Powers. The need for religion will end when man becomes sensible enough to govern himself."—quoted in *The Encyclopedia of Unbelief,* edited by Gordon Stein, under "Ferrer, Francisco"

"It is a conspicuous fact in our modern Christian society that as a result and cumulation of our patriarchal development, the woman does not belong to herself. . . . Man has made her a perpetual minor."—ibid.

"Science has shown that the story of the creation is a myth and the gods legendary."—quoted by Paul Aurich in *The Modern School Movement: Anarchism and Education in the United States* (Princeton: Princeton University Press, 1980), p. 8.

53

John Dewey
(1859–1952)

If America had an office of national philosopher, Morris Cohen once wrote, the post would go to Dewey, a champion of scientific thinking and sensible morality.

A descendant of Vermont farmers, Dewey earned a Ph.D. degree from Johns Hopkins University in 1884 and became a professor at the University of Michigan. He married, had six children, and adopted an Italian boy during a trip to Europe.

Dewey's thinking evolved as he matured, and he was deeply affected by the breakthroughs of Charles Darwin, Sigmund Freud, and other landmark scientists. He came to regard nature as the only reality, and felt that all aspects of human life—including values and beliefs—are a product of human experience in nature.

Dewey also sought to reform education, to end the old practice of rote memorization, and to incorporate new findings on child psychology. In 1894, he moved to the University of Chicago to head a department encompassing all three of his fields: philosophy, psychology, and education. His fame as a scholar spread internationally. Along with William James and Charles Peirce, Dewey formulated pragmatism, the school of thought which judges concepts by the results they produce.

Dewey joined liberal, humanitarian causes. He became a trustee of Hull House, the Chicago sanctuary for the poor created by Jane Addams. Dewey sought laws to protect minorities, legalize labor unions, and curb business monopolies. After moving to Columbia University in 1904, he helped lead the American Civil Liberties Union and other reform organizations. Feeling that members of Congress were chiefly "errand boys of big business," he attempted to organize a third political party.

Although Dewey's mother had drilled him in strict religious instruction and he had belonged to a Congregational church in Michigan, he gradually renounced conventional faith. Says biographer George Dykhuizen:

During his Chicago years and thereafter, Dewey disassociated himself more and more from organized religion. . . . When his mother, a loyal and pious Congregationalist, remonstrated, declaring that the children ought to be sent to Sunday School, Dewey's reply was that in his youth he had gone to Sunday School enough to make up for his children's failure to do so.[1]

When conservative church groups attacked University of Chicago theologians for their unorthodox beliefs, Dewey defended their right to free thought.

Dewey repudiated what he called militant atheism. He felt that people have innate religious qualities, such as compassion for sufferers, an urge to improve life, and a sense of awe before the mysteries of existence. However, by the standards of conventional religion, Dewey was an atheist.

Dewey's Comments on Religion

"Intellectually, religious emotions are not creative but conservative. They attach themselves readily to the current view of the world and consecrate it."—*The Influence of Darwin on Philosophy,* 1909

"Modern philosophy . . . certainly exacts a surrender of all supernaturalism and fixed dogma and rigid institutionalism with which Christianity has been historically associated. . . . Faith in the Divine Author and Authority in which Western civilization confided, inherited ideas of the soul and its destiny, of fixed revelation . . . have been made impossible for the cultivated mind of the Western world." —(Cardiff)

"There is nothing left worth preserving in the notions of unseen powers, controlling human destiny, to which obedience and worship are due."—ibid.

"Demons were once appealed to in order to explain bodily disease, and no such thing as a strictly natural death was supposed to happen. The importation of general moral causes to explain present social phenomena is on the same intellectual level. Reinforced by the prestige of traditional religions, and backed by the emotional force of beliefs in the supernatural, it stifles the growth of . . . social intelligence."—ibid.

"Criticism of the commitment of religion to the supernatural is thus positive in import."—ibid.

"There can be no doubt . . . of our dependence upon forces beyond our control. Primitive man was so impotent in the face of these forces that, especially in an un-

---

favorable natural environment, fear became a dominant attitude, and, as the old saying goes, fear created gods."—ibid.

"Religions have been universal in the sense that all the people we know anything about have had a religion. But the differences among them are so great and so shocking that any common element that can be extracted is meaningless. . . . The older apologists for Christianity seem to have been better advised than some modern ones in condemning every religion but one as an impostor, as at bottom some kind of demon worship or at any rate a superstitious figment."—ibid.

"I believe that many persons are . . . repelled from what exists as a religion by its intellectual and moral implications."—ibid.

"Men move between extremes. They conceive of themselves as gods, or feign a powerful and cunning god as an ally who bends the world to do their bidding and meet their wishes."—(Greeley)

"Apologists for a religion often point to the shift that goes on in scientific ideas and materials as evidence of the unreliability of science as a mode of knowledge. They often seem peculiarly elated by the great, almost revolutionary, change in fundamental physical conceptions that has taken place in science during the present generation. Even if the alleged unreliability were as great as they assume (or even greater), the question would remain: Have we any other recourse for knowledge? But in fact they miss the point. Science is not constituted by any particular body of subject matter. It is constituted by a method, a method of changing beliefs by means of tested inquiry. . . . Scientific method is adverse not only to dogma but to doctrine as well. . . . The scientific-religious conflict ultimately is a conflict between allegiance to this method and allegiance to even an irreducible minimum of belief so fixed in advance that it can never be modified."—ibid.

54

George Santayana
(1863–1952)

The great American philosopher George Santayana was an atheist, yet he was remarkably sympathetic to religion. He contended that religion, although factually untrue, should be cherished as irrational poetry. (Of course, to some believers, this may be a worse insult than a hostile attack.)

Santayana was born in Spain to unbeliever parents, who nonetheless sent him to Catholic schools and exposed him to Catholic traditions. Biographer John Lachs says this contradiction may account for the apocryphal story that Santayana "believed that there is no God, and the Virgin Mary is His mother."[1]

At age nine, Santayana was brought to America. He attended Boston Latin School and Harvard University, where he earned a Ph.D. in philosophy and joined the faculty. In the first decade of the twentieth century, he came to be regarded as one of the nation's foremost philosophers, writing superbly in several fields.

Santayana was as peculiar about his career as he was about religion. After being appointed a full professor at Harvard, he resigned during a European trip and never returned to America. He was offered a professorship at Oxford University, but declined.

Santayana lived his last years in Rome. After his death at eighty-eight, the odd atheist was buried, as he requested, in Rome's Catholic Cemetery, in a section reserved for Spaniards.

---

1. John Lachs, *George Santayana* (New York: Twayne Publishers, 1988), p. 25.

Santayana's Comments on Religion

"My atheism, like that of Spinoza, is true piety toward the universe and denies only gods fashioned by men in their own image, to be servants of their human interests."—"On My Friendly Critics," *Soliloquies in England,* 1922

"Faith in the supernatural is a desperate wager made by man at the lowest ebb of his fortunes."—"Supernaturalism," *Little Essays,* No. 108

"Christianity persecuted, tortured, and burned. Like a hound it tracked the very scent of heresy. It kindled wars, and nursed furious hatreds and ambitions. It sanctified, quite like Mohammedanism, extermination and tyranny. . . . Man, far from being freed from his natural passions, was plunged into artificial ones quite as violent and much more disappointing."—ibid., No. 107, "Christian Morality"

"Each religion . . . necessarily contradicts every other religion, and probably contradicts itself. . . . Religions, like languages, are necessary rivals. What religion a man shall have is a historical accident, quite as much as what language he shall speak."—ibid., No. 23, "Imaginative Nature of Religion"

"Prayer, among sane people, has never superseded practical efforts to secure the desired end."—ibid.

"Religious doctrines would do well to withdraw their pretension to be dealing with matters of fact. That pretension is not only the source of the conflicts of religion with science and of the vain and bitter controversies of sects; it is also the cause of the impurity and incoherence of religion in the soul."—ibid., No. 24, "Prosaic Misunderstandings"

"It is pathetic to observe how lowly the motives are that religion, even the highest, attributes to the deity. . . . To be given the best morsel, to be remembered, to be praised, to be obeyed blindly and punctiliously—these have been thought points of honor with the gods."—ibid., No. 26, "Pathetic Notions of God"

"No religion has ever given a picture of deity which men could have imitated without the grossest immorality."—ibid.

"For Shakespeare, in the matter of religion, the choice lay between Christianity and nothing. He chose nothing."—(Cardiff)

"In Shakespeare's time and country, to be religious already began to mean to be Puritanical; and in the divorce between the fullness of life on the one hand and the depth and unity of faith on the other, there could be no doubt to which side a man of imaginative instincts would attach himself. A world of passion and beauty without a meaning must seem to him more interesting and worthy than a world of empty principle and dogma, meager, fanatical, and false."—ibid.

"The brute necessity of believing something so long as life lasts does not justify any belief in particular."—*Skepticism and Animal Faith,* 1923

"Civilization is perhaps approaching one of those long winters that overtake it from time to time. Romantic Christendom—picturesque, passionate, unhappy episode—may be coming to an end. Such a catastrophe would be no reason for despair."—*Character and Opinion in the United States,* 1920

"Miracles are propitious accidents, the natural causes of which are too complicated to be readily understood."—*Introduction to the Ethics of Spinoza,* 1910

"The Bible is literature, not dogma."—ibid.

"Men have feverishly conceived a heaven only to find it insipid, and a hell to find it ridiculous."—*The Life of Reason: Reason in Art,* 1906

"No man of any depth of soul has made his prolonged existence [in heaven] the touchstone of his enthusiasms. . . . What a despicable character must a man be, and how sunk below the level of the most barbaric virtue, if he cannot bear to live for his children, for his art, or for country!"—ibid.

"We should have to abandon our vested illusions, our irrational religions and patriotisms."—ibid.

"Religion is the natural reaction of the imagination when confronted by the difficulties in a truculent world."—*Atlantic Monthly,* 1953

55

W. E. B. Du Bois (1868–1963)

Dover

For the first half of the twentieth century, William Edward Burghardt Du Bois was America's leading black intellectual and champion of racial equality.

He earned a doctorate in history at Harvard in 1895, wrote his riveting *The Souls of Black Folk* in 1903, helped establish the National Association for the Advancement of Colored People (NAACP) in 1909, and spent the next quarter century as the brilliant editor of the NAACP's journal, *Crisis.*

Du Bois's fervor for human rights drew him to socialism. His growing radicalism alienated moderates. He broke with the NAACP twice, and was banned from addressing its chapters.

During the McCarthy witch-hunt against "subversives," Du Bois's advocacy of cooperation with the Soviet Union caused him to be indicted as an unregistered agent of a foreign power. A judge declared him innocent. In 1961, however, Du Bois publicly joined the Communist party, partly as a political statement against McCarthyism.

Then in 1962 he went to Africa to create an *Encyclopedia Africana*; he renounced his American citizenship in 1963, the year he died in Ghana.

As for religion, Du Bois was an agnostic. David Howard-Pitney, a historian at San Jose State University, writes:

> Du Bois was not religious in any traditional sense; indeed, he was something of an anti-cleric. . . . Du Bois generally regarded institutional religion as a bastion of unreason and reaction that buttressed the status quo. He was a humanist and a rationalist, not a theist or a supernaturalist. Anti-rational dogma repelled him, and he ceased participating in organized worship as a young adult.[1]

---

1. In Norm R. Allen, Jr., ed., *African-American Humanism: An Anthology* (Amherst, N.Y.: Prometheus Books, 1991), p. 33 and footnote.

Du Bois's Comments on Religion

"My religious development has been slow and uncertain. . . . By the time of graduation, I was still a 'believer' in orthodox religion, but had strong questions which were encouraged at Harvard. In Germany I became a freethinker and when I came to teach at an orthodox Methodist Negro school I was soon regarded with suspicion, especially when I refused to lead the students in public prayer. . . . I flatly refused again to join any church or sign any church creed. From my thirtieth year on I have increasingly regarded the church as an institution which defended such evils as slavery, color caste, exploitation of labor, and war. I think the greatest gift of the Soviet Union to modern civilization was the dethronement of the clergy and the refusal to let religion be taught in the public schools."—"My Character," essay in *W. E. B. Du Bois Writings* (New York: Library of America, 1986), pp. 1124–25

"Half the Christian churches of New York are trying to ruin the free public schools in order to replace them by religious dogma."—"A Vista of Ninety Fruitful Years," ibid., p. 1111

". . . The severest charge that can be brought against the Christian education of the Negro in the South during the last thirty years is the reckless way in which sapheaded young fellows, without ability, and, in some cases, without character, have been urged and pushed into the ministry."—"Careers Open to College-Bred Negroes," ibid., p. 837

"White Christianity has in the twentieth century been curiously discredited. First, it is faced by the fact of the [First] World War. Here in the twentieth century of the Prince of Peace, the leading nations representing His religion have been murdering, maiming, and hurting each other on a scale unprecedented in the history of mankind. Again, into the white church of Christ, race prejudice has crept to such an extent it is openly recognized."—"On Christianity," an essay published posthumously in *Against Racism* (Amherst: University of Massachusetts Press, 1985)

"The kind of sermon which is preached in most colored churches is not today attractive to even fairly intelligent men."—ibid.

"The theology of the average colored church is basing itself far too much upon 'hell and damnation.' . . . We are still trained to believe a good deal that is simply childish in theology. . . . Our present method of periodic revival [involves] the hiring of professional and loud-mouthed evangelists and reducing people to a state of frenzy or unconsciousness. . . ."—ibid.

56

Bertrand Russell (1872–1970)

One of the twentieth century's most brilliant thinkers and writers, the iconoclastic Bertrand Russell wrought changes in many fields, from mathematics and philosophy to social protest, freethought, and sexual morality.

Russell was born into a titled English family and educated at Cambridge University, where he became a lecturer in logic and mathematics. In the early 1900s, he wrote monumental books outlining a rational basis for mathematics and repudiating idealism, i.e., the belief that objects and experiences are products of the mind.

Had he limited himself to abstractions, Russell might be remembered solely as an academic luminary. Instead, he plunged into public protest, writing attacks on religion and denunciations of all sides in World War I. For one article, he was fined; for another, he was jailed for six months and fired from his Cambridge post. (In prison, a jailer asked Russell his religion, to which Russell replied "agnostic." The jailer had never heard of such a belief, but muttered, "I guess we all worship the same God.")

After the war, Russell championed reform movements and wrote crusading books and papers at an astounding rate. His essay "Why I Am Not a Christian," first given as a speech at Battersea Town Hall in 1927, became a classic refutation of supernaturalism. He and his second wife opened an avant-garde school in which children were taught in a liberated atmosphere free from taboos and punishments. He constantly advocated scientific and liberal thinking in opposition to religion and dogmatism.

From 1938 to 1944, Russell taught at various American universities, but the New York State Supreme Court barred him from City University of New York because of his irreligion and advocacy of sexual freedom. He returned to Cambridge, and was awarded the 1950 Nobel Prize in literature as "the champion of humanity and freedom of thought."

233

Russell's sense of moral urgency never slackened. At age eighty-nine he was arrested for demonstrating against thermonuclear weapons.

A dozen years before Russell's death, biographer Alan Wood summarized him: "He is certainly the leading questioner of our times. He started by asking questions about mathematics and religion and philosophy, and he went on to question accepted ideas about war and politics and sex and education, setting the minds of men on the march, so that the world could never be quite the same as if he had not lived."[1]

(I include Russell here in "The Early Twentieth Century" largely for convenience's sake, since the quotes from his writings range from the 1920s to the 1960s.)

Russell's Views on Religion

"Religion is based, I think, primarily and mainly upon fear . . . fear of the mysterious, fear of defeat, fear of death. Fear is the parent of cruelty, and therefore it is no wonder if cruelty and religion have gone hand in hand."—*Why I Am Not a Christian,* 1927

"The whole conception of God is a conception derived from the ancient Oriental despotisms. It is a conception quite unworthy of free men. When you hear people in church debasing themselves and saying that they are miserable sinners, and all the rest of it, it seems contemptible and not worthy of self-respecting human beings."—ibid.

"One is often told that it is a very wrong thing to attack religion, because religion makes men virtuous. So I am told; I have not noticed it. . . . You find this curious fact, that the more intense has been the religion of any period and the more profound has been the dogmatic belief, the greater has been the cruelty and the worse has been the state of affairs. In the so-called ages of faith, when men really did believe the Christian religion in all its completeness, there was the Inquisition, with its tortures; there were millions of unfortunate women burned as witches; and there was every kind of cruelty practiced upon all sorts of people in the name of religion."—ibid.

"You find as you look around the world that every single bit of progress in humane feeling, every improvement in the criminal law, every step toward the diminution of war, every step toward better treatment of the colored races, or every mitigation of slavery, every moral progress that there has been in the world, has been consistently opposed by the organized churches of the world. I say quite deliberately that the Christian religion, as organized in its churches, has been and still is the principal enemy of moral progress in the world."—ibid.

---

1. Alan Wood, *Bertrand Russell: The Passionate Skeptic* (New York: Simon & Schuster, 1958).

"Historically it is quite doubtful whether Christ ever existed at all, and if he did, we do not know anything about him. . . . I am concerned with Christ as he appears in the gospels, taking the gospel narrative as it stands, and there one finds some things that do not seem to be very wise. For one thing, he certainly thought that his second coming would occur in clouds of glory before the death of all the people who were living at that time. . . . There is one very serious defect to my mind in Christ's moral character, and that is that he believed in hell. I do not myself feel that any person who is really profoundly humane can believe in everlasting punishment. . . . This doctrine, that hell-fire is a punishment for sin, is a doctrine of cruelty. It is a doctrine that put cruelty into the world and gave the world generations of cruel torture."—ibid.

"We can now begin a little to understand things, and a little to master them by the help of science, which has forced its way step by step against the Christian religion, against the churches, and against the opposition of all the old precepts. Science can help us to get over this craven fear in which mankind has lived for so many generations. Science can teach us, and I think our own hearts can teach us, no longer to look around for imaginary supports, no longer to invent allies in the sky, but rather to look to our own efforts here below to make this world a fit place to live in, instead of the sort of place that the churches in all these centuries have made it."—ibid.

"There is something feeble and a little contemptible about a man who cannot face the perils of life without the help of comfortable myths. Almost inevitably some part of him is aware that they are myths and that he believes them only because they are comforting. But he dares not face this thought! Moreover, since he is aware, however dimly, that his opinions are not rational, he becomes furious when they are disputed."—*Human Society in Ethics and Politics,* 1954

"My own view on religion is that of Lucretius. I regard it as a disease born of fear and as a source of untold misery to the human race."—*Has Religion Made Useful Contributions to Civilization?* 1930

"Christ taught that you should give your goods to the poor, that you should not fight, that you should not go to church, and that you should not punish adultery. Neither Catholics nor Protestants have shown any strong desire to follow his teaching in any of these respects. . . . What is true of Christianity is equally true of Buddhism. The Buddha was amiable and enlightened; on his deathbed he laughed at his disciples for supposing that he was immortal. But the Buddhist priesthood—as it exists, for example, in Tibet—has been obscurantist, tyrannous, and cruel in the highest degree."—ibid.

"The intolerance that spread over the world with the advent of Christianity is one of its most curious features. . . . From the age of Constantine to the end of the seventeenth century, Christians were far more fiercely persecuted by other Christians than they were by the Roman emperors."—ibid.

"It is no credit to the orthodox that they do not now believe all the absurdities that were believed 150 years ago. The gradual emasculation of the Christian doctrine has been effected in spite of the most vigorous resistance, and solely as the result of the onslaughts of freethinkers."—ibid.

"So far as I can remember, there is not one word in the gospels in praise of intelligence."—(Peter)

"Christians hold that their faith does good, but other faiths do harm. . . . What I wish to maintain is that all faiths do harm. . . . We only speak of faith when we wish to substitute emotion for evidence. . . . We are told that faith could remove mountains, but no one believed it; we are now told that the atomic bomb can remove mountains, and everyone believes it."—ibid.

"Most people whose intelligence is much above the average are, nowadays, openly or secretly agnostic."—(Cardiff)

"Throughout history, increase of civilization has been correlated with decrease of religiosity."—ibid.

"Religion encourages stupidity, and an insufficient sense of reality."—ibid.

"I am myself a dissenter from all known religions and I hope that every kind of religious belief will die out."—ibid.

"A good world needs knowledge, kindliness, and courage; it does not need a regretful hankering after the past, or a fettering of this free intelligence by the words uttered long ago by ignorant men."—ibid.

"Religions, which condemn the pleasures of sense, drive men to seek the pleasures of power. Throughout history, power has been the vice of the ascetic."—1938 (Wilcox/George)

"More and more people are becoming unable to accept traditional beliefs. If they think that, apart from these beliefs, there is no reason for kindly behavior, the results may be needlessly unfortunate. That is why it is important to show no supernatural reasons are needed to make men kind and to prove that only through kindness can the human race achieve happiness."—"The Faith of a Rationalist," BBC broadcast, 1953

"We read in the Old Testament that it was a religious duty to exterminate conquered races completely, and that to spare even their cattle and sheep was an impiety. Dark terrors and misfortunes in the life to come oppressed the Egyptians and Etruscans, but never reached their full development until the victory of Christianity."—"Ideas That Have Harmed Mankind," *Unpopular Essays* (New York: Simon & Schuster, 1950), p. 149

"Most of the greatest evils that man has inflicted upon man have come through people feeling quite certain about something which, in fact, was false."—ibid.

"Dogma demands authority, rather than intelligent thought, as the source of opinion; it requires persecution of heretics and hostility to unbelievers; it asks of its disciples that they should inhibit natural kindliness in favor of systematic hatred."
—"Philosophy and Politics," *Unpopular Essays,* p. 20

"The essence of the liberal outlook lies not in *what* opinions are held, but in *how* they are held: instead of being held dogmatically, they are held tentatively, and with a consciousness that new evidence may at any moment lead to their abandonment. This is the way opinions are held in science, as opposed to the way in which they are held in theology."—ibid., p. 15

"The most savage controversies are those about matters as to which there is no good evidence either way. Persecution is used in theology, not in arithmetic."
—"An Outline of Intellectual Rubbish," *Unpopular Essays,* p. 104

". . . Life on this planet is almost certainly temporary. The earth will grow cold, or the atmosphere will gradually fly off, or there will be an insufficiency of water, or, as Sir James Jeans genially prophesies, the sun will burst and all the planets will be turned into gas. . . . Of course, such an event is of little importance from the point of view of orthodox theology, since men are immortal, and will continue to exist in heaven and hell when none are left on earth."—ibid., p. 84

"Man is a credulous animal, and must believe *something*; in the absence of good grounds for belief, he will be satisfied with bad ones."—ibid.

"The twin concepts of sin and vindictive punishment seem to be at the root of much that is most vigorous, both in religion and politics."—*Unpopular Essays*

"Belief in a Divine Mission is one of the many forms of certainty that have afflicted the human race."—ibid.

"The opinions that are held with passion are always those for which no good ground exists; indeed, the passion is the measure of the holder's lack of rational conviction. Opinions in politics and religion are almost always held passionately."—*Skeptical Essays,* 1961

"Fanaticism is a camouflage for cruelty. Fanatics are seldom humane, and those who sincerely dread cruelty will be slow to adapt to a fanatical creed."—*Theory and Practice of Bolshevism,* 1920

"The fact that an opinion has been widely held is no evidence whatever that it is not utterly absurd; indeed, in view of the silliness of the majority of mankind, a widespread belief is more likely to be foolish than sensible."—"Christian Ethics," *Marriage and Morals,* 1929

"The fundamental cause of trouble in the world today is that the stupid are cocksure while the intelligent are full of doubt."—(Wilcox/George)

"As Christianity became more firmly established, its hostility to the religion of the Old Testament grew fiercer. The Jews, it held, had failed to recognize the Messiah announced by the prophets of old, and therefore must be evil. From Constantine onward, anti-Semitism became a respectable form of Christian fervor, though in fact the religious motive was not the only one. It is odd that Christianity, which had itself been suffering appalling persecution, should, once in power, turn with equal ferocity on a minority which was just as steadfast in its beliefs."—*Wisdom of the West* (New York: Doubleday & Co., 1959), p. 130

"The Chinese said they would bury me by the Western Lake and build a shrine to my memory. I might have become a god, which would have been very chic for an atheist."—quoted in McWilliams, *Ain't Nobody's Business If You Do*

"The church attacked the habit of the bath on the ground that everything which makes the body more attractive tends toward sin. Dirt was praised, and the odor of sanctity became more and more penetrating."—(Vernon)

57

Albert Einstein (1879–1955)

A rguably, Albert Einstein was the greatest scientist who ever lived. He single-handedly transformed humanity's grasp of reality and the universe. As a quiet clerk in the Swiss patent office, with no instrument but his mind, he pondered riddles of physics and conceived astonishing answers.

Einstein's famous equation $E=mc^2$ showed that matter and energy are inter-changeable, ushering in the age of nuclear power. His theory of special relativity showed that time, space and mass change with speed, while his theory of general relativity revealed that gravity warps space, causing light to bend. Einstein's work on the photoelectric effect showed that light travels as particles (photons) as well as waves. His groundbreaking paper on Brownian Motion demonstrated that molecules in gas or liquid are in eternal, chaotic movement. From his principles, scientists developed multitudes of modern devices, from hydrogen bombs to fluorescent lights.

Yet, in later years, Einstein hindered another advance: quantum explanations of functions within the atom. In his resistance, he said, "God does not play dice with the universe." This and other references to God caused many clergymen to declare Einstein a religious believer, but that was untrue.

Einstein used the word God, as some physicists do, to symbolize the mysterious laws that govern all matter, energy, and movement. He felt what he called a "cosmic religion," a sense of awe before the immensity of the universe and the unfathomable forces that make it function. (Einstein's espousal of cosmic faith caused Catholic Bishop Fulton J. Sheen to quip: "Who ever wanted to die for the Milky Way?")

Einstein's opposition to supernaturalism is clear in his personal writing and in testimony of his intimate friends. Peter Bucky, a young confidant of the genius, wrote a charming memoir that illuminated Einstein's romantic pursuit of women, his enchantment with sailing, and his utter lack of interest in organized religion. Bucky wrote:

Einstein told me many times that he did not believe in a single God. He said he could not imagine how God could manifest himself in a human countenance. Rather, he believed that there was a cosmic force that could develop things that mortal men could not even begin to comprehend. . . .

I recall his telling me that, during his earlier years, when he would apply for various positions and come to a column asking for details about his religion, he would mark down "dissident," thus demonstrating his disinterest in any one faith. . . .

During an interview with Professor William Hermanns, Einstein once said that he could never accept any conceptualization of God that was based on fear, either fear of life or fear of death, or one that required a blind belief, totally removed from logic. Nor did he envision God in any personal sense. In that respect, he said that if he were to talk about a personal God, he would consider himself to be a liar.[1]

Einstein's Views on Religion

"I cannot imagine a God who rewards and punishes the objects of his creation, whose purposes are modeled after our own—a God, in short, who is but a reflection of human frailty. Neither can I believe that the individual survives the death of his body, although feeble souls harbor such thoughts through fear or ridiculous egotism."—"Religion and Science," *New York Times Magazine,* November 9, 1930

"I cannot conceive of a God who rewards and punishes his creatures, or has a will of the kind that we experience in ourselves."—*Ideas and Opinions*

"A man's ethical behavior should be based effectively on sympathy, education and social ties and needs; no religious basis is necessary. Man would indeed be in a poor way if he had to be restrained by fear of punishment and hope of reward after death."—ibid.

"The man who is thoroughly convinced of the universal operation of the law of causation cannot for a moment entertain the idea of a being who interferes in the course of events. . . . He has no use for the religion of fear and equally little for social or moral religion."—ibid.

"It was the experience of mystery—even if mixed with fear—that engendered religion."—*Living Philosophies,* 1931

"The idea of a Being who interferes with the sequence of events in the world is absolutely impossible."—quoted by E. H. Cotton in *Has Science Discovered God?* 1931

"During the youthful period of mankind's spiritual evolution, human fantasy created gods in man's own image, who, by the operations of their will were supposed to determine, or at any rate to influence, the phenomenal world. . . . The idea of God in the religions taught at present is a sublimation of that old conception of the

---

1. Peter A. Bucky, *The Private Albert Einstein* (Kansas City: Andrews & McMeel, 1992), p. 82.

gods. Its anthropomorphic character is shown, for instance, by the fact that men appeal to the Divine Being in prayers and plead for the fulfillment of their wishes. . . . In their struggle for the ethical good, teachers of religion must have the stature to give up the doctrine of a personal God, that is, give up that source of fear and hope which in the past placed such vast power in the hands of priests."—remarks at a 1940 New York panel discussion, reported in *Science, Philosophy and Religion: A Symposium*, edited by L. Bryson and L. Finkelstein

"I do not believe in the God of theology who rewards good and punishes evil." —Einstein as quoted in a memoir by *Life* editor William Miller, *Life*, May 2, 1955

"I believe in mystery and, frankly, I sometimes face this mystery with great fear. In other words, I think that there are many things in the universe that we cannot perceive or penetrate, and that also we experience some of the most beautiful things in life only in a very primitive form. Only in relation to these mysteries do I consider myself to be a religious man. But I sense these things deeply. What I cannot understand is how there could possibly be a God who would reward or punish his subjects or who could induce us to develop our will in our daily life."—interview with Peter A. Bucky, quoted in *The Private Albert Einstein*, p. 85

"Actually, my first religious training of any kind was in the Catholic catechism. A fluke, of course, only because the primary school that I first went to was a Catholic one. I was, as a matter of fact, the only Jewish child in the school. This actually worked to my advantage, since it made it easier for me to isolate myself from the rest of the class and find the comfort in solitude that I so cherished." —ibid., p. 86

". . . There was religion, which is implanted into every child by way of the traditional education-machine. Thus I came—despite the fact that I was the son of entirely irreligious (Jewish) parents—to a deep religiosity, which, however, found an abrupt ending at the age of twelve. Through the reading of popular scientific books I soon reached the conviction that much in the stories of the Bible could not be true. The consequence was a positively fanatic freethinking, coupled with the impression that youth is intentionally being deceived by the state through lies; it was a crushing impression. Suspicion against every kind of authority grew out of this experience, a skeptical attitude toward the convictions which were alive in any specific social environment—an attitude which has never again left me."—autobiographical notes written for *Albert Einstein: Philosopher-Scientist*, 1946

"It has not done so up to now."—Einstein's reply, after an interviewer asked him if religion will promote peace (Cardiff)

"Strange is our situation here on earth. Each of us comes for a short visit, not knowing why, yet sometimes seeming to divine a purpose. From the standpoint of daily life, however, there is one thing we do know: that man is here for the sake of other men—above all for those upon whose smiles and well-being our own happiness depends."—(Greeley)

58

H. L. Mencken
(1880–1956)

Library of Congress Collection

Newspaper people have a reputation for cynicism—but few carry it to the pinnacle attained by Henry Louis Mencken. A brilliant writer with a sardonic wit, he delighted some readers and outraged others by lampooning much that is "respectable" in American life.

Born in Baltimore to an agnostic German-American father and a Lutheran mother, Mencken attended Sunday school enough, as he later told Will Durant, to learn that Christianity "was full of palpable absurdities."

As a youth, he landed a job with the *Baltimore Morning Herald* and soon switched to the *Baltimore Sun,* where he spent most of his working life. Mencken's iconoclastic columns and editorials electrified readers and drew furious denunciations. When Mencken began a column titled "The Free Lance" in 1911, the *Sun*'s publisher made him promise not to attack religion. But after Methodist ministers assailed Mencken for ridiculing the Anti-Saloon League, the publisher released the writer from his pledge.

In addition to newspaper work, Mencken also wrote twenty-eight books and was editor of the *Smart Set* and *American Mercury* magazines. He once published a book consisting entirely of denunciations of him. He attacked sentimental novelists and encouraged gifted newcomers such as Theodore Dreiser and Sinclair Lewis.

Mencken scorned middle-class pretensions and conformity. His appeal stemmed partly from his audacity: In a time when politicians lavished fulsome praise on America, skeptical readers found it refreshing for Mencken to call Americans "the most timorous, sniveling, poltroonish, ignominious mob of serfs and goose-steppers ever gathered under one flag in Christendom since the end of the Middle Ages."[1] Contemptuously, Mencken asserted that the majority of Americans lacked the intelligence and will to become skeptical and scientific-minded.

---

1. "On Being An American," *Prejudices: Third Series,* 1922.

Menken's language was delightful, prompting author Marion Rodgers to state that he had "a style of great force." For example, Mencken wrote that political conventions "are not without a certain charm to connoisseurs of the obscene."

Mencken's popularity faded somewhat during the Depression, when satire was less welcome. In 1948, a stroke left him unable to read or write until his death seven years later.

Mencken's Comments on Religion

"Religion is fundamentally opposed to everything I hold in veneration—courage, clear thinking, honesty, fairness, and, above all, love of the truth."—*Autobiographical Notes,* 1925

"I believe that religion, generally speaking, has been a curse to mankind."—*New York Times Magazine,* September 11, 1955

"Faith may be defined briefly as an illogical belief in the occurrence of the improbable."—ibid.

"What I got in Sunday school . . . was simply a firm conviction that the Christian faith was full of palpable absurdities, and the Christian God preposterous. . . . The act of worship, as carried on by Christians, seems to me to be debasing rather than ennobling. It involves groveling before a being who, if he really exists, deserves to be denounced instead of respected."—letter to Will Durant

"Christian endeavor is notoriously hard on female pulchritude."—"The Aesthetic Recoil," *American Mercury,* July 1931

"The chief contribution of Protestantism to human thought is its massive proof that God is a bore."—*Minority Report,* 1956

"God is the immemorial refuge of the incompetent, the helpless, the miserable. They find not only sanctuary in his arms, but also a kind of superiority, soothing to their macerated egos; He will set them above their betters."—ibid.

"The essence of science is that it is always willing to abandon a given idea for a better one; the essence of theology is that it holds its truths to be eternal and immutable. To be sure, theology is always yielding a little to the progress of knowledge, and only a Holy Roller in the mountains of Tennessee would dare to preach today what the popes preached in the thirteenth century."—ibid.

"The difference between the smartest dog and the stupidest man—say a Tennessee Holy Roller—is really very small."—ibid.

"Metaphysics is almost always an attempt to prove the incredible by an appeal to the unintelligible."—ibid.

"Moral certainty is always a sign of cultural inferiority. The more uncivilized the man, the surer he is that he knows precisely what is right and what is wrong. All human progress, even in morals, has been the work of men who have doubted the current moral values, not of men who have whooped them up and tried to enforce them. The truly civilized man is always skeptical and tolerant."—ibid.

"There is no possibility whatsoever of reconciling science and theology, at least in Christendom. Either Jesus rose from the dead or he didn't. If he did, then Christianity becomes plausible; if he did not, then it is sheer nonsense. I defy any genuine scientist to say that he believes in the Resurrection, or indeed in any other cardinal dogma of the Christian system."—ibid.

"The effort to reconcile science and religion is almost always made, not by theologians, but by scientists unable to shake off altogether the piety absorbed with their mother's milk."—ibid.

"Whenever a reporter is assigned to cover a Methodist conference, he comes home an atheist."—newspaper proverb quoted by Mencken (and probably invented by him) (Mencken)

". . . Christian theology, like every other theology, is not only opposed to the scientific spirit, it is opposed to all other attempts at rational thinking."—(Gray)

"The most costly of all follies is to believe passionately in the palpably not true." —*A Mencken Chrestomathy*, 1949

"Archbishop: A Christian ecclesiastic of a rank superior to that attained by Christ."—ibid.

"Progress: The process whereby the human race has got rid of whiskers, the vermiform appendix, and God."—ibid.

"Sunday school: A prison in which children do penance for the evil conscience of their parents."—ibid.

"Theology: An effort to explain the unknowable by putting it into terms of the not worth knowing."—ibid.

"The curse of man, and cause of nearly all of his woes, is his stupendous capacity for believing the incredible."—ibid.

"There is only one honest impulse at the bottom of Puritanism, and that is the impulse to punish the man with a superior capacity for happiness—to bring him down to the miserable level of 'good' men, i.e., of stupid, cowardly, and chronically unhappy men."—*The Vintage Mencken*, edited by Alistair Cooke (New York: Alfred A. Knopf, 1959)

"Men become civilized, not in proportion to their willingness to believe, but in proportion to their readiness to doubt."—(Seldes)

"The Catholic clergy seldom bother to make their arguments plausible; it is plain that they have little respect for human intelligence, and indeed little belief in its existence."—ibid.

"The truth is, as everyone knows, that the great artists of the world are never puritans, and seldom ever ordinarily respectable. No virtuous man—that is, virtuous in the YMCA sense—has ever painted a picture worth looking at, or written a symphony worth hearing, or a book worth reading, and it is highly improbable that the thing has ever been done by a virtuous woman."—ibid.

"To sum up: (1) The cosmos is a gigantic flywheel making 10,000 revolutions a minute. (2) Man is a sick fly taking a dizzy ride on it. (3) Religion is the theory that the wheel was designed and set spinning to give him the ride."—in *Smart Set*, December 1920

"The Jews fastened their religion upon the Western world, not because it was more reasonable than the religions of their contemporaries—as a matter of fact, it was vastly less reasonable than many of them—but because it was far more poetical."—in *American Mercury*, January 1924

"The most curious social convention of the great age in which we live is the one to the effect that religious opinions should be respected."—ibid., March 1930

"Religion, like poetry, is simply a concerted effort to deny the most obvious realities."—*Prejudices: Third Series*

"The liberation of the human mind has been best furthered by gay fellows who heaved dead cats into sanctuaries and then went roistering down the highways of the world, proving to all men that doubt, after all, was safe—that the god in the sanctuary was a fraud. One horse-laugh is worth 10,000 syllogisms."—in *The American Mercury*, January 1924

"Puritanism: The haunting fear that someone, somewhere, may be happy." —"Sententiae," *A Book of Burlesques*, 1920

"The scent of frying astronomers long ago ceased to ascend to Yahweh." —(Cardiff)

"When I die, I shall be content to vanish into nothingness.... No show, however good, could conceivably be good forever. . . . I do not believe in immortality, and have no desire for it."—(Peter)

"It is now quite lawful for a Catholic woman to avoid pregnancy by a resort to mathematics, though she is still forbidden to resort to physics and chemistry." —ibid.

59

Other Figures of the Early Twentieth Century

William Howard Taft: Dover

B y the first half of the twentieth century, the Western world grudgingly had accepted the right of doubters to doubt. Yet the tumultuous skepticism of the
1800s gradually receded, and many freethinker organizations dwindled. Meanwhile, social pressure for conformity increased: politicians could hardly hope for
election without proper Christian credentials.

Consider William Howard Taft (1857–1930), America's twenty-seventh president and later chief justice of the Supreme Court. He was a Unitarian, but kept his
unorthodoxy to himself. At the turn of the century, Taft was offered the presidency
of Yale University, but felt he couldn't accept, because all previous presidents had
been Congregationalists. In an explanatory letter to Yale, Taft wrote: ". . . I do not
believe in the divinity of Christ, and there are many other of the postulates of the
orthodox creed to which I cannot subscribe."

Had this letter become public, Taft might have lost the presidential election
of 1908, especially since his rival was the sanctimonious, Bible-championing
William Jennings Bryan. When Taft unsuccessfully sought reelection in 1912, foes
attacked his lack of faith. One accuser said he "does not believe that Jesus Christ
was the Son of God, but looks upon our immaculate Savior as a common bastard
and a low, cunning impostor!"

Taft optimistically thought such intolerance would fade. He once remarked:
"We, as Unitarians, may feel that the world is coming our way."

Social disapproval of doubt persisted—but so did skepticism. As the twentieth century proceeded, a large number of Western thinkers, scientists, writers, leaders, and other outstanding people declared varying degrees of disbelief. In addition to those already profiled, here are comments by others.

Scientists

"The whole religious complexion of the modern world is due to the absence from Jerusalem of a lunatic asylum."—Havelock Ellis (1859–1939), British psychologist, *Impressions and Comments,* 1914

"There is a very intimate connection between hypnotic phenomena and religion."—Ellis (Noyes)

"If faith cannot be reconciled with rational thinking, it has to be eliminated as an anachronistic remnant of earlier stages of culture and replaced by science dealing with facts and theories which are intelligible and can be validated."—Erich Fromm (1900–1980), American psychologist, *Man for Himself,* 1947

"Scientific education and religious education are incompatible. The clergy have ceased to interfere with education at the advanced state, with which I am directly concerned, but they have still got control of the children. This means that the children have to learn about Adam and Noah instead of about evolution; about David who killed Goliath, instead of Koch who killed cholera; about Christ's ascent into heaven instead of Montgolfier's and Wright's. Worse than that, they are taught that it is a virtue to accept statements without adequate evidence, which leaves them a prey to quacks of every kind in later life, and makes it very difficult for them to accept the methods of thought which are successful in science."—J. B. S. Haldane (1892–1964), English biologist

"I, personally, am unable to accept any revealed religion, Christian or not."—Bronislaw Malinowski (1884–1942), Polish-born American anthropologist, quoted by Martin E. Marty in *Varieties of Unbelief* (New York: Holt, Rinehart & Winston, 1964), p. 127

"The Good Book—one of the most remarkable euphemisms ever coined."—Ashley Montagu (1905–), British anthropologist (Peter)

"Religion belongs to that realm that is inviolable before the law of causation and therefore is closed to science."—Max Planck (1858–1947), German physicist, *Where is Science Going?* 1932

"In the realm of science, all attempts to find any evidence of supernatural beings, of metaphysical conceptions, as God, immortality, infinity, etc., thus have failed, and if we are honest, we must confess that in science there exists no God, no immortality, no soul or mind as distinct from the body."—Charles P. Steinmetz (1865–1923), inventor and engineer, quoted in *American Freeman,* July 1941

"I consider Christian theology to be one of the great disasters of the human race. . . . It would be impossible to imagine anything more un-Christlike than theology. Christ probably couldn't have understood it."—Alfred North Whitehead (1861–1947), British-American mathematician and philosopher (Peter)

Writers

"The gods of men are sillier than their kings and queens, and emptier and more powerless."—Maxwell Anderson (1888–1959), American playwright (Cardiff)

"Of all possible sexual perversions, religion is the only one to have ever been scientifically systematized."—Louis Aragon (1897–1982), French poet, *Treatise on Style,* part 1, 1928

" 'Theocracy' has always been the synonym for a bleak and narrow, if not a fierce and blood-stained, tyranny."—William Archer (1856–1924), English journalist (Cardiff)

"The pursuit of happiness belongs to us, but we must climb around or over the church to get to it."—Heywood Broun (1888–1939), journalist and leader of the American Newspaper Guild (Peter)

". . . Precarious is the position of the New York newspaperman who ventures any criticism of the Catholic Church. There is not a single New York editor who does not live in mortal terror of the power of this group. . . . If the church can bluff its way into a preferred position, the fault lies not with the Catholics but with the editors."—Broun (Cardiff)

"It may be that religion is dead, and if it is, we had better know it and set ourselves to try to discover other sources of moral strength before it is too late."—Pearl S. Buck (1892–1973), American novelist and Nobel Prize winner, *What America Means to Me,* 1947

"I feel no need for any other faith than my faith in human beings. Like Confucius of old, I am so absorbed in the wonder of earth and the life upon it that I cannot think of heaven and the angels."—Buck (Seldes)

"Believing in Hell must distort every judgment on this life."—Cyril Connolly (1903–1974), English critic and writer, *The Unquiet Grave,* 1945

"Those of us who were brought up as Christians and who have lost our faith have retained the Christian sense of sin without the saving belief in redemption. This poisons our thought and so paralyzes us in action."—Connolly, ibid.

"The ethical view of the universe involves us in so many cruel and absurd contradictions that I have come to suspect that the aim of creation cannot be ethical at all."—Joseph Conrad (1857–1924), Polish-English novelist (Cardiff)

"It isn't true that the laws of nature have been capriciously disturbed; that snakes have talked; that women have been turned into salt; that rods have brought water out of rocks."—Sir Arthur Conan Doyle (1859–1930), creator of Sherlock Holmes, discussing Bible miracles (Noyes)

"Dogmas of every kind put assertion in the place of reason and give rise to more contention, bitterness, and want of charity than any other influence in human affairs."—Doyle, ibid.

"Assure a man that he has a soul and then frighten him with old wives' tales as to what is to become of him afterward, and you have hooked a fish, a mental slave."—Theodore Dreiser (1871–1945), American novelist (Gray)

"If I were personally to define religion, I would say that it is a bandage that man has invented to protect a soul made bloody by circumstance."—attributed to Dreiser in *The New York Public Library Book of 20th-Century Quotations*

"All forms of dogmatic religion should go. The world did without them in the past and can do so again."—Dreiser (Seldes)

"Men in the nineteenth century were sad that they could no longer believe in God; they are more deeply saddened now by the fact that they can no longer believe in man."—Irwin Edman (1896–1954), American philosopher, *Candle in the Dark,* 1939

"To die for an idea is to set a rather high price upon conjecture."—Anatole France (1844–1924), French writer, *The Revolt of the Angels,* 1914

"Humanism is the creed of those who believe that in the circle of enwrapping mystery, men's fates are in their own hands—a faith that for modern man is becoming the only possible faith."—John Galsworthy (1867–1933), English novelist and playwright, quoted in Corliss Lamont, *The Philosophy of Humanism* (New York: Continuum Publishing Co., 1988), p. 71

"In times of death and famine, reason is on the side of the priests—who have their own kind of logic which cries for miracles and, on occasion, invents them."—Jean Giraudoux (1882–1944), French writer, *Judith,* 1931

"Grandfather . . . knew to a dot everything that God wanted, but with all that he was greedy, malicious, and lied constantly."—Maxim Gorky (1868–1936), Russian playwright (Noyes)

"No priestcraft can longer make man content with misery here in the hope of compensation hereafter."—G. Stanley Hall (1844–1924), American psychologist and educator, *Senescence,* 1922

"Fashions in sin change."—Lillian Hellman (1905–1984), American playwright, *Watch on the Rhine,* 1941

"All mystics set out to say . . . that the incomprehensible is uncomprehensible, and that we knew before."—Franz Kafka (1883–1924), Austrian writer

"In Jerusalem . . . the angry face of Yahweh is brooding over the hot rocks which have seen more holy murder, rape and plunder than any other place on earth. Its inhabitants are poisoned by religion."—Arthur Koestler (1905–1983), British philosopher who lived in Jerusalem in the late 1920s, quoted by Amos Elon in *Jerusalem: City of Mirrors* (Boston: Little, Brown & Co., 1989), p. 64.

"When a culture feels that its end has come, it sends for a priest."—Karl Kraus (1874–1936), Austrian satirist, *Pro Domo et Mundo,* 1912

". . . [P]oetry, mythology, and religion represent the world as a man would like to have it, while science represents the world as he gradually comes to discover it."—Joseph Wood Krutch (1893–1970), American critic and naturalist, *The Modern Temper*

"There is nothing more innately human than the tendency to transmute what has become customary into what has been divinely ordained."—Suzanne LaFollette (1893–1983), American editor, *The Beginnings of Emancipation,* 1926

"Here [in Jerusalem], no mercy is shown. One hates one's fellow man to the glory of God."—Selma Lagerlof (1858–1940), Nobel Prize-winning Swedish novelist, *Jerusalem,* 1901

"Sing then the core of dark and absolute oblivion where the soul at last is lost in utter peace."—D. H. Lawrence (1885–1930), English novelist and poet (Cardiff)

"I know the greatness of Christianity; it is a past greatness. . . . I live in 1924, and the Christian venture is done."—Lawrence, in *Phoenix: The Posthumous Papers of D. H. Lawrence* (New York: Viking, 1936), p. 734

"It is, I think, an error to believe that there is any need of religion to make life seem worth living."—Sinclair Lewis (1885–1851), Nobel Prize-winning American novelist, quoted in Will Durant's *On the Meaning of Life,* 1932, p. 37

". . . There is too much undissolved wrath and punishment in most religions." —Joshua Liebman, *Peace of Mind,* 1946

"I am a hopeless materialist. I see the soul as nothing else than the sum of activities of the organism plus personal habits—plus inherited habits, memories, experiences, of the organism. I believe that when I am dead, I am dead. I believe that with my death I am just as much obliterated as the last mosquito you and I squashed."—Jack London (1876–1916), American novelist (Cardiff)

"I know that a creed is the shell of a lie."—Amy Lowell (1874–1925), American poet and critic, "What's O'Clock," 1925

"Ah, snug lie those that slumber / Beneath Conviction's roof. / Their floors are sturdy lumber / Their windows weatherproof. / But I sleep cold forever / And cold sleep all my kind / For I was born to shiver / in the draft from an open mind." —Phyllis McGinley (1905–1978), *A Pocket Full of Wry,* 1940

"Give up the dream that Love may trick the fates / To live again somewhere beyond the gleam / Of dying stars, or shatter the strong gates / Some god has builded high; give up the dream."—Don Marquis (1878–1937), American journalist and humorist, "Transient"

". . . Old godheads sink in space and drown / Their arks like foundered galleons sucked down."—Marquis (Cardiff)

"Many books have been written to show that Christianity has emasculated the world, that it shoved aside the enlightenment and wisdom of Hellas for a doctrine of superstition and ignorance."—Edgar Lee Masters (1869–1950), American poet (Cardiff)

"Hebraic and Christian anthropomorphism . . . has done so much to curse the world."—Masters, ibid.

"The arguments for immortality, weak when you take them one by one, are no more cogent when you take them together. . . . For my part, I cannot see how consciousness can persist when its physical basis has been destroyed, and I am too sure of the interconnection of my body and my mind to think that any survival of my consciousness apart from my body would be in any sense a survival of myself."—W. Somerset Maugham (1874–1965), English novelist, *The Summing Up* (New York: Doubleday, 1938), p. 275

"It has been said that metaphysics is the finding of bad reasons for what we believe on instinct."—Maugham, ibid.

"What mean and cruel things men do for the love of god."—Maugham, *A Writer's Notebook,* 1949

"I thought it was only in revealed religion that a mistranslation improved the sense."—Maugham (Cardiff)

"The man who has no mind of his own lends it to the priests."—George Meredith (1828–1909), English novelist, quoted in *Fortnightly Review,* July 1909

"The Old Testament is responsible for more atheism, agnosticism, disbelief—call it what you will—than any book ever written; it has emptied more churches than all the counterattractions of cinema, motor bicycle and golf course."—A. A. Milne (1882–1956), English playwright, novelist, and children's writer

"Heaven may be for the laity, but this world is certainly for the clergy."—George Moore (1852–1933), Irish novelist, *Epigrams*

"One may sigh for all that one loses in giving up the old religion. . . . But the new irreligion is the manlier, honester and simpler thing, and affords a better theory of life and a more solid basis for morality."—Charles Eliot Norton (1827–1908), American author and educator, letter to Goldwin Smith, January 31, 1905

"The existence of a world without God seems to me less absurd than the presence of a God, existing in all his perfection, creating an imperfect man in order to make him run the risk of Hell."—Armand Salacrou, "Certitudes et Incertitudes," in *Theatre,* 1943

"To work hard, to live hard, to die hard, and then to go to hell after all would be too damned hard."—Carl Sandburg (1878–1967), American poet, *The People, Yes,* 1936

"Martyrdom has always been a proof of the intensity, never of the correctness of a belief."—Arthur Schnitzler (1862–1931), Austrian playwright, *Buch der Sprüche und Bedenken,* 1927

"Martyrdom has always been a proof of the intensity, never of the correctness, of a belief."—Schnitzler, ibid.

"It is no cynical joke, it is literally true, that the Christian churches would not recognize Christianity if they saw it."—Lincoln Steffens (1866–1936), crusading journalist (Cardiff)

"Why is it that the less intelligence people have, the more spiritual they are? They seem to fill all the vacant, ignorant spaces in their heads with soul. Which explains how it is that the less knowledge they have, the more religion."—Steffens, ibid.

"There ain't no answer. There ain't going to be any answer. There never has been an answer. That's the answer."—Gertrude Stein (1874–1946), American writer, quoted by Robert Byrne in *The Fourth 637 Best Things Anybody Ever Said*

"That which has been believed by everyone, always and everywhere, has every chance of being false."—Paul Valéry (1871–1945), French poet, *Tel quel I,* 1943

"The race of men, while sheep in credulity, are wolves for conformity."—Carl Van Doren (1885–1950), American editor and writer, *Why I Am an Unbeliever*

"I was indeed a prodigy of Early Impiety. . . . There was a time when I believed in the story and the scheme of salvation, so far as I could understand it, just as there was a time when I believed there was a Devil. . . . Suddenly the light broke through to me and I knew this God was a lie. . . . I sensed it was a silly story long before I dared to admit even to myself that it was a silly story. For indeed it is a silly story, and each generation nowadays swallows it with greater difficulty. . . . Why do people go on pretending about this Christianity?"—H. G. Wells (1866–1946), English novelist and critic (Cardiff)

". . . Indeed Christianity passes. Passes—it has gone! It has littered the beaches of life with churches, cathedrals, shrines and crucifixes, prejudices and intolerances, like the sea urchin and starfish and empty shells and lumps of stinging jelly upon the sands here after a tide. A tidal wave out of Egypt. And it has left a multitude of little wriggling theologians and confessors and apologists hopping and burrowing in the warm nutritious sand. But in the hearts of living men, what remains of it now? Doubtful scraps of Arianism. Phrases. Sentiments. Habits."—Wells, ibid.

"I do not believe in the least that either the body of H. G. Wells or his personality is immortal."—Wells, ibid.

"The most evil thing in the world today is the Roman Catholic Church."—Wells, ibid.

"So many gods, so many creeds / So many paths that wind and wind / While just the art of being kind / Is all the sad world needs."—Ella Wheeler Wilcox (1850–1919), American journalist and poet, "The World's Need"

"The world has a thousand creeds, and never a one have I / Nor a church of my own, though a million spires are pointing the way on high."—Wilcox, "Heresy"

"It is time that outraged public sentiment cry out in detestation of the outrages committed in the name of religion."—Wilcox (Noyes)

"The acute delight Americans have always got from denying themselves joy and maiming others that they might be 'saved' from some obliquity of moral carriage is only lately understood. One step further and it leads to persecutions."—William Carlos Williams (1883–1963), American physician and writer, "The Virtue of History," *In the American Grain,* 1925

"Once every people in the world believed that trees were divine, and could take a human or grotesque shape and dance among the shadows; and that deer, and ravens and foxes, and wolves and bears, and clouds and pools, almost all things under the sun and moon, and the sun and moon, were not less divine and changeable. They saw in the rainbow the still-bent bow of a god thrown down in his negligence; they heard in the thunder the sound of his beaten water jar, or the tumult of his chariot wheels; and when a sudden flight of wild ducks, or of crows, passed over their heads, they thought they were gazing at the dead hastening to their rest. . . ."—William Butler Yeats (1865–1939), Irish poet

"Once you attempt legislation upon religious grounds, you open the way for every kind of intolerance and religious persecution."—Yeats, remarks on the adoption of the Irish Constitution of 1937

Reformers and Educators

"The predominant emphasis on the motive of fear for the enforcement of absolute commands has made religious morality develop the most intense cruelty that the human heart has known."—Morris R. Cohen (1880–1947), philosopher and educator, in *Religion Today,* 1933

"There are no more metaphysics among the educated Japanese. Why should there be among us?—Michael J. Dee, *Conclusions,* 1917

"It was the 'heresy' of . . . Joan of Kent, in the reign of Edward IV, that Jesus did not take his body from his mother, but only passed through her as light through a glass. For entertaining this opinion she was committed to prison for twelve months, during which time her conversion was taken in hand by many famous

Protestant divines . . . [who], finding it impossible to effect her conversion to the true doctrine—that is to say, *their* doctrine—determined that she should be put to death as an incorrigible heretic. . . . The unhappy woman was committed to the flames."—George Foote, *The Mother of God,* 1932.

"Whatever may be true of men's creed, nothing is clearer than the fact that the personality and the sovereignty of God are not a large factor in the practical life and thought of our age."—Charles W. Garman, *Letters, Lectures, Addresses,* 1909

"Religion is a superstition that originated in man's inability to solve natural phenomena. The Church is an organized institution that has always been a stumbling block to progress."—Emma Goldman (1869–1940), American anarchist, jailed and deported to Russia, *What I Believe*

"Long-haired preachers come out every night / And they tell you what's wrong and what's right / Till they get all your coin on the drum / Then they tell you when you're on the bum: / You will eat, bye and bye / In that beautiful land in the sky— 'way up high / Work and pray, live on hay / You'll get pie in the sky when you die—That's a lie."—Joe Hill, labor organizing song to the tune of "The Sweet Bye and Bye," 1906

"Christianity . . . made, for nearly 1,500 years, persecution, religious wars, massacres, theological feuds and bloodshed, heresy huntings and heretic burnings, prisons, dungeons, anathemas, curses, opposition to science, hatred of liberty, spiritual bondage, the life without love or laughter. . . ."—M. M. Mangasarian, "The Martyrdom of Hypatia," in *The Rationalist,* May 15, 1915

"Science has gone on from strength to strength; position after position, once occupied by religion, has been captured until the whole of science has been emancipated from the bondage of the supernatural."—Walter Mann, *The Religion of Famous Men,* 1916

"Christianity as an institutionalized religion has laid no stress on the pursuit of truth. Indeed, for the most part it has been suspicious of the truthseeking process. The truthseeker might overturn accepted beliefs."—Harry A. Overstreet, American philosopher (Cardiff)

"We consider prayer as nothing but a fervent wish."—A. Philip Randolph (1889–1979), civil rights leader and founder of the railway porters union, quoted in *American Atheist,* February 1987, p. 26

"The name of Christ has caused more persecutions, wars, and miseries than any other name has caused."—John E. Remsburg, *The Christ,* 1910

"I do not want church groups controlling the schools of our country. They must remain free."—Eleanor Roosevelt (1884–1962), American author, diplomat, and humanitarian, "My Day" column, July 8, 1949

Judges

"The greatest dangers to liberty lurk in insidious encroachment by men of zeal, well-meaning but without understanding."—U.S. Supreme Court Justice Louis D. Brandeis (1856–1941), *Olmstead* v. *United States,* 1928

"The churches used to win their arguments against atheism, agnosticism, and other burning issues by burning the ismists, which is fine proof that there is a devil but hardly evidence that there is a God."—Judge Ben B. Lindsey (1869–1943), *The Revolt of Modern Youth,* with Wainwright Evans (New York: Boni & Liveright, 1925), p. 180

"I cannot admit that any man born of woman has either the knowledge or authority to tell other men, as a statement of ascertained fact, what God's purposes are in this or any other matter."—Lindsey, ibid., p. 285

"No chapter in human history has been so largely written in terms of persecution and intolerance as the one dealing with religious freedom. From ancient times to the present day, the ingenuity of man has known no limits in its ability to forge weapons of oppression for use against those who dare to express or practice unorthodox religious beliefs."—Frank Murphy (1890– 1949), U.S. Supreme Court Justice, *Prince* v. *Massachusetts,* 1944

"Parents may be free to become martyrs themselves. But it does not follow they are free, in identical circumstances, to make martyrs of their children before they have reached the age of full and legal discretion when they can make that choice for themselves."—Wiley Rutledge (1894–1949), U.S. Supreme Court Justice, ibid.

"There are those who feel more deeply over religious matters than they do about secular things. It would be almost unbelievable, if history did not record the tragic fact, that men have gone to war and cut each other's throats because they could not agree as to what was to become of them after their throats were cut. Many sins have been committed in the name of religion. Alas! The spirit of proscription is never kind. It is the unhappy quality of religious disputes that they are always bitter. For some reason, too deep to fathom, men contend more furiously over the road to heaven, which they cannot see, than over their visible walks on earth."
—Walter P. Stacy, Chief Justice North Carolina Supreme Court, *State* v. *Beal,* 1930

Government Leaders

"As a result of quarrels over heresies, what massacres followed among Christians in the name of the common God of universal charity."—Georges Clemenceau (1841–1929), premier of France (Cardiff)

"In the experiences of a year of the presidency, there has come to me no other such unwelcome impression as the manifest religious intolerance which exists among many of our citizens. I hold it to be a menace to the very liberties we boast and cherish."—U.S. President Warren G. Harding (1865–1923), address, March 24, 1922

"I am not merely an opponent of Christianity; I am a heathen—and proud of it."—Gen. Erich Ludendorff (1865–1937), German political leader, press interview, 1935

"Religion is a species of mental disease. It has always had a pathological reaction on mankind."—Benito Mussolini (1883–1945), Italian dictator, speech in Lausanne, July 1904

"The God of the theologians is the creation of their empty heads."—Mussolini, ibid.

"The history of the saints is mainly the history of insane people."—Mussolini, ibid.

"When we claim that 'God does not exist,' we mean to deny by this declaration the personal God of theology, the God worshiped in various ways and divers modes by believers the world over . . . that God of absurd attributes who is an affront to human reason."—Mussolini, l'Homme et la divinité, published by Bibliothèque Internationale de propagande rationaliste, Geneva, 1904

"Science is now in the process of destroying religious dogma. The dogma of the divine creation is recognized as absurd."—Mussolini, ibid.

"Religious morality shows the original stigmata of authoritarianism precisely because it pretends to be the revelation of divine authority. In order to translate this authoritarianism into action and impose it upon humanity, the priestly caste of revealers has sprung up and with it the most atrocious intolerance."—Mussolini, ibid.

"The thousands of gods that man has worshiped are myths born of his fears and his imaginations."—Culbert Olson, governor of California, 1938–43 (Gray)

"I wouldn't say that religion has promoted the social progress of mankind. I say that it has been a detriment to the progress of civilization, and I would also say this: that the emancipation of the mind from religious superstition is as essential to the progress of civilization as is emancipation from physical slavery."—Olson, ibid.

"I don't see how anybody can read the Bible and believe it's the word of God, or believe that it is anything but a barbarous story of a barbaric people."—Olson, ibid.

"May it not suffice for me to say . . . that of course like every other man of intelligence and education I do believe in organic evolution. It surprises me that at this late date such questions should be raised."—U.S. President Woodrow Wilson (1856–1924), letter to an academic, August 29, 1922

Historians

"History has shown that on no subject can human passions be aroused to such a murderous frenzy as on that of man's relation to his Maker."—historian Claude G. Bowers, *Jefferson in Power,* 1936

"There can be no doubt that the Bible ... became a stumbling-block in the path of progress, scientific, social and even moral. It was quoted against Copernicus as it was against Darwin."—Preserved Smith (1880–1941), American historian

"The common assumption, hardly disputed even now, that the moral influence of the Bible has been wholly good, and that all that is needed to improve our society is to 'spread the gospel,' is not borne out by a candid study of history."—Smith, *A History of Modern Culture,* 1930

Others

"I don't believe in God. My God is patriotism. Teach a man to be a good citizen and you have solved the problem of life."—Andrew Carnegie (1837–1919), American steel magnate and philanthropist (Cardiff) (Noyes)

"I have not bothered Providence with my petitions for about forty years." —Carnegie (Cardiff)

"I will give a million dollars for any convincing proof of a future life."—Carnegie, ibid.

"I give money for church organs in the hope that the organ music will distract the congregation's attention from the rest of the service."—Carnegie, ibid.

"One never knows, do one?"—Thomas "Fats" Waller (1904–1943), jazz pianist, quoted by Roger Angell in *The New Yorker,* August 5, 1985

"I believe in God, only I spell it Nature."—Frank Lloyd Wright (1867–1959), American master architect, *Quote,* August 14, 1966

Part Seven

The Mid- and Late
Twentieth Century

60

Margaret Sanger (1883–1966)

If ever a hero fought a lonely struggle, scorned by the clergy and "respectable" society, and won final vindication, such a hero was Margaret Sanger, who brought birth control to America.

She was jailed eight times, and lacked organized support, yet she never faltered in her determination to free women from the perpetual pregnancy that had been their fate in the past.

Sanger was born in upstate New York, the daughter of a freethinker. When she was a little girl, her father invited "the Great Agnostic," Robert Ingersoll, to speak at a local hall. But angry believers barred them from the hall and flung tomatoes at Ingersoll, Margaret, and her father. Afterward, her family was taunted as "heathens" and "devil's children." Her father had difficulty finding work.

She received nurse training at White Plains and married an artist, William Sanger. In her work among the dingy tenements of New York City's Lower East Side, Sanger saw poor women broken by constant childbearing and families unable to feed teeming broods. Birth control was unknown.

Sanger recounted a 1912 incident in which a desperate mother botched a self-induced abortion and nearly died. When the woman begged for advice on how to avoid pregnancy, her doctor could suggest only that her husband "sleep on the roof." Three months later, Sanger was called to the woman's home, to find her pregnant again and dying.

At that time, almost any mention of sex was a crime in America. Puritanical fundamentalist Anthony Comstock had induced Congress to pass the "Comstock Law" banning sexual material from the mail, including discussion of birth control. When Comstock became the nation's chief postal inspector, Sanger fell victim to him repeatedly. In 1912, she began writing a series titled "What Every Girl Should Know" in a socialist paper. One article mentioned syphilis and gonorrhea. Comstock's agents censored the article, so the newspaper printed the headline, "What

Every Girl Should Know," followed by: "Nothing! By order of the Post Office Department."

Determined to combat unwanted pregnancy and venereal disease, Sanger went to Holland and learned of a new invention, the diaphragm. She returned to the United States in 1913 to launch her crusade. In 1914, she began publishing the periodical *The Woman Rebel,* which was indicted under the Comstock Law because it mentioned contraception. In 1916, she opened America's first birth-control clinic—and was jailed thirty days for "maintaining a public nuisance."

As she was booked into jail, the warden asked Sanger her religion, to which she replied, "Humanity." She later recounted in her autobiography: "He had never heard of this form of belief, and rephrased the question, 'Well, what church do you go to?' None. He looked at me in sharp surprise. All inmates of the penitentiary went to church."[1]

Biographer Virginia Coigney recorded that Sanger "was an atheist and the daughter of an atheist," yet she was driven by compassion "to free women from biological slavery."[2]

In the early years of Sanger's struggle, few groups came to her aid, because sex itself was taboo. Churches called her evil for attempting to thwart God's will. But she persisted.

In 1921, Sanger founded the American Birth Control League, a forerunner to the Planned Parenthood Federation. In 1929, police raided her clinic and seized her files. But by then, some doctors, social workers, and reformers had begun to support her cause. The battle moved into courts and legislatures, in a long campaign for women's freedom.

In 1965, a year before Sanger's death, a major victory was won. The U.S. Supreme Court struck down a Connecticut law that had outlawed contraception, even for married couples. In 1972, the high court killed a Massachusetts law which had made it a crime to sell birth-control devices to unmarried people. Thereafter, all American adults enjoyed the right to choose birth control—a right that Margaret Sanger had begun seeking six decades earlier.

Sanger's Comments on Religion

"No Gods, No Masters."—masthead motto of Sanger's newsletter, *The Woman Rebel*

"Cannibals at least do not hide behind the sickening smirk of the Church. . . . Their tastes are not so fastidious, so refined, so Christian, as those of our great American coal operators. . . . Remember the men and women and children who were sacrificed in order that John D. Rockefeller, Jr., might continue his noble career of charity and philanthropy as a supporter of the Christian faith. . . ."—(Gray)

---

1. *Margaret Sanger: An Autobiography* (New York: W. W. Norton & Co., 1938).
2. Virginia Coigney, *Margaret Sanger: Rebel with a Cause* (New York: Doubleday, 1969).

61

Will Durant
(1885–1981)

America's beloved tutor and mentor Will Durant taught millions of intelligent readers the outline of philosophy and the intertwined forces of history. But few of his devotees knew he was a youthful candidate for the Catholic priesthood who turned to atheism and was excommunicated.

Durant was born to devout French-Canadian parents. His father could neither read nor write, yet became a superintendent in a New Jersey celluloid mill. The son later remarked that he was named William James Durant "by parents who had never heard of the philosopher William James."

Durant's pious mother constantly steered him toward the priesthood. At age fifteen, he entered a Jesuit college in Jersey City and spent seven years of intense study. But reading science and philosophy gradually destroyed his belief in the supernatural.

Durant later wrote, "By the end of my sophomore year, I had discovered . . . that Christianity was only one of a hundred religions claiming special access to truth and salvation; and that myths of virgin births, mother goddesses, dying and resurrected deities, had appeared in many pre-Christian faiths. . . . I could no longer think of becoming a priest."[1]

Durant said he "relinquished my belief in heaven" and felt the smug "pride of belonging to the elite few who had liberated themselves from the falsehoods that had kept most Europeans and Americans in bondage for fifteen centuries."[2]

However, Durant concealed his skepticism from relatives and family friends, who glowed proudly at the prospect of his ordination. Under constant emotional pressure, he made what he later called the "lunatic" decision to hide his disbelief, proceed through seminary, become a priest, and work from within to lead the

---

1. Will and Ariel Durant, *A Dual Autobiography* (New York: Simon & Schuster, 1977), p. 32.
2. Ibid.

Catholic Church to socialistic goals. But further study made him see "the absurdity of my dream of a socialist Catholic Church." Durant told church superiors he
had to withdraw. They allowed him to serve as a teacher at Seton Hall University
in New Jersey, while hiding his agnosticism from his family.

Then he was invited to speak on "The Origins of Religion" at a New York assembly of the Francisco Ferrer Association, named for the radical who defied
Spain's semi-theocracy (see chapter 52). Durant told the group that sex is a sub-
current in religion, and "the phallus had in many places and forms been worshiped
as a symbol of divine power." Immediately, the New Jersey bishop excommunicated Durant and announced the action to newspapers. Durant's mother collapsed
in shock and his father ordered him to move out of their home.

Durant was hired as sole teacher in a discipline-free, grade-free, religion-free
New York school established by the Francisco Ferrer Association. A vivacious
fourteen-year-old Jewish student, Ada Kaufman, developed a crush on the twenty-
seven-year-old teacher, pursuing him with pubescent abandon. Durant reassured
the girl's family that he would not molest her. Yet Durant was drawn to the charming, impulsive Ada. He wrote her a letter saying he was vulnerable because he was
lonely and "hungered for affection, since I was compelled to leave mother and sisters, a year ago this week, because of my socialism and atheism." A year later, they
were married and remained a devoted couple for more than half a century, their
deaths occurring only two weeks apart. Ada eventually took the pen name Ariel
and wrote jointly with her husband.

Durant published *Philosophy and the Social Problem* in 1917. Then he wrote
biographies of philosophers which were printed as five-cent Little Blue Books by
agnostic publisher Emanuel Haldeman-Julius. He scored world success in 1926
with *The Story of Philosophy,* which sold two million copies. Much of the rest of
Durant's life was spent writing the colossal, eleven-volume *Story of Civilization,*
which won a Pulitzer Prize.

Durant's Comments on Religion

"Does history support a belief in God? If by God we mean not the creative vital-
ity of nature but a supreme being intelligent and benevolent, the answer must be
a reluctant negative."—*The Lessons of History,* 1968 (with Ariel Durant)

". . . In France the Church was a powerful organization owning a large share of the
national wealth and soil. . . . It refused to pay taxes beyond its occasional 'gratuitous gift'; it held thousands of peasants in practical serfdom on its lands; it maintained monks in what seemed to be fruitless idleness. It had repeatedly profited
from false documents and bogus miracles. It controlled nearly all schools and universities, through which it inoculated the minds of the young with stupefying ab-

surdities. It denounced as heresy any teaching contrary to its own, and used the state to enforce its censorship over speech and press. It had done its best to choke the intellectual development of France. It had urged Louis XIV into the inhuman persecution of the Huguenots, and the heartless destruction of Port Royal. It had been guilty of barbarous campaigns against the Albigenses, and of sanctioning massacres like that of St. Bartholomew's Day; it had fomented religious wars that had almost ruined France. And amid all these crimes against the human spirit it had pretended, and made millions of simple people believe, that it was above and beyond reason and questioning, that it had inherited a divine revelation, that it was the infallible and divinely inspired vicegerent of God, and that its crimes were as much the will of God as were its charities."—*The Story of Civilization,* vol. 9, *The Age of Voltaire* (New York: Simon & Schuster, 1965), p. 608

". . . Behind the support that Christianity had given to morality, they saw a thousand heretics burned at the stake, the Albigensians crushed out in a homicidal crusade, Spain and Portugal darkened with autos-da-fe, France torn apart by rival mythologies, and all the future of the human spirit subject in every land to the repeated resurrection of superstition, priestcraft, and persecution."—ibid., p. 737

"*Sapere aude*—'to dare to know'—became the motto of this *éclairissement,* or enlightenment, this Age of Reason triumphant and fulfilled. . . . Man could at last liberate himself from medieval dogmas and Oriental myths; he could shrug off that bewildering, terrifying theology, and stand up free, free to doubt, to inquire, to think, to gather knowledge and spread it, free to build a new religion around the altar of reason and the service of mankind."—ibid., pp. 606–607

"The greatest question of our time is not communism vs. individualism, not Europe vs. America, not even the East vs. the West; it is whether men can bear to live without God."—*On the Meaning of Life,* 1932

"Is Christianity dying? Is the religion that gave morals, courage, and art to Western civilization suffering slow decay through the spread of knowledge, the widening of astronomic, geographical, and historical horizons, the realization of evil in history and the soul, the decline of faith in an afterlife and of trust in the benevolent guidance of the world? If this is so, it is the basic event of modern times, for the soul of a civilization is its religion, and it dies with its faith."—*The Age of Reason Begins,* 1961

62

Walter Lippmann
(1889–1974)

Often called "the greatest journalist of his age," Walter Lippmann was an American phenomenon for six decades, a political and social commentator read by millions.

Born into a New York Jewish family, Lippmann became a bright socialist maverick at Harvard, rubbing elbows with George Santayana, William James, and other great liberal thinkers. After graduation, he helped found *The New Republic* and rose so rapidly in stature that President Woodrow Wilson appointed him assistant secretary of war, sent him to help negotiate the end of World War I, and heeded him in creating the League of Nations.

Through the 1920s, Lippmann wrote for the New York *World.* He never took Judaism seriously, and became a secular seeker of human advancement.

In 1929, Lippmann published a book that became an international sensation: *A Preface to Morals* analyzed the values vacuum of the 1920s. It observed that thinking modern people no longer could embrace religion or totally trust human institutions, and thus were left in a limbo of uncertainty. According to Lippmann, humanity, "having ceased to believe without ceasing to be credulous, hangs, as it were, between heaven and earth and is at rest nowhere." While previous generations lived by orthodox dogmas, new times had brought "brave and brilliant atheists who have defied the Methodist God and have become very nervous." Similarly, women were gaining liberation, but were unsure if they wanted it. To cure the unease of the times, then, intelligent people must use their reason to find purely humanistic values and systems they can trust.

Even before the stock market crash underscored its message, *A Preface to Morals* was a runaway best-seller and eventually was translated into a dozen languages. Writes biographer Ronald Steel: "Readers embraced the book's stoicism, its bleak humanism, and its rewarding conclusion that he who had lost his religious faith could find salvation in a secular humanism that only innately superior sensibilities could glimpse."[1]

Through the 1930s, Lippmann wrote for the *New York Herald Tribune* and began a syndicated column published in 250 newspapers. He eventually won two Pulitzer Prizes, continued to produce books, and was a confidant of several presidents.

As he aged, the onetime socialist grew increasingly conservative. Near the end of his life, Lippmann endorsed Richard Nixon in the 1968 election—and lived just long enough to see Nixon driven from office in disgrace.

As Lippmann lay dying, Steel writes, he had "no complaints, no fears, no regrets. Never did he speak of prayer, or of God, or of an afterlife. To the end he was like the mature man who, as he had once written 'would take the world as it comes.' . . . As he had long ago shed his Judaism and had no other religion, his friends did not know where to hold a service. . . ."[2]

They resolved their dilemma by conducting a secular memorial in a Ford Foundation auditorium.

Lippmann's Views on Religion

"There is no arguing with the pretenders to a divine knowledge and to a divine mission. They are possessed with the sin of pride, they have yielded to the perennial temptation."—*The Public Philosophy,* 1955

"No more than the kings before them should the people be hedged with divinity."—ibid.

"The radical novelty of modern science lies precisely in the rejection of the belief, which is at the heart of all popular religion, that the forces which move the stars and atoms are contingent upon the preferences of the human heart."—(Peter)

"As long as all evils are believed somehow to fit into a divine, if mysterious, plan, the effort to eradicate them must seem on the whole futile, and even impious. The history of medical progress offers innumerable instances of how men have resisted the introduction of sanitary measures because they dreaded to interfere with the providence of God. It is still felt, I believe, in many quarters, even in medical circles, that to mitigate the labor pains in childbirth is to blaspheme against the commandment that in pain children shall be brought forth. An aura of dread surrounds evil as long as evil situations remain entangled with a theory of divine government."—*A Preface to Morals,* 1929

---

1. Ronald Steel, *Walter Lippmann and the American Century* (Boston: Little, Brown & Co., 1980), p. 263.
2. Ibid., p. 599.

"When men can no longer be theists, they must, if they are civilized, become humanists."—ibid.

"Insofar as men have now lost their belief in a heavenly king, they have to find some other ground for their moral choices than the revelation of his will. It follows necessarily that they must find the tests of righteousness wholly within human experience."—ibid.

"The teachers of theistic morality, when the audience is devout, have only to fortify the impression that the rules of conduct are certified by God the invisible King. . . . But the teachers of humanism have no credentials. Their teaching is not certified. They have to prove their case by the test of mundane experience. . . . Yet with all its difficulties, it is to a morality of humanism that men must turn when the ancient order of things dissolves. When they find that they no longer believe seriously and deeply that they are governed from heaven, there is anarchy in their souls until by conscious effort they find ways of governing themselves."—ibid.

"The greatest of all perplexities in theology has been to reconcile the infinite goodness of God with his omnipotence. Nothing puts a greater strain upon the faith of the common man than the existence of utterly irrational suffering in the universe."—ibid.

63

Langston Hughes
(1902–1967)

Growing up black in the worst days of American segregation—when African Americans were lynched regularly in the South, and were confined to menial status in the North—was an embittering experience.

Writer-poet Langston Hughes was keenly intelligent, and keenly resentful of the unfair society. Like many black intellectuals, he was drawn to socialism as an avenue to equality.

After graduating from high school in Cleveland, Hughes wrote teenage poetry of such power that it was published and drew attention. He entered Columbia University, but dropped out to explore life in Harlem. He became a steward on a freighter to Africa, then a busboy in a Washington hotel. When the great poet Vachel Lindsay dined at the hotel, Hughes slipped his own poems under the visitor's plate—and Lindsay proclaimed that he had discovered a profound busboy poet.

Books, plays, and poems began pouring from Hughes, but he earned barely enough for survival. In 1932, he went to Russia with several young blacks to make a movie about racism in America. While there, he wrote "Goodbye Christ," a sarcastic poem telling "Christ Jesus Lord God Jehova" to depart and "make way for a new guy with no religion at all—. . . ME!"

The poem was published, but drew little notice. Hughes returned to America and continued his struggle. In 1940, as he addressed a California audience about his autobiography, *The Big Sea,* the meeting was disrupted by followers of evangelist Aimee Semple McPherson, who had been incited to anger over "Goodbye Christ."

The Saturday Evening Post reprinted the poem, along with an attack on Hughes by McPherson. The poet's already shaky career seemed doomed, so he issued an apology saying that "Goodbye Christ" was an error of youthful immaturity.

Later, when Hughes spoke at Wayne University in Detroit, he was picketed by a hundred members of the right-wing America First party of Gerald L. K. Smith. They distributed leaflets denouncing the university for inviting "an atheistic communist . . . a notorious blasphemous poet." Subsequent appearances in other cities were blocked by bomb threats and protests by white churchmen.

Hughes began writing plays in cooperation with church theater groups. Biographer Arnold Rampersad said this step was "strategic, as he [Hughes] sought to counter, as best he could, his almost ineradicable reputation as an atheist. However, he made no effort to appear pious in public, and attached himself to no church."[1]

By the time of his death, Hughes had written twenty-eight books and many plays, and was known around the world as a gifted voice against social injustice.

Hughes' Comments on Religion

"Goodbye, Christ Jesus Lord God Jehova / Beat it on away from here now / Make way for a new guy with no religion at all—/ A real guy named / Marx Communist Lenin Peasant Stalin Worker ME—/ I said, ME!"—"Goodbye Christ," 1932

"I was saved from sin when I was going on thirteen. But not really saved. It happened like this: There was a big revival at my Auntie Reed's church. Every night for weeks there had been much preaching, singing, praying, and shouting. . . . Finally all the young people had gone to the altar and were saved, but one boy and me. He was a rounder's son named Westley. Westley and I were surrounded by sisters and deacons praying. It was very hot in the church, and getting late now. Finally Westley said to me in a whisper, 'God damn! I'm tired o' sitting here. Let's get up and be saved.' So he got up and was saved. Then I was left all alone on the mourners' bench. My aunt came and knelt at my knees and cried, while prayers and songs swirled all around me in the little church. The whole congregation prayed for me alone, in a mighty wail of moans. . . . God had not struck Westley dead for taking his name in vain or for lying in the temple. So I decided that maybe to save further trouble, I'd better lie, too, and say that Jesus had come, and get up and be saved. So I got up. Suddenly the whole room broke into a sea of shouting, as they saw me rise. . . . I couldn't bear to tell her that I had lied, that I had deceived everybody in the church, that I hadn't seen Jesus, and that now I didn't believe there was a Jesus any more. . . ."—"Salvation," from *The Big Sea,* 1940

1. Arnold Rampersad, *The Life of Langston Hughes* (New York: Oxford University Press, 1988), vol. 2, p. 306.

64

Ayn Rand
(1905–1982)

Courtesy Ayn Rand Institute

A yn Rand was born Alissa Rosenbaum into a nominally Jewish family in czarist Russia, and came of age during the horrors of World War I and the Bolshevik Revolution. As a little girl, she read heroic novels and came to idealize the bold individual who defies the timid majority—an identity that later became her own.

At age thirteen, she declared herself an atheist. Biographer James Baker recounts:

> In long conversations with her father during this period of confusion and danger, she came to the conclusion that the idea of a God who dictates his will to man and demands that man humble himself in his presence, is degrading to man and antithetical to the image of man as hero. . . . Man can never achieve greatness so long as he is burdened by a humiliating theism.[1]

When the victorious Bolsheviks seized her father's business, the Rosenbaum family was reduced to poverty, and their daughter turned bitterly against collectivism. Thus, during the twentieth century's long struggle between "godly capitalism and godless communism," Alissa had one foot in each camp.

". . . She was the oddest of birds, an atheist who believed in free enterprise," Baker comments. ". . . She held firmly to atheism throughout her life; and she believed it just as important to fight the witch doctor's mysticism as Atilla's collectivism. . . . Already she was identifying religion and communism as brothers under the skin. . . . Both subordinated man to a higher power: religion to god, communism to the state."[2]

---

1. James T. Baker, *Ayn Rand* (New York: Twayne Publishers, 1987), p. 3.
2. Ibid., pp. 140, 114, and 115.

After graduating from a Russian university, she went to Hollywood in 1926, worked in the film industry, and began writing novels under the name Ayn Rand. *The Fountainhead* (1943), featuring a heroic architect somewhat like Frank Lloyd Wright, became a best-seller. So did *Atlas Shrugged* (1957), about heroic, self-made corporate executives.

Meanwhile, Rand also achieved stature as a philosopher, an exponent of Objectivism, dedicated to individualism and capitalism. Critics contend that her followers became rather like a cult. Psychotherapist Albert Ellis even called Objectivism a dogmatic, absolutist, intolerant, unrealistic faith—not a liberator from religion but a substitute for it.

Rand was aggressively outspoken, sometimes calling the Christian cross a torture symbol, sometimes denouncing American conservatives such as William F. Buckley, Jr., who combined capitalism and Christianity.

Whatever else she was, Rand was unusual in America. No other woman has attained her degree of success as both a serious novelist and a serious philosopher.

Rand's Comments on Religion

"Existence exists, and only existence exists. So if you are to postulate something beyond existence—some supernatural realm—you must do it by openly denying reason, dispensing with definitions, proofs, arguments, and saying flatly, 'To hell with argument, I have faith.' That, of course, is a willful rejection of reason. Objectivism advocates reason as man's sole means of knowledge, and therefore . . . it is atheist. It denies any supernatural dimension presented as a contradiction of nature, of existence. This applies not only to God, but also to every variant of the supernatural ever advocated or to be advocated. In other words, we accept reality, and that's all."—"The Philosophy of Objectivism," lecture, 1976

"Religion . . . is the first enemy of the ability to think. That ability is not used by men to one-tenth of its possibility, yet before they learn to think they are discouraged by being ordered to take things on faith. Faith is the worst curse of mankind, as the exact antithesis and enemy of thought."—private notes, 1934, reported in Barbara Brandon, *The Passion of Ayn Rand*

"For centuries, the mystics of spirit had existed by running a protection racket—by making life on earth unbearable, then charging you for consolation and relief, by forbidding all the virtues that make existence possible, then riding on the shoulders of your guilt, by declaring production and joy to be sins, then collecting blackmail from the sinners."—*For the New Intellectual,* 1961

65

Jean-Paul Sartre (1905–1980)

The horrors of World War II and the Nazi Holocaust caused reflective people everywhere to ponder the madness in human life. Thus, in the postwar years, the time was ripe for a philosophy that focused on the world's irrationality and the fragility of each person's existence.

That philosophy—existentialism—became an international craze in the decade after the war, and its chief exponent, the shy French intellectual Jean-Paul Sartre, was propelled to a permanent place in history.

Previous philosophers had contended that people can know little except their own existence. Germany's Martin Heidegger declared that we are born into an incomprehensible, uncaring universe, and are doomed to die without ever knowing why we are here. The best each person can do, Heidegger said, is to choose values and work for them until death.

Some Christian thinkers expounded a religious version of existentialism; but that which seized the world's imagination was the bleak, stark, godless existentialism preached by novelist-playwright-professor Sartre and his colleagues, including his lifelong lover, Simone de Beauvoir, and the writer Albert Camus.

Life has no meaning in a cosmic sense, Sartre taught. Nature does not care whether people are kind or cruel, or if they slaughter each other. There is no God to dictate right or wrong behavior. People are "condemned to be free"—left entirely on their own to decide how to live. The only meaning to life is that devised by people as they fashion codes for themselves. To attain an "authentic" existence, each one of us must select goals and strive tirelessly for them.

Sartre advocated humanism—constant effort to relieve human suffering and improve the quality of life—but with a gloomy awareness of the senseless destruction and random tragedy that often cripple the most earnest work.

As the nightmare of World War II receded from public attention, the fervor for existentialism also faded. Sartre was voted the Nobel Prize in Literature in 1964,

273

but rejected it—the only person ever to do so—on grounds that he did not want to be turned into a cultural icon.

Like many intellectuals, Sartre flirted with communism, but renounced it as Soviet oppression grew evident. He was so thoroughly an atheist that he rarely mentioned it, considering the topic of God to be beneath discussion. In his autobiography, *The Words,* Sartre recalled deciding at about age twelve that God does not exist, and hardly thinking about it thereafter.

Throughout his life, Sartre suffered from a failure of his eyes to coordinate. At about seventy, his vision disintegrated and his health failed. He tried to continue work, but died in 1980. All France mourned, and fifty thousand came to his funeral.

Sartre's Views on Religion

". . . There are two kinds of existentialists. There are, on the one hand, the Christians . . . and on the other the existential atheists, amongst whom we must place Heidegger as well as the French existentialists and myself."—lecture at the Club Maintenant, Paris, October 29, 1945

"Atheistic existentialism, of which I am a representative, declares... that if God does not exist, there is at least one being whose existence comes before its essence, a being which exists before it can be defined by any conception of it. That being is man."—ibid.

". . . There is no human nature, because there is no God to have a conception of it. Man simply is."—ibid.

"The existentialist . . . finds it extremely embarrassing that God does not exist, for there disappears with him all possibility of finding values in an intelligible heaven. . . . Dostoevsky once wrote, 'If God did not exist, everything would be permitted,' and that, for existentialism, is the starting point. Everything is indeed permitted if God does not exist, and man is in consequence forlorn, for he cannot find anything to depend upon either within him or outside himself."—ibid.

"When we speak of 'abandonment'—a favorite word of Heidegger—we mean only to say that God does not exist, and that it is necessary to draw the consequences of his absence right to the end."—ibid.

"Existentialism is nothing less than an attempt to draw all the consequences of a coherent atheistic position. It isn't trying to plunge man into despair at all. But if one calls every attitude of unbelief despair, like the Christians, then the word is not being used in its original sense. Existentialism isn't so atheistic that it wears itself out showing that God doesn't exist. Rather, it declares that even if God did exist, that would change nothing. There you've got our point of view. Not that we believe that God exists, but we think that the problem of his existence is not the issue. . . ."—ibid.

". . . Illusion has been smashed to bits; martyrdom, salvation and immortality are falling to pieces; the edifice is going to rack and ruin; I collared the Holy Ghost in the basement and threw him out; atheism is a cruel and long-range affair; I think I've carried it through."—*The Words,* 1964

"Respectable society believed in God in order to avoid having to speak about him."—ibid.

"We have lost religion, but we have gained humanism. The ideal now is to liberate and to help emancipate mankind, with the result that man becomes really an absolute for man."—quoted in *Life* magazine, November 6, 1964

66

A. J. Ayer
(1910–1989)

For centuries, philosophers struggled over attempts to prove the existence of God through logic. But a brilliant young English thinker in the 1930s showed the world that this effort is a waste of brainpower, because statements about God have no meaning in a scientific sense.

Alfred Jules Ayer, who had studied philosophy at Oxford and in Vienna, was only twenty-six when he published *Language, Truth and Logic,* a landmark book in the advance of thought.

His central point—developed earlier by his colleagues in the short-lived "Vienna Circle" of thinkers—was that statements have scientific meaning only if they are verifiable. For example, a claim that life exists on Mars is meaningful, because astronauts eventually may land on Mars and either verify or disprove it.

But unverifiable statements—such as "God exists" or "human life has a distinct purpose" or "abortion is evil"—are scientifically meaningless, even though hotly debated, because they cannot be tested, Ayer observed. They are pure opinion. Unless the heavens open and Jehovah steps forth, no reliable evidence is available to verify that God exists. Claims of miraculous healings and the like cannot be deemed evidence of God, because patients die despite all the prayers that are offered.

Conversely, an absolute denial of God's existence is equally meaningless, since verification is impossible. However, despite this assertion, Ayer may be considered a practical atheist: one who sees no reason to worship an invisible deity.

Ayer brought the work of the Vienna Circle—known as logical positivism—to world attention. The group held that the scientific method is the only viable position. This approach banished "woolly uplift" from philosophy, Ayer said.

Ayer became a professor at London University and Oxford University, and

---

*Reprinted from The *Philosophy of A. J. Ayer,* edited by Lewis Edwin Hahn (LaSalle, Ill.: Open Court Publishing Company, 1992).

was knighted in 1970. Married four times, Ayer also had torrid love affairs, including one in the 1940s with Hollywood columnist Sheilah Graham, best known as the 1930s soulmate of novelist F. Scott Fitzgerald. In 1992, Graham's daughter, Dr. Wendy Fairey, dean of liberal arts and sciences at Brooklyn College, wrote a book detailing how Ayer acknowledged, just before his death from lung disease, that he was her father.[1]

Ayer's Comments on Religion

"The fact that people have religious experiences is interesting from the psychological point of view, but it does not in any way imply that there is such a thing as religious knowledge. . . . Unless he can formulate his 'knowledge' in propositions that are empirically verifiable, we may be sure that he is deceiving himself."—*Language, Truth and Logic,* 1936

"I do not find Christianity credible, but I am not sure that it is a more absurd myth than the religion of Zoroaster. Undoubtedly it has bred many fanatics, but so have the Hindu religions, and so has Islam. It would be difficult to find a more obnoxious cult than that of the Aztecs, of which human sacrifice on a large scale was an integral part. Even so, Christianity might be considered worse if its threat of damnation is understood to imply a threat of eternal suffering."—*Thomas Paine* (New York: Athenaeum, 1988), p. 151

". . . If one takes full account of the persecution of heretics, the frequency and savagery of the religious wars which Christianity had engendered, the harm caused, especially to children, by the pernicious doctrine of original sin, a case could be made for saying that the world would have been better off without Christianity." —ibid., p. 151

". . . The misfortunes which God is represented in the book of Job as allowing Satan to inflict on Job, merely to test his faith, are indications, if not of positive malevolence, at least of a suspicious and ruthless insecurity, which is characteristic more of a tyrant than of a wholly powerful and benevolent deity."—ibid., p. 141

---

1. Wendy W. Fairey, *One of the Family* (New York: W. W. Norton & Co., 1992).

67

Isaac Asimov
(1920–1992)

Isaac Asimov's amazing mind was unstoppable. He had vast knowledge in many fields, and churned out as many as twenty-one books a year, writing as fast as he could type. In four decades, he produced 470 books, an incredible amount of work.

Asimov called himself "an explainer" of science, and multitudes of Americans like me studied his lucid volumes like Bibles, trying to grasp the reality of quarks and quasars, radiation and relativity, gravity and galaxies. He also used his scientific comprehension to spin fascinating science fiction, which brought his greatest fame. And he wrote mysteries, histories, humor, critiques of opera and Shakespeare, and even bawdy poetry he labeled "Lecherous Limericks." Asimov also was a national leader of Mensa, the society for people with high IQs. And he made nearly fifty speeches a year.

Asimov's mental outpourings were so prodigious that a librarian remarked at his death, "He was the only author in the world who had at least one book in each of the major classifications of the old Dewey decimal system."

Asimov was born in Russia to Jewish parents who brought him to New York at age three. A brilliant student, he graduated from Columbia University at age nineteen and earned a doctorate in biochemistry at twenty-seven. He taught at Boston University until writing became a full-time occupation.

Asimov was a self-declared atheist who scorned the supernatural, not only in religion but in astrology, occultism, spiritualism, and other mystical fields. He signed the *Humanist Manifesto II,* and chose an Ethical Culture leader to perform his second marriage. The American Humanist Association (AHA) named Asimov "Humanist of the Year" in 1984. He later became president of the AHA.

Through it all, the shaggy-sideburned thinker was funny, lusty, opinionated, self-deprecating, self-laudatory, and truly remarkable.

Asimov's Comments on Religion

"It seems to me that God is a convenient invention of the human mind."—*Columbus Dispatch,* July 20, 1991

"Don't you believe in flying saucers? they ask me. Don't you believe in telepathy?—in ancient astronauts?—in the Bermuda Triangle?—in life after death? No, I reply. No, no, no, no, and again no."—*The Roving Mind,* 1983

"I have never, in all my life, not for one moment, been tempted toward religion of any kind. The fact is that I feel no spiritual void. I have my philosophy of life, which does not include any aspect of the supernatural."—*I. Asimov: A Memoir* (New York: Doubleday, 1994), p. 13

"I certainly don't believe in the mythologies of our society, in heaven and hell, in God and angels, in Satan and demons. I've thought of myself as an 'atheist,' but that simply described what I *didn't* believe in, not what I did. Gradually, though, I became aware there was a movement called 'humanism,' which used that name because, to put it most simply, humanists believe that human beings produced the progressive advance of human society and also the ills that plague it. They believe that if the ills are to be alleviated, it is humanity that will have to do the job. They disbelieve in the influence of the supernatural on either the good or the bad of society."—ibid., p. 498

". . . Those of us who are willing to identify ourselves as humanists are few. I suspect that huge numbers of people of Western tradition are humanists as far as the way they shape their lives is concerned, but that childhood conditioning and social pressures force them to pay lip-service to religion."—ibid., p. 499

"Humanists, out of respect for science, are skeptical of paranormal claims and have no belief in the supernatural. They see insufficient reason to believe in a life after death and to put reliance upon supposed cosmic guarantees, rewards, or punishments."—recruiting statement Asimov wrote for the AHA

". . . The fundamentalists deny that evolution has taken place; they deny that the earth and the universe as a whole are more than a few thousand years old, and so on. There is ample scientific evidence that the fundamentalists are wrong in these matters, and that their notions of cosmogony have about as much basis in fact as the Tooth Fairy has."—*'X' Stands for Unknown* (New York: Doubleday & Co., 1984), p. 196

"Many people who know nothing about science will dismiss the theory of evolution because it is 'just a theory.' No less a brain than Ronald Reagan, in the course of his 1980 campaign, when addressing a group of fundamentalists, dismissed evolution as 'just a theory.' "—ibid., p. 214

68

Gene Roddenberry (1921–1991)

"Star Trek" is an entertainment blockbuster. For three decades, the futuristic television series, successor series, and films have enjoyed global popularity. Today the TV shows and movies appear on more than two hundred American stations daily and in dozens of foreign nations. Billions of people know Captain Kirk and his crew of the starship *Enterprise*. Devoted "Trekkies" join clubs and attend conventions.

Unlike much TV fare, "Star Trek" has a high level of intelligence, and the characters are engagingly human. The episodes often are morality plays upholding the best human values. But the morality in "Star Trek" is rooted solely in secular, humanistic beliefs, not church dictates. The show's creator-writer-producer, Gene Roddenberry, declared himself a disbeliever in supernatural religion.

Roddenberry, born in Texas in 1921, was a decorated flier in World War II who became an airline pilot, and eventually a Los Angeles police sergeant who moonlighted by writing scripts for the new television industry. Finally he became head writer of the Western show "Have Gun, Will Travel."

Then Roddenberry conceived "Star Trek." After a modest start in the late 1960s, it blossomed in reruns to become the most successful TV series in history.

Later in life, Roddenberry decided to "come out" and express his agnosticism publicly. He joined the American Humanist Association (AHA) in 1986, and later was given the organization's Humanist Arts Award.

In 1991, the AHA's magazine devoted almost an entire issue to a long interview with Roddenberry. He died of a heart attack a few months later.

Roddenberry was a humanist convinced that people have enough intelligence, compassion and spirit to find solutions to life's difficulties. After his death, Leonard Nimoy, who played the stoic Vulcan, Mr. Spock, said of Roddenberry: "He had an extraordinary vision about mankind and the potential of mankind's future."

Roddenberry's Views on Religion

"My family was from the South. My mother was very religious. Every Sunday we went to church—Baptist church. . . . I guess I was around fourteen and emerging as a personality. . . . I listened to the sermon, and I remember complete astonishment because what they were talking about were things that were just crazy. It was communion time, where you eat this wafer and are supposed to be eating the body of Christ and drinking his blood. My first impression was, 'This is a bunch of cannibals. . . .' I guess from that time it was clear to me that religion was largely nonsense—largely magical, superstitious things. In my own teen life, I just couldn't see any point in adopting something based on magic, which was obviously phony and superstitious."—*The Humanist,* March–April 1991, p. 6

"They said God was on high and he controlled the world and therefore we must pray against Satan. Well, if God controls the world, he controls Satan. For me, religion was full of misstatements and reaches of logic that I just couldn't agree with. . . . Religion was so full of inconsistencies that I could see no point in arguing each inconsistency out. It was background noise that you ignore."—ibid.

"Santa Claus doesn't exist. Yes, I think back now that there were all sorts of reasons he could not exist and maybe have a little sadness that he is gone, but then I think the same thing about Jesus and the church."—ibid.

"My brother and sister are nonreligious. In fact, the whole family is. You don't see religious stuff in my family when you are around them. This, in a family that fifteen years before had Tuesday prayer meetings in the house. Mom began that in her early twenties and just drifted out of it in later years."—ibid.

"If people need religion, ignore them and maybe they will ignore you, and you can go on with your life. It wasn't until I was beginning to do 'Star Trek' that the subject of religion arose again. What brought it up was that people were saying that I would have to have a chaplain on board the *Enterprise.* I replied, 'No, we don't.' "—ibid.

69

Steve Allen
(1921–)

Tens of millions of Americans know Steve Allen as (1) the hilarious host of the original NBC "Tonight" show, (2) a gifted jazz pianist who has recorded forty albums, (3) a movie actor who portrayed Benny Goodman, (4) a Broadway actor who played the lead in "The Pink Elephant," (5) a songwriter who has composed a record-setting four thousand melodies, (6) a screenwriter who created the PBS "Meeting of Minds" series, and (7) an author of forty-three books.

"Steve Allen does so many things, he's the only man I know who's listed on every one of the Yellow Pages," Andy Williams once cracked. But Allen's fans in the popular entertainment realm may not realize that he is an intense biblical scholar who has agonized for twenty years over the horrors and absurdities of religion. This aspect of him emerged chiefly in three recent books, in which he outlines the cruelties attributed to God in the Bible. (Quotations from them will follow.)

Allen was raised Catholic, but was automatically excommunicated when he remarried in his early thirties. His second wife, Jayne Meadows, is the daughter of a Presbyterian minister, and so they attended this church for a while. Later, he sometimes visited Unitarian congregations.

After his son Brian joined a cult in the 1970s, Allen related the family crisis in a book, *Beloved Son: A Story of the Jesus Cults* (New York: Bobbs-Merrill, 1982).

An entertainer lives in hotel rooms, and Allen passed many nights reading the Gideon Bibles in hotel nightstands. From that, he says, he saw the ghastly nature of God as portrayed in the Old Testament.

Allen isn't an atheist. He says he accepts "the probability that there is some kind of divine force." But he disdains the supernatural and intolerant components of religion.

Allen's Comments on Religion

". . . From my mid-twenties I began to have certain doubts about one aspect or another of the Catholic and/or Christian teachings and record. I do not refer here only to the obvious atrocities found in Christian history, of which there are more than enough to gratify the prejudice of the antireligious and to shame all decent Christians. Nor did learning of the vulgar, sinful, corrupt, or warlike behavior of certain popes weaken my faith. The troubling questions arose from one source only: my intellect. To the extent that one has some respect for the rules of evidence, one cannot ignore those moments when a biblically based religious opinion comes into flat contradiction with either factual evidence or logical reasoning."—*Steve Allen on the Bible, Religion, & Morality* (Amherst, N.Y.: Prometheus Books, 1990), p. xxiii

"During all the years of my fervent belief, I simply had no idea how many sorry and embarrassing passages there are in the scriptural record. I had encountered a few instances of critical literature, but it had largely bounced off the armored shell of my bias and loyalty to the Catholic church."—ibid., p. 411

". . . There is scarcely a page of the Bible on which an open mind does not perceive a contradiction, an unlikely story, an obvious error, an historical impossibility of one sort or another."—ibid., p. 413

". . . Consider the wave of revulsion that floods the average person when he or she hears of the practice of human sacrifice by the Aztecs and other so-called primitive peoples. How savage and barbaric such practices seem. But when a Christian or Jew comes across human sacrifice in the Bible (see Jephthah's immolation of his daughter in Judges 11:30–40), is he or she repulsed?"—ibid., p. 416

"In every single instance where churchmen placed themselves squarely athwart the path of science, as regards a particularly knotty question, the religious forces were eventually defeated for the very sound reason that they were wrong."—ibid., p. xxiv

"During many years as a churchgoer, I often heard or read Catholic or Protestant commentaries strongly critical of atheists or other persons who, it was said, 'hated God.' Only later did I come to realize that an atheist does not hate God; he simply is one who is unable to believe that a God exists."—ibid., p. xxv

"I believe it is the imposition of a dictatorship that increasing numbers on the Christian Right now wish to construct in the United States. . . . They believe that Christianity should be the official religion of the United States and that American laws should be specifically Christian."—ibid., p. xxxii

"The proposition that the entire human race—consisting of enormous hordes of humanity—would be placed in serious danger of a fiery eternity characterized by unspeakable torments purely because a man disobeyed a deity by eating a piece of fruit offered him by his wife is inherently incredible."—ibid., p. xiv

"If we start with the unquestioned assumption that there is a God and that he is, by definition, good, then it inescapably follows that the countless atrocities attributed to him in the Old Testament are not only lies, but insulting lies at that. . . . This is something the fundamentalist cannot even consider, much less concede."
—ibid., p. xvi

". . . There will inevitably be a certain amount of destructive, superstitious nonsense preached. Many of our nation's fundamentalist Christians, who, by and large, believe that the Bible is reliable as history and science, are no longer content with teaching their freely gathered congregations. . . . The freedom to preach unscientific superstition deserves to be limited when it attempts to impose itself on those who have not requested it and who may, in fact, hold contrary religious opinions, or none at all. When, for example, America's fundamentalist believers in the inerrancy of the Bible insist on having historical and scientific errors taught in our nation's public schools, then they must be opposed by all legal means."
—ibid., p. xxix

"In the end, then, it all comes down to Pascal's Gamble and the individual freedom to opt for faith. Pure science, pure reason are very largely on the side of the rationalists, agnostics, and atheists."—ibid., p. 420

". . . Both the existence and nonexistence of God seem in some respects preposterous. I accept the probability that there is some kind of divine force, however, because that appears to me the least preposterous assumption of the two."—ibid., p. xxix

". . . I cannot see how it can be argued that one should speak in tones of reverence and awe about the alleged divine instruction—in Psalms—to grab the defenseless bodies of innocent infants and dash their brains out against the nearest rocks or walls."—*More Steve Allen on the Bible, Religion, & Morality* (Amherst, N.Y.: Prometheus Books, 1993), p. xvi

"The Bible has been interpreted to justify such evil practices as slavery, the slaughter of prisoners of war, the sadistic murders of women believed to be witches, capital punishment for hundreds of offenses, polygamy, and cruelty to animals. It has been used to encourage belief in the grossest superstition and to discourage the free teaching of scientific truths."—ibid., p. xviii

"It was only when I finally undertook to read the Bible through from beginning to end that I perceived that its depiction of the Lord God—whom I had always viewed as the very embodiment of perfection—was actually that of a monstrous, vengeful tyrant, far exceeding in bloodthirstiness and insane savagery the depredations of Hitler, Stalin, Pol Pot, Attila the Hun, or any other mass murderer of ancient or modern history."—ibid., p. xix

"It is not hardness of heart or evil passions that drive certain individuals to atheism, but rather a scrupulous intellectual honesty."—*Reflections* (Amherst, N.Y.: Prometheus Books, 1994), p. 24

"Few if any articulate atheists, agnostics, or secular humanists have been attracted to cults."—ibid., p. 76

"Where does faith come from? Most believers will answer that it comes from God, but such an answer produces more confusion than clarity, since it is an absurdity to assume that God endorses every one of the thousand-and-one religions of the world, many of whose dogmas are mutually exclusive, and some of which are idiotic."—ibid., p. 111

"Millions of Germans had absolute faith in Hitler. Millions of Russians had faith in Stalin. Millions of Chinese had faith in Mao. Billions have had faith in imaginary gods."—ibid., p. 112

"The Old Testament condones slavery and bigotry against outsiders, whereas the American system outlaws slavery and discrimination."—ibid., p. 138

". . . Humans develop myths, each generation adding or subtracting details. . . . There is no particular harm in all of this—until the point is reached at which such creative interweaving of fact and fantasy, history and dreams becomes codified and perceived . . . as The Word of God. At that fateful point, the clouds of time darken, and the tribe marches forward to misunderstanding, hatred, and, inevitably, bloodshed."—ibid., pp. 218–19

"If you pray for rain long enough, it eventually does fall. If you pray for floodwaters to abate, they eventually do. The same happens in the absence of prayers." —ibid., p. 245

"I do not understand those who take little or no interest in the subject of religion. If religion embodies a truth, it is certainly the most important truth of human existence. If it is largely error, then it is one of monumentally tragic proportions— and should be vigorously opposed."—ibid., p. 273

"We hear much, in recent years, of a return to religion. . . . There is also an especially disturbing proliferation of bizarre cults and freako churches, large and small, whose belief systems are intellectually on a par with the mindset of supermarket tabloids. And even within religious groups that are respectful of scientific evidence, not to mention common sense, it is the irrational and superstitious wings of such congregations that are flourishing. . . . Among the hundreds of millions of believers in Islam, it is the most violent and fanatical elements that are flourishing. Before, therefore, we indulge in unconditional enthusiasm about the present 'return to religion,' we should attempt to assess it in its totality."—ibid., p. 277

"Some religious opinions are beautiful, moral, enlightening, uplifting; others are bizarre, crazy, socially dangerous, vengeful, personally destructive. There are millions of religious fanatics in the world. Some of them act crazy. You wouldn't want them in your house. You wouldn't want your daughter to marry one of them."—ibid., p. 280

70

Kurt Vonnegut, Jr. (1922–)

AP/Wide World Photos

O ne of America's most brilliant postwar novelists, Kurt Vonnegut is so unusual as to be almost unique. His horrible, hilarious, bizarre, tender tales—sometimes including himself, the writer, mingling with his fictional characters—subtly cry for kindness amid the cruel chaos of life.

His books have sold millions of copies in many languages, and have made Vonnegut a cult hero. His popularity shows how well he fits the alienated mood of bright modern readers.

Critic Robert Group says Vonnegut "offers a mixture of wistful humanism and cynical existentialism that implies a way of dealing with modern realities completely different from that of most American writers. . . . One must cry out against absurdity, even if one is ignored. Vonnegut creates a vision so preposterous that indignation might provide the basis for change—while laughter allows one to cope with the moment." Writer Michael Crichton calls Vonnegut's novels attacks against "our deepest fears of automation and the bomb, our deepest political guilts, our fiercest hatreds and loves. Nobody else writes books on these subjects; they are inaccessible to normal novelistic approaches. But Vonnegut, armed with his schizophrenia, takes an absurd, distorted, wildly funny framework. . . ."[1]

Vonnegut declares himself an atheist. He was born in Indianapolis, son of a German immigrant family that ignored religion. He didn't learn until late in life that his great-grandfather wrote a freethinker book in 1900 titled *Instruction in Morals,* saying the notion of God was concocted from "the fantasy of man."

As an aviator in World War II, Vonnegut was captured by Germans and imprisoned at Dresden. Although the lovely, historic city played no military role, it was destroyed in a hideous 1945 Allied firebomb raid that killed perhaps 100,000

---

1. Michael Crichton, "The Critic as Artist: Essays on Books, 1920–1970," in *Contemporary Authors New Revision Series,* vol. 25, p. 472.

civilians. Vonnegut survived, and incorporated the raid in his famous novel, *Slaughterhouse Five.* He says, rather cold-bloodedly, that the senseless massacre benefited nobody—except himself, in that he profited from writing about it.

Vonnegut wrote that his first marriage collapsed because his wife became a born-again Christian, and that her "alliances with the supernatural" pained and distressed him. He quoted from his great-grandfather's book: "Whoever entertains liberal views and chooses a consort who is captured by superstition risks his liberty and his happiness."[1]

While busy with his writing, Vonnegut has become a leader of agnostic efforts. After the death of Isaac Asimov created a vacancy, Vonnegut became honorary president of the American Humanist Association. And he was named Humanist Laureate of the Academy of Humanism established by the Council for Democratic and Secular Humanism.

Vonnegut's Views on Religion

"I am an atheist (or at best a Unitarian who winds up in churches quite a lot)."
—*Fates Worse Than Death: An Autobiographical Collage of the 1980s* (New York: G. P. Putnam's Sons, 1991), p. 86

"I am a fourth-generation German-American religious skeptic (freethinker). Like my essentially puritanical forebears, I believe that God has so far been unknowable and hence unservable, hence the highest service one can perform is to his or her community, whose needs are quite evident. I believe that virtuous behavior is trivialized by carrot-and-stick schemes, such as promises of highly improbable rewards or punishments in an improbable afterlife."—letter to the chapel dean at Transylvania University, Lexington, Ky., 1991, after the dean had asked Vonnegut his "religious persuasion"

"I am of course a skeptic about the divinity of Christ and a scorner of the notion that there is a God who cares how we are or what we do. . . . Religious skeptics often become very bitter toward the end, as did Mark Twain. . . . I know why I will become bitter. I will finally realize that I have had it right all along: that I will not see God, that there is no heaven or Judgment Day."—address at Twain's home in Hartford, Conn., April 30, 1979

"Interviewer: Did the study of anthropology later color your writings? Vonnegut: It confirmed my atheism, which was the faith of my fathers anyway. Religions were exhibited and studied as the Rube Goldberg inventions I'd always thought they were."—imaginary interview with himself Vonnegut wrote for *The Paris Review,* No. 69, 1977

---

1. *Palm Sunday: An Autobiographical Collage* (New York: Delacorte Press, 1991), pp. 192–93.

"Might we not do without religion entirely? . . . A lot of people have been forced to do without it—because the old-time religions they know are too superstitious, too full of magic, too ignorant about biology and physics to harmonize with the present day."—commencement address, Geneva, N.Y., May 26, 1974

"How on earth can religious people believe in so much arbitrary, clearly invented balderdash? . . . The acceptance of a creed, any creed, entitles the acceptor to membership in the sort of artificial extended family we call a congregation. It is a way to fight loneliness. Any time I see a person fleeing from reason and into religion, I think to myself, There goes a person who simply cannot stand being so goddamned lonely anymore."—address to Unitarian congregation, Cambridge, Mass., January 27, 1980

"Say what you will about the sweet miracle of unquestioning faith, I consider a capacity for it terrifying and absolutely vile!"—(Peter)

71

Other Recent
Scientists

Richard Feynman: AP/Wide World
Photos

From Hypatia to Bruno, from Galileo to Darwin, scientists have been attacked by the clergy for scientific findings that contradicted religious dogmas. In virtually every confrontation, history later proved the church wrong.

The long struggle between science and religion was unavoidable, because two opposite mind-sets were at work: one demanding tangible evidence, the other accepting miracle claims on faith.

Today, scientists generally disbelieve in the supernatural, but many do not bother to state their doubts. Following are a few who did.

Scientists' Comments on Religion

"What gods are there, what gods have there ever been, that were not from man's imagination?"—Joseph Campbell (1904–1987), American anthropologist, *Myths to Live By,* 1972

". . . Devout belief, dogmatism, and religiosity distinctly contribute to, and in some ways are equal to, mental or emotional disturbance."—Albert Ellis, American psychotherapist, *Free Inquiry,* spring 1988, p. 27

"Devout deity-inspired religionists tend to sacrifice human love for godly love. . . . They foment religious fights, feuds, wars, and terrorism, in the course of which orthodox believers literally batter and kill rather than cooperatively help each other."—Ellis, ibid., p. 28

". . . Religious creeds encourage some of the craziest kinds of thoughts, emotions, and behaviors and favor severe manifestations of neurosis, borderline personality states, and sometimes even psychosis."—Ellis, ibid., p. 31

"Religious fanaticism has clearly produced, and in all probability will continue to produce, enormous amounts of bickering, fighting, violence, bloodshed, homicide, feuds, wars, and genocide."—Ellis, ibid., p. 32

"In those days, in Far Rockaway, there was a youth center for Jewish kids at the temple. . . . Somebody nominated me for president of the youth center. The elders began getting nervous, because I was an avowed atheist by that time. . . . I thought nature itself was so interesting that I didn't want it distorted like that [by miracle stories]. And so I gradually came to disbelieve the whole religion."— Richard P. Feynman (1918–1988), Nobel Prize-winning American physicist, *What Do You Care What Other People Think?* (New York: W. W. Norton & Co., 1988), pp. 25–28

"Sometimes I think we're alone. Sometimes I think we're not. In either case, the thought is quite staggering."—R. Buckminster Fuller (1895–1983), American inventor-engineer-architect-philosopher

"I don't see any god up here."—Yury Gagarin (1934–1968), atheist Soviet cosmonaut, speaking from orbit in 1961

"We are here because one odd group of fishes had a peculiar fin anatomy that could transform into legs for terrestrial creatures; because the earth never froze entirely during an ice age; because a small and tenuous species, arising in Africa a quarter of a million years ago, has managed, so far, to survive by hook and by crook. We may yearn for a 'higher' answer—but none exists."—Stephen Jay Gould, American paleontologist, *Life* magazine, December 1988

"The fundamentalists, by 'knowing' the answers before they start [examining evolution], and then forcing nature into the straitjacket of their discredited preconceptions, lie outside the domain of science—or of any honest intellectual inquiry."—Gould, *Bully for Brontosaurus,* 1990

"Religion is but a desperate attempt to find an escape from the truly dreadful situation in which we find ourselves. Here we are in this wholly fantastic universe with scarcely a clue as to whether our existence has any real significance. No wonder then that many people feel the need for some belief that gives them a sense of security, and no wonder that they become very angry with people like me who say that this is illusory."—Fred Hoyle, British astronomer. *The Nature of the Universe,* 1950

If some good evidence for life after death were announced, I'd be eager to examine it; but it would have to be real scientific data, not mere anecdote. . . . Better the hard truth, I say, than the comforting fantasy."—Carl Sagan, *The Demon-Haunted World: Science as a Candle in the Dark* (New York: Random House, 1996), p. 204

"If you want to save your child from polio, you can pray or you can inoculate. . . . Try science."—Sagan, ibid., p. 30

"Think of how many religions attempt to validate themselves with prophecy. Think of how many people rely on these prophecies, however vague, however unfulfilled, to support or prop up their beliefs. Yet has there ever been a religion with the prophetic accuracy and reliability of science? . . . No other human institution comes close."—Sagan, ibid., p. 30

"Since World War II, Japan has spawned enormous numbers of new religions featuring the supernatural. . . . In Thailand, diseases are treated with pills manufactured from pulverized sacred Scripture. 'Witches' are today being burned in South Africa. . . . The worldwide TM [Transcendental Meditation] organization has an estimated valuation of $3 billion. For a fee, they promise to make you invisible, to enable you to fly."—Sagan, ibid., p. 16

"In Italy, the Inquisition was condemning people to death until the end of the eighteenth century, and inquisitional torture was not abolished in the Catholic Church until 1816. The last bastion of support for the reality of witchcraft and the necessity of punishment has been the Christian churches."—Sagan, ibid., p. 413

"What chiefly concerns and alarms many of us are the problems arising from religious fanaticism. As long as large numbers of militant enthusiasts are persuaded that they alone have access to the truth, and that the rest of us are infidels, we remain under threat. Lord Acton's famous phrase about power can be used of another danger. Dogma tends to corrupt, and absolute dogma corrupts absolutely."—Anthony Storr, British psychiatrist, *Human Destructiveness* (New York: Grove Weidenfeld, 1991), p. 156

72

Other Recent
Literary Figures

Gore Vidal: Library of Congress Collection

Writing is thinking on paper (or, in the new age, on a computer screen). Something in the mental processes of writers must incline them to nonconformity, because a remarkable number of writers are religious misfits. British researcher David Tribe once listed about a hundred skeptics among authors, including the following, in alphabetical order: Edward Albee, William Archer, James Baldwin, Charles Baudelaire, Samuel Beckett, Ambrose Bierce, Bertold Brecht, Anton Chekhov, Joseph Conrad, Theodore Dreiser, Alexandre Dumas fils, Ralph Waldo Emerson, William Faulkner, Edward FitzGerald, Gustave Flaubert, Anatole France, John Galsworthy, Andre Gidé, Maxim Gorky, Thomas Hardy, A. E. Housman, Victor Hugo, James Joyce, D. H. Lawrence, T. E. Lawrence, Sinclair Lewis, Jack London, W. Somerset Maugham, Guy de Maupassant, Herman Melville, Arthur Miller, A. A. Milne, Iris Murdoch, Sean O'Casey, Eugene O'Neill, John Osborne, Ouida (Marie Louise de la Ramée), Harold Pinter, Marcel Proust, Edmond Rostand, George Sand, Ivan Turgenev, Peter Ustinov, Walt Whitman, Tennessee Williams, and Virginia Woolf.[1]

Actually, this list might be doubled. Tribe failed to include H. G. Wells, Upton Sinclair, Edgar Allan Poe, Edgar Lee Masters, Peter de Vries, Kurt Vonnegut, Gore Vidal, James A. Michener, and scores of others included in this book.

Following is a survey of skepticism among various postwar writers.

*　　*　　*

"The patrons of such establishments as the Angelus Temple and the Rev. Billy Sunday's tabernacles are of the type who make up the vast memberships of various fanatical religious bodies, reform leagues, and mobs of all sorts. They are the

---

1. David H. Tribe, *One Hundred Years of Freethought* (London: Elek Books Ltd., 1967), p. 195.

folks whom the Lord blessed with a lot of feelings and scant reasoning power, making them thus abnormally suggestible to dynamic personalities—spellbinders, demagogues, bunk-shooters, bunco-steerers of all sorts. They make life rosy for the evangelistic faith manufacturer, the salvationist, the 'divine healer,' the flag-waving politician, the blue-sky promoter. They fill our churches and our jails. They shout hallelujahs at Aimee Semple McPherson's temple. . . ."—Louis Adamic (1899–1951), American novelist (Cardiff)

"One of the many burdens of the person professing Christianity has always been the odium likely to be heaped upon him by fellow Christians quick to smell out, denounce and punish fraud, hypocrisy and general unworthiness among those who assert the faith. In ruder days, disputes about what constituted a fully quali-fied Christian often led to sordid quarrels in which the disputants tortured, burned and hanged each other in the conviction that torture, burning and hanging were Christian things to do. . . ."—Russell Baker, American columnist, *The New York Times,* December 1988

"God has been replaced, as he has all over the West, with respectability and air conditioning."—Imamu Amiri Baraka (b. LeRoi Jones), "What Does Non-Vio-lence Mean?" *Home,* 1966

"I cannot be angry at God, in whom I do not believe."—Simone de Beauvoir (1908–1986), French writer and political activist

"For those who believe in God, most of the big questions are answered. But for those of us who can't readily accept the God formula, the big answers don't remain stone-written. We adjust to new conditions and discoveries. We are pliable. Love need not be a command or faith a dictum. I am my own God. We are here to un-learn the teachings of the church, state and our education system. We are here to drink beer. We are here to kill war. We are here to laugh at the odds and live our lives so well that Death will tremble to take us."—Charles Bukowski (1920–1994), American writer, *Life* magazine, December 1988

"The trouble with born-again Christians is that they are an even bigger pain the second time around."—Herb Caen, *San Francisco Chronicle,* July 20, 1981

"I shall not, as far as I am concerned, try to pass myself off as a Christian in your presence. I share with you the same revulsion from evil. But I do not share your hope, and I continue to struggle against this universe in which children suffer and die."—Albert Camus (1913–1960), Nobel Prize-winning French novelist, ad-dressing Dominican priests in 1948, quoted by himself in "The Unbeliever and Christians," *Resistance, Rebellion, and Death* (New York: Alfred A. Knopf, 1961), p. 70

"Capital punishment . . . has always been a religious punishment and is irrecon-cilable with humanism."—Camus (Peter)

"For every credibility gap, there is a gullibility fill."—Richard Clopton, ibid.

"Wherever they've gone / they're not here anymore / and all they stood for is empty also."—Robert Creeley, American poet, "Heaven," *Echoes* (New York: New Directions, 1993)

"Fanaticism is . . . overcompensation for doubt."—Robertson Davies, Canadian playwright and novelist, *Manticore,* 1972

"Religion has shifted to take in every change in the winds, so that its obedience to American culture and political trends is apparent. As lifestyles have changed, so has the theology of the churches. Manifest destiny became social gospel with barely a backward glance."—Vine Deloria, Jr., *We Talk, You Listen,* 1970

"I read about an Eskimo hunter who asked the local missionary priest, 'If I did not know about God and sin, would I go to hell?' 'No,' said the priest, 'not if you did not know.' 'Then why,' asked the Eskimo earnestly, 'did you tell me?' "—Annie Dillard, *Pilgrim at Tinker Creek,* 1974

"By dipping us children in the Bible so often, they hoped, I think, to give our lives a serious tint, and to provide us with quaintly magnificent snatches of prayer to produce as charms while, say, being mugged for our cash or jewels."—Dillard, *An American Childhood,* 1987

"Science may have come a long way, but as far as religion is concerned, we are first cousins to the !Kung tribesmen of the Kalahari Desert. Except for the garments, their deep religious trances might just as well be happening at a revival meeting or in the congregation of a fundamentalist TV preacher. . . . As we move further from the life of ignorance and superstition in which religion has its roots, we seem to need it more and more. . . . Why has religion become a force just when we'd have thought it would be losing ground to secularism?"—Phil Donahue, *The Human Animal* (New York: Simon & Schuster, 1985), pp. 382–89

"The God-loving people who fashioned the soaring vaults and delicate windows of Chartres had murder on their minds. Some of the workers may well have been veterans of the First Crusade, an expedition to save the Holy Land from the Muslims that was part religious frenzy, part military adventure and part social fad. On that excursion, begun four years after work on Chartres began, the Crusaders slaughtered thousands of noncombatants, leveled whole communities, and finally 'saved' the holy city of Jerusalem by massacring all its inhabitants—men, women, children, Muslims, Jews: everybody. . . . We can pray one minute and kill the next. . . . We like to think that our erratic behavior is a thing of the past, that we've outgrown the excesses of the Crusades. But nothing could be further from the truth. There are people in Belfast today who will repeat the catechism, then go toss a bomb into a crowded pub. . . ."—Donahue, ibid., p. 21

"In Jerusalem, the various modes of worship essentially stood for the same cause but were equally hateful to one another. They never served as a unifying factor. Their adherents were equally manipulated by the clergies to regard the others as wicked infidels or idolaters. The centuries passed in constant pious agitation and in frequent religious wars."—Amos Elon, *Jerusalem: City of Mirrors* (Boston: Little, Brown & Co.), 1989, p. 27

"Local psychiatrists now speak of a Jerusalem syndrome. A hundred-odd pilgrims and tourists are treated each year at Kfar Shaul Hospital, the government mental-health center serving the Jerusalem area, for breakdowns related to this syndrome, which involves messianic fantasies and delusions of being Mary Magdalene, John the Baptist, or other biblical characters. They are mostly Americans and almost all are Protestant. Many have a strong grounding in the Bible. In Jerusalem, they suddenly take off their clothes or shout prophecies on street corners, only to revert to normal after a few days' treatment."—Elon, ibid., p. 147

". . . Jerusalem has been—and for many, still is—a metaphor for destruction and the vengeance of an offended God. She is the city where believers have killed unbelievers to give life to faith."—Elon, ibid., p. 149

"I am waiting for them to prove that God is really American."—Lawrence Ferlinghetti, "I Am Waiting," *A Coney Island of the Mind,* 1958

"Faith, to my mind, is a stiffening process, a sort of mental starch, which ought to be applied as sparingly as possible. . . . I do not believe in it for its own sake at all."—E. M. Forster (1879–1970), English novelist, *Two Cheers for Democracy,* 1951

"I left the Catholic Church almost thirty years ago. It is relevant to my present attitudes that even though I rejected the Church . . . I clearly remain a 'cultural Catholic,' much as an atheist Jew is culturally Jewish. . . . To complicate matters further, I consider myself to be—in Max Weber's phrase—'religiously musical' even though I do not believe in God. . . . I am, then, what Georg Simmel called a 'religious nature without religion,' a pious man of deep faith, but not in the supernatural."—Michael Harrington, *The Politics at God's Funeral,* 1983

"That God has managed to survive the inanities of the religions that do Him homage is truly a miraculous proof of His existence."—Ben Hecht (1894–1964), in *Bartlett's Unfamiliar Quotations* (Chicago: Cowles, 1971), p. 113

"Men rarely (if ever) managed to dream up a god superior to themselves. Most gods have the manners and morals of a spoiled child."—Robert A. Heinlein (1907–1988), science fiction writer, quoted in McWilliams, *Ain't Nobody's Business If You Do,* p. 375

"The faith in which I was brought up assured me that I was better than other people; I was *saved,* they were *damned.* . . . Our hymns were loaded with arrogance—self-congratulation on how cozy we were with the Almighty and what a high opinion he had of us, what hell everybody else would catch come Judgment Day."—Heinlein (Peter)

"Good God, how much reverence can you have for a Supreme Being who finds it necessary to include such phenomena as phlegm and tooth decay in his divine system of creation?"—Joseph Heller, *Catch 22,* 1961

"Every judgment teeters on the brink of error. To claim absolute knowledge is to become monstrous. Knowledge is an unending adventure at the edge of uncertainty."—Frank Herbert, *Dune,* 1965

"Gullibility and credulity are considered undesirable qualities in every department of human life—except religion. . . . Why are we praised by godly men for surrendering our 'godly gift' of reason when we cross their mental thresholds? . . . Atheism strikes me as morally superior, as well as intellectually superior, to religion. Since it is obviously inconceivable that all religions can be right, the most reasonable conclusion is that they are all wrong. Does this leave us shorn of hope? Not a bit of it. Atheism, and the related conviction that we have just one life to live, is the only sure way to regard all our fellow creatures as brothers and sisters. . . . Even the compromise of agnosticism is better than faith. It minimizes the totalitarian temptation, the witless worship of the absolute and the surrender of reason."—Christopher Hitchens, "The Lord and the Intellectuals," *Harper's,* July 1982, p. 60

"Self-righteousness is a loud din raised to drown the voice of guilt within us." —Eric Hoffer, *The True Believer,* 1951

"It was the craving to be a one and only people which impelled the ancient Hebrews to invent a one and only God whose one and only people they were to be."—Hoffer, cited in Eugene Brussell, *Dictionary of Quotable Definitions* (New York: Prentice-Hall, 1970)

"Writing for a penny a word is ridiculous. If a man really wants to make a million dollars, the best way would be to start his own religion."—L. Ron Hubbard, science fiction writer who later created Scientology, quoted in the *New York Times,* July 11, 1984

"In the name of religion, one tortures, persecutes, builds pyres. . . ."—Eugene Ionesco (1912–1994), French playwright, *Esquire* magazine, 1974

"Christianity was a great religion. It has been over for a hundred years now; whatever the twentieth century knows of it can be thought of as a lingering unreality preserved in the church. When something even so small as a lightbulb goes out, the eyes for a moment still see it; and a sound after it is made will have, in the right places, an echo. So it is not at all strange that when something so huge as a world religion goes out, there remains for a century or more in certain places some notion that it is still there."—Mary Jean Irion, *From the Ashes of Christianity,* 1968

"Organized Christianity has probably done more to retard the ideals that were its founder's than any other agency in the world."—Richard Le Gallienne (Peter)

"Several months ago, I received a letter from the Bishop of Durham in England inviting me to participate in a public debate about God and religion. . . . I wrote back to say that God wasn't my line of work: that I did not believe in him, that I thought the church had done more harm than good. . . ."—Michael Lewis, *The New Republic,* November 8, 1993, p. 46

"To me, a man committed to no creed, and more uncertain than I should be of certain ultimate beliefs. . . ."—Archibald MacLeish (1892–1982), American poet and playwright, on the Broadway opening of his play *J. B., Time* magazine, December 22, 1958, p. 56

"The infantile cowardice of our time which demands an external pattern, a non-human authority. . . ."—MacLeish, quoted by Bergen Evans, regarding his play *J. B.*

"Piety's hard enough to take among the poor who *have* to practice it. A rich man's piety stinks. It's insufferable."—MacLeish, *J. B.*

"The Old Testament is tribal in its provinciality; its god is a local god, and its village police and sanitary regulations are erected into eternal laws."—John Macy (Peter)

"I am terrified of restrictive religious doctrine, having learned from history that when men who adhere to any form of it are in control, common men like me are in peril. . . . So I am a humanist. And if you want to charge me with being the most virulent kind—a secular humanist—I accept the accusation, but I do not want to be accused of atheism. No man who loves the book of Deuteronomy and the first chapter of the General Epistle of St. James, as I do, can be totally anti-religious. A charge that *can* be lodged against me is that I am a knee-jerk liberal, for I confess that sin."—James A. Michener, *The World Is My Home,* 1991

"Jerusalem is . . . the fabled city which for the Western mind is as much dream as stone . . . a compressed symbol of our most sublime aspirations along with our most disgusting, hatefully brainless excursions into religious bigotry and fratricide."—Arthur Miller, American playwright, comment on dust jacket of *Jerusalem: City of Mirrors*

"If you scratch any aggressive tribalism, or nationalism, you usually find beneath its surface a religious core, some older binding energy of belief or superstition . . . that is capable of transforming itself into a death-force, with the peculiar annihilating energies of belief. Faith, the sweetest refuge and consolation, may harden, by perverse miracle, into a sword—or anyway into a club or a torch or an assault rifle. Religious hatreds tend to be merciless and absolute."—Lance Morrow, *Time,* March 15, 1993, p. 24

"Our existence is but a brief crack of light between two eternities of darkness." —Vladimir Nabokov (1899–1977), Russian-American novelist (Peter)

"Religious ideologies and their fanaticisms are dangerous enough, but when these or other ideologies become frenzied elements of the political area, the only area of absolute power over human lives ... they become potentially dangerous in their impact on a free society."—Robert Nisbet, *Prejudices: A Philosophical Dictionary,* 1982

"She was a good Christian woman with a large respect for religion, though she did not, of course, believe any of it was true."—Flannery O'Connor (1925–1964), "Greenleaf," in *Everything That Rises Must Converge,* published posthumously in 1965

" 'I'm going to preach there was no Fall because there was nothing to fall from, and no Redemption because there was no Fall, and no Judgment because there wasn't the first two. Nothing matters but that Jesus was a liar.' "—O'Connor, *Wise Blood,* 1949

"No doubt alcohol, tobacco, and so forth, are things that a saint must avoid, but sainthood is also a thing that human beings must avoid. . . . Many people genuinely do not wish to be saints, and it is probable that some who achieve or aspire to sainthood have never felt much temptation to be human beings."—George Orwell (Eric Arthur Blair) (1903–1950), "Reflections on Gandhi," *Shooting an Elephant,* 1950

"God must have loved the people in power, for he made them so much like their own image of him."—Kenneth Patchen (1911–1972), American poet, *Some Little Sayings and Observations,* 1956

"I never cease being dumbfounded by the unbelievable things people believe." —Leo Rosten (Peter)

"The idea of the sacred is quite simply one of the most conservative notions in any culture, because it seeks to turn other ideas—uncertainty, progress, change—into crimes."—Salman Rushdie, Herbert Reade Memorial Lecture, February 6, 1990, written in hiding a year after Shi'ite mullahs offered a two-million-dollar reward for Rushdie's murder for "blasphemy"

"For Catholics before Vatican II, the land of the free was preeminently the land of Sister Says—except, of course, for Sister, for whom it was the land of Father Says."—Wilfrid Sheed, *Frank and Maisie: A Memoir with Parents,* 1985

"There are a score of great religions in the world, each with scores or hundreds of sects, each with its priestly orders, its complicated creed and ritual, its heavens and hells. Each has its thousands or millions or hundreds of millions of 'true believers'; each damns all the others with more or less heartiness—and each is a mighty fortress of graft."—Upton Sinclair (1878–1968), American novelist and socialist (Cardiff)

"Various Catholic societies . . . in every city and town in America, are pushing and plotting to get Catholics upon library boards, so that the public may not have a chance to read scientific books; to get Catholics into the public schools and on school boards, so that children may not hear about Galileo, Bruno, and Ferrer; to have Catholics in control of police and on magistrates' benches, so that priests who are caught in brothels may not be exposed or punished."—Sinclair, ibid.

"Belief in Some One's right to punish you is the fate of all children in Judaic-Christian culture. But nowhere else, perhaps, have the rich seedbeds of Western homes found such a growing climate for guilt as is produced in the South by the combination of a warm moist evangelism and racial segregation."—Lillian Smith, *Killers of the Dream,* 1949

"Camp meetings and revivals are the South's past, and once were a heroic part of that past. Today, though often cheapened and vulgarized to the point of obscenity, they are still part of the South's present. Guilt was then and is today the biggest crop raised in Dixie."—Smith, ibid.

"I regard monotheism as the greatest disaster ever to befall the human race. I see no good in Judaism, Christianity, or Islam—good people, yes, but any religion based on a single, well, frenzied and virulent god, is not as useful to the human race as, say, Confucianism, which is not a religion but an ethical and educational system."—Gore Vidal, American novelist, *At Home,* 1988

"Christianity is such a silly religion."—Vidal, in *Time* magazine, September 28, 1992, p. 66

"It is the final proof of God's omnipotence that he need not exist in order to save us."—Peter de Vries, *Mackeral Plaza,* 1958

" 'You don't believe in God,' I said to Stein.
    'God is a word banging around in the human nervous system. He exists about as much as Santa Claus.'
    'Santa Claus has had a tremendous influence, exist or not.'
    'For children.'
    'Lots of saints have died for God with a courage that's hardly childish.'
    'That's part of the horror. It's all a fantasy. It's all for nothing.' . . ."
    —de Vries, *The Blood of the Lamb* (Boston: Little, Brown, 1961), p. 182

" 'You ought to be ashamed,' a woman in an Easter bonnet told Stein. 'Your race gave us our religion. . . . From ancient polytheism, the belief in lots of gods,' the woman continued a little more eruditely, 'the Hebrew nation led us on to the idea that there is only one.'
    'Which is just a step from the truth,' said Stein. . . ."
    —de Vries, ibid., p. 207

"As early as 382 A.D., the church officially declared that any opposition to its own creed in favor of others must be punished by the death penalty."—Barbara G. Walker, *The Woman's Encyclopedia of Myths and Secrets,* 1983

"Why do born-again people so often make you wish they'd never been born the first time?"—Katherine Whitehorn, British journalist, *The Observer,* May 20, 1979

"When has religion ever been unifying? Religion has introduced many wars in this world, enough bloodshed and violence."—Elie Wiesel, Nobel Prize-winning novelist

"All fanaticism is a strategy to prevent doubt from becoming conscious."—H. A. Williams, *The True Wilderness,* 1965

"All your Western theologies, the whole mythology of them, are based on the concept of God as a senile delinquent."—Tennessee Williams (1911–1983), Pulitzer Prize-winning American playwright, *The Night of the Iguana,* 1961

"I abhor the very notion of mysticism. . . ."—Richard Wright (1908–1960), American novelist, *Blueprint for Negro Writing*

73

Other Recent Scholars and Reformers

Gloria Steinem: Courtesy *Ms.* magazine

Philosophers naturally are at odds with religion: they ask "What is the meaning of life?" They wouldn't need to ask if they accepted the church's explanation that the purpose of life is to serve invisible deities and go to invisible heavens.

Social reformers, too, can run afoul of religion when they seek to change established orders reinforced by entrenched faiths. For example, the struggle for women's equality, birth control, and the right to choose abortion has pitted feminists against the conservative clergy.

Following are skeptical views by recent scholars, historians, philosophers, reformers, advocates of democracy, intellectual activists, and other combatants in the never-ending battle of ideas.

*　　*　　*

"The Catholic wife is under great pressure. . . . If she uses contraceptives, she is called wicked by her parish priest. If she follows the advice of her priest and refrains from sexual intercourse, she is called cold by her husband. If she doesn't take steps, she is called mad by society at large."—Anne Biezanek, *The New York Times,* May 21, 1964

"God is the Celebrity-Author of the World's Best Seller. We have made God into the biggest celebrity of all, to contain our own emptiness."—Daniel J. Boorstin, Librarian of Congress, *The Image,* 1962

"I've steered clear of God. He was an incredible sadist."—John Collier (1884–1968), American sociologist (Peter)

"Zealous groups threaten to infringe civil liberties when they seek government support to impose their own religious views on nonadherents. This has taken many forms, including attempts to introduce organized prayer in public schools, to outlaw birth control and abortion, and to use public tax revenues to finance religious schools."—Norman Dorsen, *Civil Liberties,* 1986

". . . Stuff is all there is; while everything which is not stuff is nonsense." —Antony Flew, British philosopher, *The Encyclopedia of Unbelief* (Amherst, N.Y.: Prometheus Books, 1985)

"We go to sea repeatedly from Melville's time on—and the image of men at sea, like the image of men in the wilderness, seems to me to be almost an archetypal image of human beings on their own, human beings making their own way, guiding themselves by the stars they can see—rather than by faith or prayer or invisible forces."—Dr. Maxine Greene, Columbia University professor, "Man without God in American Fiction," a paper read to the New York chapter of the American Humanist Association, December 14, 1962

"As a set of cognitive beliefs, religion is a speculative hypothesis of an extremely low order of probability."—Sidney Hook (1902–1989), American philosopher, *The Partisan Review,* March 1950

"Religious tolerance has developed more as a consequence of the impotence of religions to impose their dogmas on each other than as a consequence of spiritual humility. . . ."—Hook, "Religious Liberty from the Viewpoint of a Secular Humanist," in *Religious Conflict in America,* 1964, p. 141

". . . [T]raditional dogmatic or authoritarian religions that place revelation, God, ritual, or creed above human needs and experience do a disservice to the human species. Any account of nature should pass the tests of scientific evidence; in our judgment, the dogmas and myths of traditional religions do not do so. . . . We find insufficient evidence for belief in the existence of a supernatural; it is either meaningless or irrelevant to the question of the survival and fulfillment of the human race. . . . [W]e can discover no divine purpose or providence for the human species. While there is much that we do not know, humans are responsible for what we are or will become. No deity will save us; we must save ourselves."—*Humanist Manifesto II,* edited by Paul Kurtz and signed by many scientists and scholars (Amherst, N.Y.: Prometheus Books, 1973), p. 16

"*Homo religiosus* invents religious symbols, which he venerates and worships to save him from facing the finality of his death and dissolution. He devises paradise fictions to provide succor and support. . . . In acts of supreme self-deception, at various times and in various places he has been willing to profess belief in the most incredible myths because of what they have promised him. . . ."—Paul Kurtz, American philosopher, *The Transcendental Temptation* (Amherst, N.Y.: Prometheus Books, 1986), preface

". . . The beginning of wisdom is the awareness that there is insufficient evidence that a god or gods have created us and the recognition that we are responsible in part for our own destiny. Human beings can achieve this good life, but it is by the cultivation of the virtues of intelligence and courage, not faith and obedience, that we will most likely be able to do so."—Kurtz, ibid.

"The skeptic has no illusions about life, nor a vain belief in the promise of immortality. Since this life here and now is all we can know, our most reasonable option is to live it fully."—Kurtz, ibid.

"Supernatural entities simply do not exist. This nonreality of the supernatural means, on the human level, that men do not possess supernatural and immortal souls; and, on the level of the universe as a whole, that our cosmos does not possess a supernatural and eternal God."—Corliss Lamont, *The Philosophy of Humanism* (New York: Continuum, 1988), p. 116

"God, once imagined to be an omnipresent force throughout the whole world of nature and man, has been increasingly tending to seem omniabsent. Everywhere, intelligent and educated people rely more and more on purely secular and scientific techniques for the solution of their problems. As science advances, belief in divine miracles and the efficacy of prayer becomes fainter and fainter."—Lamont, ibid., p. 129

"As a social and as a personal force, religion has become a dependent variable. It does not originate; it reacts. It does not denounce; it adapts. It does not set forth new models of conduct and sensibility; it imitates. Its rhetoric is without deep appeal; the worship it organizes is without piety. It has become less a revitalization of the spirit in permanent tension with the world than a respectable distraction from the sourness of life."—C. Wright Mills (1916–1962), American sociologist, *The Nation,* March 8, 1958

"The First Crusade . . . set off on its two-thousand-mile jaunt by massacring Jews, plundering and slaughtering all the way from the Rhine to the Jordan. 'In the temple of Solomon,' wrote the ecstatic cleric Raimundus de Agiles, 'one rode in blood up to the knees and even to the horses' bridles, by the just and marvelous judgment of God.'"—Herbert J. Muller, American scholar (1905–1980) (Peter)

"Religion has ever been anti-human, anti-woman, anti-life, anti-peace, anti-reason and anti-science. The god idea has been detrimental not only to humankind but to the earth. It is time now for reason, education and science to take over."—Madalyn Murray O'Hair, speech in St. Petersburg, Florida, April 14, 1990

"Unlike Christianity, which preached a peace it never achieved, Islam unashamedly came with a sword."—Steven Runciman, British scholar and diplomat, "The First Crusade," *A History of the Crusades*

"Everything Hitler did to the Jews, all the horrible, unspeakable misdeeds, had already been done to the smitten people before by the Christian churches. . . . The isolation of Jews into ghetto camps, the wearing of the yellow spot, the burning of Jewish books, and finally the burning of the people—Hitler learned it all from the church. . . . Wherever there are Christian churches, there is anti-Semitism."

—Dagobert Runes, historian whose mother was killed by Nazis, *The War against the Jews* (New York: Philosophical Library, 1968), p. xvii

"The most malicious kind of hatred is that which is built upon a theological foundation."—George Sarton (1884–1955), Harvard science historian, *History of Science*

"As a historian, I confess to a certain amusement when I hear the Judeo-Christian tradition praised as the source of our present-day concern for human rights. . . . In fact, the great religious ages were notable for their indifference to human rights . . . not only for acquiescence in poverty, inequality, exploitation and oppression, but also for enthusiastic justifications for slavery, persecution, abandonment of small children, torture, and genocide. Religion during most of the history of the West saw the trials visited on mankind in this world as ordained by the Almighty to test and purify sinful mortals. . . . Moreover, religion enshrined hierarchy, authority, and inequality; hated blasphemy; and feared heresy. . . . It was the age of equality that brought about the disappearance of such religious appurtenances as the *auto-da-fe* and burning at the stake. . . ."—Arthur Schlesinger, Jr., speech at the inauguration of Vartan Gregorian as president of Brown University, 1989

". . . Belief in God is irrational to the point of absurdity; and . . . this irrationality, when manifested in specific religions such as Christianity, is extremely harmful."—George H. Smith, *Atheism: The Case against God* (Amherst, N.Y.: Prometheus Books, 1979)

"Those who regard the fundamentalist revival as a harmless return to religious values would do well to take a closer look. There is a deep, underlying revolt here—a rejection of the rationalism and humanism in modern society."—Smith, *Atheism, Ayn Rand, and Other Heresies* (Amherst, N.Y.: Prometheus Books, 1991)

"By the year 2000 we will, I hope, raise our children to believe in human potential, not God."—Gloria Steinem, American feminist leader (Peter)

"We will live to see the day that St. Patrtick's Cathedral is a child-care center and the pope is no longer a disgrace to the skirt that he has on."—Steinem, addressing protesters at Columbus Circle in New York City, October 6, 1995, during a visit by Pope John Paul II

"Today we are witnessing such a resurgence of religious bigotry that one cannot help wondering how long it will be before 'equal time' in our schools is demanded for geocentrism and flat-earthism as well as for creationism."—Dr. Thomas S. Vernon, professor emeritus of philosophy, *Great Infidels,* 1989, p. 105

"The priesthoods of whatever stripe can never live down, nor make amends for, their disgraceful role in retarding the development of modern science during the past millennium in Christendom. . . . Supernaturalism is, in its social functions and consequences, a dangerous opiate. And, what is perhaps even worse, it discourages objective attempts at intelligent social trial-and-error, planning, and even research, and undermines man's faith in his own resources."—George B. Vetter, *Magic and Religion,* 1973

74

Others in the Arts and Entertainment

Katharine Hepburn: AP/Wide World Photos

The world of stage, screen, music, and painting—art high and low—contains a goodly number of religious nonconformists.

British researcher David Tribe listed these major composers as skeptics: Hector Berlioz, Georges Bizet, Johannes Brahms, Benjamin Britten, Claude Debussy, Frederick Delius, Jules Massenet, Richard Strauss, Peter Tchaikovsky, Giuseppe Verdi, and Richard Wagner. Among painters, he added: Kate Greenaway, Henri Matisse, Pablo Picasso, Auguste Rodin, Dante Gabriel Rossetti, and James McNeill Whistler.[1]

Those whose irreverent remarks draw wide circulation usually are figures of popular culture. Following are comments by some recent entertainers.

*　　*　　*

"Not only is there no God, but try getting a plumber on weekends."—Woody Allen, "My Philosophy," *The New Yorker,* December 27, 1969

"I do occasionally envy the person who is religious naturally, without being brainwashed into it or suckered into it by all the organized hustles."—Allen, *Rolling Stone,* 1987

"How can I believe in God when just last week I got my tongue caught in the roller of an electric typewriter?"—Allen, *Without Feathers,* 1975

"The Vatican is against surrogate mothers. Good thing they didn't have that rule when Jesus was born."—Elayne Boosler, comedienne quoted by Robert Byrne in *The Fourth 637 Best Things Anybody Ever Said*

---

1. David H. Tribe, *One Hundred Years of Freethought* (London: Elek Books Ltd., 1967), p. 196.

"Christ and Moses standing in the back of St. Pat's, looking around. Confused, Christ is, at the grandeur of the interior, the baroque interior, the rococo baroque interior. Because his route took him through Spanish Harlem, and he was wondering what the hell fifty Puerto Ricans were doing living in one room when that stained glass window is worth 10 G's a square foot."—Lenny Bruce (1926–1966), *The Essential Lenny Bruce,* 1967

"If there is a supreme being, he's crazy."—Marlene Dietrich (1901–1992), quoted in *Rave* magazine, November 1986

"Like many people, I have no religion, and I am just sitting in a small boat drifting with the tide. I live in the doubts of my duty. . . . I think there is dignity in this, just to go on working. . . . Today we stand naked, defenseless, and more alone than at any time in history. We are waiting for something, perhaps another miracle, perhaps the Martians. Who knows?"—Federico Fellini (1920–1993), Italian movie director, quoted by Martin E. Marty in *Varieties of Unbelief* (New York: Holt, Rinehart & Winston, 1964), p. 54

"I'm an atheist, and that's it. I believe there's nothing we can know except that we should be kind to each other and do what we can for other people."—Katharine Hepburn, in *Ladies' Home Journal,* October 1991

"Praying is like a rocking chair—it'll give you something to do, but it won't get you anywhere."—Gypsy Rose Lee (1914–1970), stripper, quoted by E. Haldeman-Julius

"Imagine there's no heaven; it's easy if you try / No hell below us, above us only sky / Imagine all the people living for today—Ah . . . / Imagine there's no countries; it isn't hard to do / Nothing to kill or die for, and no religion too / Imagine all the people living life in peace. . . ."—John Lennon (1940–1980), "Imagine"

"I'm an atheist, and Christianity appears to me to be the most absurd imposture of all the religions, and I'm puzzled that so many people can't see through a religion that encourages irresponsibility and bigotry."—Butterfly McQueen, actress who played a slave girl in the film version of *Gone with the Wind,* quoted in the *Charleston Gazette* after her death, January 11, 1996

"I'm one of those cliff-hanging Catholics. I don't believe in God, but I do believe that Mary was his mother."—Martin Sheen, quoted in McWilliams, *Ain't Nobody's Business If You Do,* p. 429

"Why is it when we talk to God, we're said to be praying, but when God talks to us, we're schizophrenic."—Lily Tomlin, quoted in *Dictionary of Contemporary Quotation* (J. G. Burke Publisher, 1981)

"Beliefs are what divide people. Doubt unites them."—Peter Ustinov

75

Recent Political Figures

Indira Gandhi: Library of Congress
Collection

Political leaders need popular support, so they rarely make skeptical remarks that might anger religious believers.

For example, both Prime Minister Indira Gandhi and her father, Prime Minister Jawaharlal Nehru, had no faith in India's maze of mysticism, but were cautious about expressing their views. Once, Gandhi was asked by a news reporter if she thought India's holy men actually could perform the miracles they claimed. She merely smiled—and her hint of public disbelief caused a flurry of outrage. Tragically, she later became a victim of religious hate: In India's never-ending bloodshed between Hindus, Muslims, and Sikhs, she was assassinated by Sikh extremists.

In the United States, federal judges are appointed for life; therefore, they are less dependent upon public popularity and are freer to challenge religion. For instance, Supreme Court justices ruled in 1962 that public schools may not impose mandatory prayers upon pupils, because the Constitution forbids the government to enforce religious conformity. The decision triggered a storm that still rages. The unpopular action never would have been taken by elected members of Congress, who must please voters.

Following are some statements by various public leaders.

Government Officials

"There exists no politician in India daring enough to attempt to explain to the masses that cows can be eaten."—Indian Prime Minister Indira Gandhi (1917–1984), quoted by Oriana Fallaci in "Indira's Coup," *New York Review* of *Books*

"I'm frankly sick and tired of the political preachers across this country telling me as a citizen that if I want to be a moral person, I must believe in A, B, C and D. Just who do they think they are? And from where do they presume to claim the right to dictate their moral beliefs to me? And I am even more angry as a legislator who must endure the threats of every religious group who thinks it has some God-granted right to control my vote on every roll call in the Senate."—Sen. Barry Goldwater, R-Ariz., floor speech, September 1981

"Religious factions will go on imposing their will on others unless the decent people connected to them recognize that religion has no place in public policy."
—Goldwater, speech, 1981

"I want nothing to do with any religion concerned with keeping the masses satisfied to live in hunger, filth, and ignorance."—Indian Prime Minister Jawaharlal Nehru (1889–1964), quoted by Edgar Snow in *Journey to the Beginning*

"The spectacle of what is called religion, or at any rate organized religion, in India and elsewhere, has filled us with horror, and I have frequently condemned it and wished to make a clean sweep of it."—Nehru (Cardiff)

"It is not God that is worshiped but the group or authority that claims to speak in His name. Sin becomes disobedience to authority, not violation of integrity."
—Sir Sarvepalli Radhakrishnan (1888–1975), Indian statesman and philosopher, quoted in J. A. C. Brown, *Techniques of Persuasion,* 1965

Judges

"In efforts to force loyalty to whatever religious group happened to be on top and in league with the government of a particular time and place, men and women had been fined, cast in jail, cruelly tortured, and killed. Among the offenses for which these punishments were inflicted were such things as speaking disrespectfully of the views of ministers of government-established churches, nonattendance at those churches, expressions of nonbelief in their doctrines, and failure to pay taxes and tithes to support them."—Hugo L. Black (1886–1971), U.S. Supreme Court Justice, *Emerson* v. *Board of Education,* 1947

"We repeat and again reaffirm that neither a state nor the federal government can constitutionally force a person 'to profess a belief or disbelief in any religion.' Neither can constitutionally pass laws or impose requirements which aid all religions as against nonbelievers. . . ."—Black, *Torcaso* v. *Watkins,* 1961

"Religious conflicts can be the bloodiest and cruelest conflicts that turn people into fanatics."—William J. Brennan, U.S. Supreme Court Justice, on National Public Radio, January 29, 1987

"Religious experiences which are as real as life to some may be incomprehensible to others."—William O. Douglas (1898–1980), U.S. Supreme Court Justice, *U.S.* v. *Ballard,* 1944

"The religiously used real estate of the churches today constitutes a vast domain. Their assets total over $141 billion and their annual income at least $22 billion. And the extent to which they are feeding from the public trough in a variety of ways is alarming."—Douglas, *Walz* v. *Tax Commission,* 1970

"The mounting wealth of the churches makes ironic their incessant demands on the public treasury."—Douglas, *Tilton* v. *Richardson,* 1971

"The day that this country ceases to be free for irreligion, it will cease to be free for religion—except for the sect that can win political power."—Robert H. Jackson (1892–1954), U.S. Supreme Court Justice, *Zorach* v. *Clauson,* April 7, 1952

"In our country are evangelists and zealots of many different political, economic and religious persuasions whose fanatical conviction is that all thought is divinely classified into two kinds—that which is their own and that which is false and dangerous."—Jackson, quoted in McWilliams, *Ain't Nobody's Business if You Do,* p. 170

"Religious oppression is older than the pyramids of Egypt and as current as the butchering of members of the Baha'i faith in Iran today. One of the dominant themes of human history, religious intolerance, unhappily continues with the ferocity and relentlessness of all that is evil in the human spirit."—John L. Kane, U.S. District Judge, address, Denver, June 1987

"No group, no matter how large or small, may use the organs of government, of which the public schools are the most conspicuous and influential, to foist its religious beliefs on others."—William R. Overton, U.S. Judge, Eastern District of Arkansas, overturning Arkansas Act 590, 1982

". . . The problem to be considered and solved when the First Amendment was proposed was not one of hazy or comparative insignificance, but was one of blunt and stark reality, which had perplexed and plagued the nations of Western civilization for some fourteen centuries, and during that long period, the union of church and state in the government of man had produced neither peace on earth nor good will to man."—Justice Prescott of the Maryland high court, *Horace Mann League* v. *Board of Public Works,* 1966

"Teachers of science in the public schools should not be expected to avoid the discussion of every scientific issue on which some religion claims expertise."—U.S. District Court, Southern District of Texas, *Wright* v. *Houston Independent School District,* 1972

76

Troubled Believers

Albert Gore, Jr.

"We Christians must admit that our religion has propagated, in the name of Jesus, devilish acts, bloody wars, awful persecutions, hate crimes, and political chaos," a Presbyterian minister wrote in an American religious magazine in 1994.

Sometimes, denunciations of religion come from within—from idealistic believers distressed by the fruits of faith. This chapter surveys many such protests by the devout through several centuries. Since the protesters cannot be considered skeptics, they are considered a separate category and therefore grouped together here.

One troubled believer was Frederick Douglass, the runaway slave who became a brilliant crusader against the custom of light-skinned people owning dark-skinned people as property. Although a Christian, Douglass was repelled by the clergy's endorsement of that custom.

Biographer William McFeely noted that soon after Douglass "took to the field for antislavery, he wrote a candid letter to his fellow communicants of the Zion chapel, saying . . . that he had to 'cut loose from the church' because he had found the American church, writ large, to be a 'bulwark of American slavery.' "[1]

In the aftermath of World War II, several horrified American theologians saw the Nazi Holocaust as a natural result of centuries of Christian hostility to Jews in Europe. They wrote agonized rebukes of their own faith.

Even political leaders such as Vice President Albert Gore, a Southern Baptist, have spoken against the intolerance within their religion.

A sampling of criticisms by churchmen follows.

*   *   *

---

1. William S. McFeely, *Frederick Douglass* (New York: W. W. Norton & Co., 1991), p. 85.

"The principle of the Inquisition was murderous. . . . The popes were not only murderers in the great style, but they also made murder a legal basis of the Christian Church and a condition of salvation."—Lord Acton (1834–1902), English editor, historian, Catholic dissident, and member of Parliament

"Patriotism is in political life what faith is in religion, and it stands to the domestic feelings and to homesickness as faith to fanaticism and to superstition."
—Acton, quoted in *The Home and Foreign Review,* July 1932

"We must recognize that the death of God is a historical event: God has died in our time, in our history, in our existence."—Thomas J. J. Altizer, Emory University theologian, *Time* magazine, October 22, 1965

"When popes damn popes, and councils damn them all, and popes damn councils, what must Christians do?"—Richard Baxter (1615–1691), English Puritan minister, *Hypocrisy*

"The God of the Bible is a moral monstrosity."—the Rev. Henry Ward Beecher (1813–1887) (Cardiff)

"There was never such a gigantic lie told as the fable of the Garden of Eden."—Beecher, ibid.

"Of all governments, there is no other so bad as the government of an ecclesiastical class."—Beecher, ibid.

"As men look back upon nations in the olden time, and know that amid their fondest convictions they were in profound error—that their gods were myths, their histories half fables, and their theology a mere fiction—so now and then it came home to him with ghastly distinctness, that a time would come when men would look back upon him and his generation in the same manner."—reflections by a character in Beecher's novel, *Norwood,* 1868

"Doctrine is nothing but the skin of truth set up and stuffed."—Beecher, *Life Thoughts*

"God is no more in the church than in the marketplace. . . . The priests lie in pretending that they make Christ's body and give it to the people for their salvation."—Pierre de Bruys, rebellious priest and founder of the Petrobrusian sect, who doubted the doctrine of transubstantiation, burned at the stake in 1126 (Gray)

"In most if not all of the world's trouble spots, religious extremism is at the heart of the problem. In Israel, Muslims throw rocks at Jews and Jews shoot back at Muslims. In the chaos of Lebanon, religious factions are so numerous it is difficult to keep track of them. In Northern Ireland, Catholic and Protestant Christians bomb each other as they have for decades. Hindu India and Muslim Pakistan face off against each other, offering the prospect of nuclear weapons if necessary to prove their points. . . . All of this killing is done with the absolute certainty that God wants it so. If thine enemy offends thee, rub him out. Indeed, it is believed that to lose one's life in God's cause is to die a martyr's death and win a reward in heaven."—Sen. John Danforth, R-Missouri, and Episcopal priest, in *The Washington Post,* October 1990

"We have men sold to build churches, women sold to support the gospel, and babes sold to purchase Bibles for the poor heathen, all for the glory of God and the good of souls. The slave auctioneer's bell and the church-going bell chime in with each other, and the bitter cries of the heart-broken slave are drowned in the religious shouts of his pious master. Revivals of religion and revivals in the slave trade go hand in hand."—Frederick Douglass (1817–1895), *Narrative of the Life of Frederick Douglass, An American Slave, Written by Himself,* 1845

"I can see no reason, but the most deceitful one, for calling the religion of this land Christianity. I look upon it as the climax of all misnomers, the boldest of all frauds, and the grossest of all libels."—Douglass, ibid.

"I would say, welcome infidelity! welcome atheism! welcome anything . . . in preference to the gospel as preached [by persons who] convert the very name of religion into an engine of tyranny and barbarous cruelty."—Douglass, "The Meaning of the Fourth of July for the Negro"

"I prayed for freedom twenty years, but received no answer until I prayed with my legs."—Douglass (Noyes)

"Religious talk is a very feast to self-deceit."—Frederick W. Faber (1814–1863), English Catholic theologian, student of Cardinal Newman, *Spiritual Conferences*

"Science has had to struggle for life against the fury of theological dogmatists, but in every instance the dogmatists have been ignominiously defeated."—Frederic William Farrar (1831–1903), archdeacon of Westminster Cathedral, quoted in Clampett, *Luther Burbank: Our Beloved Infidel,* p. 68

"When the church has attempted to fetter human thought, it is to freethought that we owe the emancipation of the human mind."—Farrar (Cardiff)

"However skillfully the modern ingenuity of semi-belief may have tampered with supernatural interpositions, it is clear to every honest and unsophisticated mind that, if miracles be incredible, Christianity is false."—Farrar, *The Witness of History to Christ,* 1870

"The most heinous and the most cruel crimes of which history has record have been committed under the cover of religion or equally noble motives."—Mohandas Gandhi (1869–1948), *Young India,* July 7, 1927

"There's no religion so irrational but can boast its martyrs."—Joseph Glanvil (1636–1680), chaplain to Charles II, *The Vanity of Dogmatizing,* 1661

"Jefferson knew history. He could look back on centuries of religious war in Europe: on massacre, burning, rape, pillage, and hatreds that tore nations apart and soaked the earth in blood. He knew from history and human nature how easy it is to arouse mass, murderous passion when religious demagogues cry that God wills it. . . . My mother's people, the Lafons, were French Huguenots, driven out of their homeland because of their religious faith, Protestantism. They found a new home in America. . . .

"We have had narrow escapes. Americans are human beings, subject to the same temptations and the same pride and the same fears that afflict people of all nations. Puritans in Boston hanged Quakers in a grim public ceremony on the limbs of the Great Elm on Boston Common. Baptists under Roger Williams had to flee Massachusetts. . . . Joseph Smith, founder of the Church of Latter Day Saints, the Mormons, was murdered by a mob. . . . Anti-Semitism is a stain on our history. For many decades, Jews could not buy houses in some parts of town. They were banned from many organizations. . . . Their innocent children suffered the thousand daily humiliations that prejudice could heap upon them, and some suffer still. . . .

"Even as we celebrate our religious liberty today, killing in the name of religion goes on all around the world. At this moment, the Muslims of Sarajevo are being shelled by artillery from the supposedly Christian Serbs in the mountains above the helpless city. The peaceful, inoffensive adherents of the Baha'i faith in Iran are imprisoned and murdered by the Iranian government. Their crime? The Baha'is believe in the spiritual unity of humankind. Saddam Hussein carries on a campaign of terror against the Shi'ite Muslims in his Iraq. Muslim fundamentalists in Egypt machine gun tourists. Hindus and Muslims in the Indian subcontinent are at each other's throats. Northern Ireland blazes with gunfire between opposing sides who claim to worship the same Christ. . . . Throughout history, religious wars have always been the most brutal and cruel and merciless."

—Vice President Albert Gore, speaking at a Religious Freedom Day ceremony in Richmond on January 14, 1994, in a building designed by Thomas Jefferson

"To become a popular religion, it is only necessary for a superstition to enslave a philosophy."—William Ralph Inge (1860–1954), English theologian, *Outspoken Essays,* 1919

"All of them, from the highest to the lowest, do as it is said in the prophets: They are enthralled to avarice, love presents, and seek rewards; for the sake of bribes, they pronounce the godless righteous."—Pope Innocent III (1161–1216), berating Catholic clergy

"Is it not strange that the descendants of those Pilgrim Fathers who crossed the Atlantic to preserve their own freedom of opinion have always proved themselves intolerant of the spiritual liberty of others?"—General Robert E. Lee (1807–1870), letter to his wife, December 27, 1856

"The Holocaust was, of course, the bitter fruit of long centuries of Christian teaching about the Jewish people."—Dr. Franklin Littell, chairman of the religion department at Temple University, preface to Paul Grosser and Edwin Halperin, *The Causes and Effects of Anti-Semitism* (New York: Philosophical Library, 1978), p. xi

"It is becoming quite clear that religion is at the heart of so many civil wars and international struggles. People seem willing to kill, maim, torture and die for a religious or spiritual belief which moves them to believe that their source of the divine is the only source. . . . Consider: In the name of God, a *fatwa* against Salman Rushdie. In the name of God, murder in the Balkans. In the name of God, the bombing of the World Trade Center. In the name of God, the siege at Waco, Texas. In the name of God, Hindus and Muslims kill each other in India. In the name of God, bloody warfare between Protestants and Catholics in Ireland. In the name of God, Shi'ites and Sunnis are at each other's throats in Iraq and Iran, as are Arabs and Jews in the Middle East. In the name of God, a doctor is murdered because he believed in a woman's right to choose. In the name of God, what is going on?"—actress Shirley MacLaine, a New Age mystic, addressing the American Society of Newspaper Editors, Baltimore, 1993

"Look at the hotspots of the earth today: religious extremists are lighting fuses in Northern Ireland, Israel, Bosnia, and the U.S.A., and fomenting all kinds of 'culture wars.' Religion can breed harassment, bigotry, prejudice, intolerance and deception. . . . We Christians must admit that our religion has propagated, in the name of Jesus, devilish acts, bloody wars, awful persecutions, hate crimes, and political chaos. We have seen leaders of Operation Rescue harassing neighbors and demonstrating at women's clinics in most detestable and criminal ways. The hate that certain extreme elements of the Christian community have cultivated toward neighbors of a homosexual orientation resembles the environment of hell. . . . This New Right confronts us with a threat far greater than the old threat of Communism."—the Rev. Robert H. Meneilly, pastor of Village Presbyterian Church, Prairie, Kansas, in *Liberty* magazine, March–April, 1994, p. 14

"It too often happens that the religiously disposed are in the same degree intellectually deficient."—John Henry Newman (1801–1890), English cardinal, *The Idea of a University*, 1852

"Men insist most vehemently upon their certainties when their hold upon them has been shaken. Frantic orthodoxy is a method for obscuring doubt."—Reinhold Niebuhr (1892–1971), American theologian, *Does Civilization Need Religion?* 1927

"There is no social evil, no form of injustice, whether of the feudal or capitalist order, which has not been sanctified in some way or another by religious sentiment and thereby rendered more impervious to change."—Niebuhr, *Christian Realism and Political Problems*, 1953

"Religion is so frequently a source of confusion in political life, and so frequently dangerous to democracy, precisely because it introduces absolutism into the realm of relative values."—Niebuhr, quoted in *Brown Alumni Monthly*, May 1989

"The tendency to claim God as an ally for our partisan values is . . . the source of all religious fanaticism."—Niebuhr (Peter)

"Your assertion that artificial contraception is 'intrinsically evil' is rejected by the vast majority of faithful, practicing Catholics. . . . The legitimacy of teaching requires that it be embraced by the faithful. Your teaching has no such legitimacy. . . . Your statements and policies often deter, rather than promote, the advancement of women. Opposition to contraception denies the moral adulthood of women." —from a full-page *New York Times* ad addressed to Pope John Paul II, signed by 3,500 American Catholics, during the 1994 Cairo conference on population control

"Such visions [of Satan] have been incorporated into Christian tradition and have served, among other things, to confirm for Christians their own identification with God and to demonize their opponents—first other Jews, then pagans, and later dissident Christians called heretics."—Elaine Pagels, *The Origin of Satan,* 1995

"It was the Easter season, and I stood there listening to the Good Friday liturgy, all about the death of Jesus. . . . I was taken aback, really distressed, because within that story are these terrible accusations against the Jews, about the execution of Jesus. It struck me deeply, this demonic language. Animosity between groups is a human universal, but what's different here is the moral and religious dimension of the animosity."—Pagels, quoted in *The New Yorker,* April 3, 1995, p. 64

"The 11 o'clock hour on Sunday is the most segregated hour in American life." —Episcopal Bishop James A. Pike, *U.S. News & World Report,* May 16, 1960

"Two-thirds of the major conflicts in the world today have religious overtones."— the Rev. David Ramage, American Presbyterian minister and chairman of the Parliament of the World Religions

"[Catholicism's] disastrous theology had prepared the way for Hitler and his 'final solution.' [The Church published] over a hundred anti-Semitic documents. Not one conciliar decree, not one papal encyclical, bull, or pastoral directive suggests that Jesus's command, 'love your neighbor as yourself,' applied to Jews. Jews were hounded from one land to another. One pope gave them a month to quit their homes in Italy, leaving them only two places of refuge. During the Crusades, they were slaughtered in the thousands, out of devotion to Christ. A Jew who showed his nose on Good Friday was virtually committing suicide, even though the man on the cross had a Jewish nose. . . . There is, tragically, an undeniable link between . . . the papal legislation, the pogroms—and the gas chambers and crematoria of the Nazi death camps."—Jesuit theologian Peter de Rosa, who left the priesthood, *Vicars of Christ: The Dark Side of the Papacy* (New York: Crown Publishers, 1988)

". . . and hated all for love of Jesus Christ."—Christina Rossetti (1830–1894), English religious poet, *A Portrait*

"The Nazis . . . did not invent a new villain. . . . They took over the two-thousand-year-old Christian tradition of the Jew as villain. . . . The roots of the death camps must be sought in the mythic structure of Christianity. . . . Myths concerning the demonological role of the Jews have been operative in Christianity for centuries. . . . Only the terrible accusation, known and taught to every Christian in earliest childhood, that the Jews are the killers of Christ, can account for the depth and persistence of this supreme hatred. In a sense, the death camps were the terminal expression of Christian anti-Semitism."—theologian Richard Rubenstein, *After Auschwitz: Religion and the Origins of the Death Camps* (Indianapolis: Bobbs-Merrill, 1966)

"It's so obvious that it hurts—that so many of the things that are wrong in the world are actually due to religious conflicts."—Rabbi Herbert Schaalman, an organizer of the 1993 Parliament of the World Religions

"As the French say, there are three sexes—men, women and clergymen."—Sydney Smith (1771–1845), English writer and minister, recounted in his daughter's memoirs

"God appeared in some passages to be not only a nationalistic deity but also a sadistic one who delighted even in killing the firstborn in every Egyptian household (Exodus 11:4–6). . . . As the law of God unfolded in the remaining books of the Torah, I found myself more and more repelled. Slavery was assumed, and the master could beat his slave mercilessly, for the law said, 'The slave is his money' (Exodus 21:21)."—John Spong, Episcopal Bishop of the Diocese of Newark, New Jersey, *Rescuing the Bible from Fundamentalism* (San Francisco: Harper, 1991)

"Religion is a very dangerous thing. These are enormous powers we are dealing with. . . . Why has there been this dark side?"—Krister Stendahl, Harvard theologian, on religious killing, at a 1989 "Anatomy of Hate" seminar at Boston University. The seminar featured a daughter of the late Egyptian President Anwar Sadat, who was assassinated in 1981 by Muslim fanatics.

"Demonization is one of the plagues of religious tradition, because you are dealing with an intense rhetoric intensified to the voltage of the divine."—Stendahl, discussing religious hostilities, in *The New Yorker,* April 3, 1995, p. 64

"We have just enough religion to make us hate, but not enough to make us love one another.—Jonathan Swift, Anglican dean and satirist (1667–1745), *Thoughts on Various Subjects,* 1706

"Difference in opinions has cost many millions of lives; for instance, whether flesh be bread, or bread be flesh; whether the juice of a certain berry be blood or wine."—Swift (Noyes)

"Time and again we see leaders and members of religions incite aggression, fanaticism, hate and xenophobia—even inspire and legitimize violent and bloody conflicts. . . . We are filled with disgust. . . . We condemn aggression and hatred in the name of religion."—*Toward a Global Ethic,* international declaration adopted by hundreds of clergymen at the Parliament of the World Religions, Chicago, 1993

"We live in a post-Christian era because Christianity has sunk into religiosity."
—Gabriel Vahanian, *The Death of God,* 1962, afterword

"I have noticed again and again since I have been in the Church that lay interest in ecclesiastical matters is often a prelude to insanity."—Evelyn Waugh (1903–1966), English novelist who quit the Church of England and became a fervent Catholic, *Decline and Fall,* part 1, chapter 8

"There is a species of person called a 'Modern Churchman' who draws the full salary of a beneficed clergyman and need not commit himself to any religious belief."—Waugh, ibid., part 2, chapter 4

"It is a curious thing that every creed promises a paradise which would be absolutely uninhabitable for anyone of civilized taste."—Waugh, quoted in McWilliams, *Ain't Nobody's Business If You* Do, p. 405

"Christian anti-Judaism . . . prepared the way for the Holocaust. . . . The Nazis . . . are inconceivable apart from this Christian tradition. Hitler's pogrom, for all its distinctiveness, is the zenith of a long Christian heritage of teaching and practice against the Jews. . . . The Holocaust . . . discloses, among other things, the demonic results and malevolent possibilities that reside in our tradition of anti-Jewish preaching and teaching. . . . Christian anti-Judaism promoted the Nazi cause in several ways. It led the Nazis to focus initially on Jews and created attitudes which permitted them to carry out their extermination program with little resistance. It made it possible for Christians to justify either assisting or not opposing the Nazi efforts. Christian anti-Judaism is profoundly incriminated in the Final Solution."—Dr. Clark M. Williamson, Christian Theological Seminary, Indianapolis, *Has God Rejected His People?: Anti-Judaism in the Christian Church* (Nashville, Tenn.: Abingdon, 1982)

"Of the many difficulties in writing about the treatment of Jews by Christians, not least is the problem of believability. That some things could have occurred seems scarcely credible. Yet they did. . . . We have seen the collusion of Christianity with pogrom and the Holocaust. . . . What is the goodness of this world . . . when millions are killed by those baptized in the name of the Redeemer? . . . The immensity of suffering and death inflicted on Jews for 1,500 years by some who called themselves Christian, and the apparent worthlessness to Christians of the lives of those who did not convert to Christianity, fundamentally question Christian claims about the value of human life. . . . Christians have lost forever the credibility of their claim to a superior religion and a superior ethic."—Williamson, ibid.

77

The Future?

When I was a young thinker and knew *everything,* it was quite obvious to me that supernatural religion soon would vanish. How could modern people continue believing in invisible spirits, unseen heavens, otherworld hells, and such spookery? I expected the whole rigmarole to go the way of vampires and leprechauns.

So much for young thinkers. Exactly the opposite happened: Supernaturalism soared. Fundamentalism left America's fringe and gained political power. The ranks of Catholics and Southern Baptists in the United States grew by tens of millions. Militant Islam became a juggernaut in the Mideast and North Africa. American sects whose members spout the "unknown tongue" broke growth records. So did second-coming churches. Burgeoning cults wrought murder in Jonestown, Waco, Switzerland, Japan, and elsewhere. New Age mysticism blossomed. Zealots mobbed American abortion clinics and killed doctors. Religion loomed larger in stormy events.

Still, strange as it may seem, amid all this holy upheaval, religion is dying in some ways—conspicuously within certain groups, and insidiously within some cultures.

In Western Europe and Japan, faith has shrunk to a mere fringe. Pollster George Gallup, Jr., says only 19 percent of Swedes and Danes now believe in a personal God, and only 24 percent of Germans—compared to 66 percent of Americans, plus nearly 30 percent more in America who envision God as "some sort of spirit or life force." Surprisingly, in "Catholic" France and Italy, only 26 percent think there is a personal deity. In Japan, 82 percent answered no when asked if they believe in life after death. In England, where 27 million are officially listed as Anglicans, only one million attend church on a typical Sunday.

In America, despite all the religious ferment and tumult, agnosticism pervades the educated classes, and secularism has transformed society. Most scientists, scholars, writers, media professionals, university professors, and others of the "cognitive elite" live as if religion did not exist. Movies, magazines, television, newspapers, and other public outlets (except for supermarket tabloids and horror

318

films) do not treat mystical claims seriously. America is a chaotic contradiction, with 100 million people praying to invisible deities every Sunday morning, but daily life proceeding as if there were no such thing as the supernatural.

I offer some signs and portents of the growth of secularism:

- Religious and moral taboos, once dominant in America, have largely vanished. Writing about sex formerly was a crime; now nude lovemaking is common in R-rated movies. Gambling was a jail offense; now it's operated by state governments. Unmarried couples who lived together were arrested; now they're casually accepted. Drinking alcohol was a crime; now it's a social ritual. Abortion was a felony; now it's a right guaranteed by the U.S. Supreme Court. Divorce was unthinkable; now it is the end for more than half of marriages. Homosexuals were imprisoned; now they march for gay pride. Birth control was a crime; now it's championed by the United Nations. Former church "thou shalt nots" disappeared like frost in the sunshine.

- While blue-collar fundamentalism and Catholicism have swelled, liberal Protestant "mainline" denominations—which deemphasize the magic of religion, making it more acceptable to educated people—are fading. These "tall-steeple" churches (Presbyterians, Methodists, Episcopalians, Lutherans, United Church of Christ, and Disciples of Christ) have lost nearly seven million members since the 1960s, while America's population rose sixty million. Evidently, the educated feel less need for watered-down mysticism.

- In *The People's Religion: American Faith in the 1990s,* pollster Gallup wrote: "The proportion of Americans who say religion is 'very important' in their lives dropped from 75 percent in 1952 to about 55 percent in the late 1970s and 1980s. In addition, the number of Bible 'literalists' declined sharply from the early 1960s to the late 1970s, and in 1988 was half what it was in the 1965. Church attendance has declined steadily since the 1950s." Gallup added: "In 1952, only 2 percent of Americans stated no religious preference; in 1987, it was 9 percent. The figure is even higher among young people: 12 percent of those 18–24 and 14 percent of those 25–29 state no religious preference. . . . The religiously unaffiliated have steadily increased as a proportion of the population and are likely to continue to do so."

- In the same book, Gallup documented that "many religious beliefs decline as education level rises." He provided a chart indicating that 51 percent of Americans with no college experience believe in angels and devils, but only 35 percent of college graduates do. The pollster noted: "Belief in Judgment Day decreases with education. Ninety-one percent of those who had not graduated from high school, 86 percent of high school graduates, 74 percent of those with some college, and 66 percent of college graduates said they would face God on Judgment Day."

- Two generations ago, in the 1930 *Who's Who in America,* 56 percent of the outstanding people in the book identified themselves as church members. In 1992, only 34 percent of those listed in *Who's Who* did so. High achievers seem to be abandoning faith, at least to a degree.

- In the latest edition of the *Handbook of Denominations in the United States,* Dr. Samuel S. Hill, religion professor at the University of Florida, notes that while fundamentalism is booming, so is an opposing force: "the ongoing, growing, and powerful movement called secularism, a way of understanding and living that is indifferent to religion—in fact, not even concerned enough to pay it any attention, much less oppose it."

- In 1994, writer-futurist Douglas Coupland, who dubbed today's video-raised young adults "Generation X," wrote a poignant book titled *Life after God,* grieving for "the first generation raised without religion." Theologian William Willimon of Duke University said the book "gives us glimpses of what it's like to have been raised by the first generation that stopped believing in God. By the time Generation X became adults, there was nothing left not to believe in."

- According to University of California sociologist Wade Clark Roof, 60 percent of "baby boomers," the teeming generation born after World War II, dropped out of their family religion, and 42 percent never rejoined any church. Among young Jews, he said, the slippage was 70 percent. In his 1993 book, *A Generation of Seekers,* Roof observed: "Most, it seems, just quit going, not out of any strong doctrinal or moral objection, but because church or synagogue seemed irrelevant to them." Among all education levels, he said, "postgraduates abandoned the churches and synagogues more so than any of the others."

- *The Restructuring of American Religion,* by Princeton sociologist Robert Wuthnow, opens with a description of ninety thousand Protestant children marching in 1946 in Brooklyn, in the 117th annual Sunday School Union Parade—partly as a show of force against Brooklyn's Catholics. Today, a half-century later, such a parade would seem strange. Mainline Protestants no longer stage extravaganzas. Instead, Wuthnow notes, America now has spectacles such as the 1980 "Washington for Jesus" rally, arranged by television evangelists, which drew a quarter-million fundamentalists to the nation's capital.

- Brookings Institution scholar A. James Reichley, in a 1991 essay titled *Religion and American Democracy,* wrote: "The role of religion has almost surely diminished. Americans remain by all measurable criteria (testimony to belief in God, church attendance, financial support of churches, and so forth) an unusually religious people among economically developed nations. More than 90 percent of Americans tell pollsters they identify with a particular religious faith, more than 80 percent say they believe in the divinity of Jesus, and about 40 percent are found in church on any given Sunday morning—far higher figures than in any European country except Ireland or Poland. . . . Yet few would contend that religion plays the role in the moral and cultural lives of Americans today that it did around the turn of the twentieth century, or even fifty years ago."

- In his new book, *The Death of Satan*, scholar Andrew Delbanco states, "the advance of secular rationality in the United States has been relentless in the face of all resistance." He says that American culture "has gradually withdrawn its support from the old conception of a universe seething with divine intelligence and has left its members with only one recourse: to acknowledge that no story about intrinsic meaning of the world has universal validity."

- Although evangelical churches are thriving in America, they suffer a serious dropout rate. In *Christianity Today* of May 16, 1994, evangelical pastor Gordon MacDonald lamented "the disappearance of enormous numbers of people in today's church world." He said that "today's impressive figures for church growth are matched by equally impressive numbers of people who are choosing to abandon organized Christianity." Such parishioners, according to MacDonald, "grow weary of the business of religion" and eventually "conclude that the claims made in the pulpit do not fit their version of reality. Ultimately, they simply stop taking it seriously and disappear, never to be heard from again."

- Two dozen American Jewish congregations have joined the Society for Humanistic Judaism, which does not assert the existence of God. In 1991, when one of the congregations sought affiliation with the Reform Judaism union, other rabbis objected. One said that recognizing the congregation "would mean that atheism is a legitimate Reform option."

- Senior television newsman Walter Cronkite hosted a 1994 show titled "Christianity Reborn: Prayer and Politics." Later, Cronkite said in an interview with *Christian Century* magazine: "I know from experience that church attendance in England, France, and the rest of Western Europe is way down. In the United States we have something of a boom. Why? What makes religiosity in this country different from that in the rest of the developed world?" When asked about allegations that news reporters "trivialize" faith, Cronkite replied: "I wouldn't say media trivialize religion; I'd say instead that they don't pay attention to religion at all. . . . They don't think religion is a broad-based interest among readers and viewers."

- In 1993, devout Yale law professor Stephen Carter wrote a bitter lament, *The Culture of Disbelief*, protesting that America's trend-setters ignore and belittle religion. In an interview at Harvard Divinity School, Carter complained: "There is less respect for religion, less of an appreciation of it as an important force in people's lives without being somehow a symptom of something neurotic. That's what has been lost."

I think Carter's message is correct—but not in the way he intended. He is right that a culture of disbelief is growing among the educated elite. This, however, is a sign not of moral decay but of intellectual honesty. It's occurring because scientific-minded people no longer can subscribe to unseen gods and devils, heavens and hells. And fewer of them want to embrace liberal theology that blurs these magical concepts into vague symbols.

Compared to the culture of belief, the culture of disbelief remains small. The lure of the supernatural still has great power: Fundamentalist rallies continue to fill large American arenas. Almost daily around the globe, Catholics sight the Virgin Mary or report that statues of saints are weeping. (As the old wisecrack goes, some things must be believed to be seen.) California evangelist Harold Camping sold thousands of books outlining his prediction that the world would end in 1994—and the next worthless forecast probably will draw just as many followers. Astrologers, flying saucer "experts," and mystical seers attract devoted throngs.

Members of David Koresh's Branch Davidians were so committed they died with their children in his Texas compound in 1993. Muslim suicide-bombers sacrifice their lives, sure of instant transport to a paradise full of Houri nymphs. Adherents of the Solar Temple cult believed its mumbo jumbo until they perished in a mass murder-suicide in 1994. Even in secularized Japan, members of the lethal Supreme Truth cult were so committed that they kissed their guru's big toe, paid two thousand dollars each for a sip of his bathwater, and ten thousand dollars for a drink of his blood. Reason and logic have little power against such impregnable belief.

With all this zealotry in the daily news, and with hundreds of millions of people still attending "respectable" churches, it seems clear that religion will remain a potent force among many groups for many years to come. But the advance of secularism is real, too. So the two-tiered society—believing masses and doubting elite—may become more polarized.

As this book has shown, the doubting elite isn't new. For two thousand years, the brightest thinkers and keenest reformers—the "greats" who changed the world—largely have been religious nonconformists. To one degree or another, they questioned extablished dogmas. Some of them were jailed or executed for it. Gradually, they secured the right to disbelieve (in the West, but not in the Muslim world, where doubt remains a capital offense today).

This two-thousand-year struggle for the freedom to think independently is a sweeping epic. Much progress has been achieved, but the battle is not won, and may never be. Supernaturalism is rooted deep in dark, fearful, irrational recesses of the human mind. It exerts a powerful grip on societies; to oppose it involves risk. Courage is required to dispute the prevailing beliefs of fellow citizens.

Nonetheless, resisting religion is an honorable cause for people who care about integrity. It is dishonest to recite solemn creeds about hells, Holy Ghosts, and the like, when there's not a shred of evidence that the hells and Holy Ghosts exist. It is dishonest to teach children there's a realm of spirits, with punishment or bliss for eternity, when nobody has any proof that the realm is anything but imaginary.

To doubt is to be honest. To say "I don't know" is to tell the truth. That is the heart of two thousand years of disbelief.

Afterthought

The Great American Think-Off is a philosophy competition held each year by the New York Mills Arts Retreat and Regional Cultural Center in Minnesota. The 1996 debate topic was "Does God Exist?" Here is the entry I submitted:

Does God exist?

Well, it depends on what you mean by God.

The universe is a maze of mysteries. How can gravity—an invisible, unexplainable force—pull the Milky Way into a spiral? How can atoms contain such awesome power that an amount of matter smaller than a dime produced the energy in the bomb that killed one hundred thousand Hiroshima residents? How can the double-helix thread of DNA create all living things, from bacteria to trees to Beethoven? How can electrons, dormant in every atom of your body, explode into violent lightning bolts when they're detached? Finally, why does anything exist at all?

If you say that the power of gravity, atoms, DNA, lightning and all the rest is God—that God is $E = mc^2$—then God exists. Those baffling forces are undeniably real.

Or if you say, as some do, that God is the love and pity in every human heart, then God exists. Those feelings are undeniably real—just like the paranoid capacity for suspicion, hate, jealousy, anger, and the like.

But if you mean church-type deities—the three gods of the Christian Trinity, the 330 million gods of Hinduism, the wrathful Jehovah of the Old Testament, the multitudinous Greek and Roman gods, the invisible feathered serpent of the Aztecs, and so on—you've entered the Twilight Zone.

Human logic can find no trustworthy evidence to prove, or disprove, the existence of unseen spirits. Weeping statues and holy apparitions aren't reliable proof. So the only truthful answer for an honest person is: I don't know.

But honest people can go farther and speculate intelligently: Do demons exist? Angels? Leprechauns? Fairies? Vampires? Werewolves? Lack of tangible evidence leads educated people to laugh off these imaginary beings. It's a small step to apply the same rationale to holy ghosts, resurrected saviors, blessed virgins, and patron saints. You can't *prove* they aren't hovering invisibly in the room with you—but it's unlikely.

Sigmund Freud said the widespread belief in a father-god arises from psychology. Tiny children are awed by their fathers as seemingly all-powerful protectors and punishers. As maturity comes, fathers grow less awesome. But the infantile image remains buried in the subconscious, and attaches to an omnipotent, supernatural father in an invisible heaven. Without knowing it, Freud said, believers worship their hidden toddler impression of the biological father, "clothed in the grandeur in which he once appeared to the small child."

That makes sense to me. It says the father-god is just a figment of the imagination. But you can't prove it's true.

Through logic, you can see that the church concept of an all-loving heavenly creator doesn't hold water. If a divine Maker fashioned everything that exists, he designed breast cancer for women, childhood leukemia, cerebral palsy, leprosy, AIDS, Alzheimer's disease, and Down's syndrome. He mandated foxes to rip rabbits apart (bunnies emit a terrible shriek at that moment) and cheetahs to slaughter fawns. No human would be cruel enough to plan such horrors. If a supernatural being did so, he's a monster, not an all-merciful father.

When you get down to it, the only evidence of God's existence is that holy men, past and present, *say* he exists.

Priests have built worldwide, trillion-dollar empires on their claim that an unseen deity waits to reward or punish people after death. But such priests once said that witches exist, and burned thousands of women on charges that they flew through the sky, copulated with Satan, changed into animals, and so forth. Priests later dropped this claim (but never apologized for the witch-hunts). If their assertion about God is as valid as their assertion about witches, their trillion-dollar empires rest on fantasy.

The universe is a vast, amazing, seething dynamo which has no discernible purpose except to keep on churning. From quarks to quasars, it's alive with incredible power. But it seems utterly indifferent to any moral laws. It destroys as blindly as it nurtures.

The philosopher Martin Heidegger stated that we know only that we exist for a while, and that we are doomed to die without knowing why we are here. If you are scrupulously honest, you cannot say much more than that.

Are the profound forces of the universe God? I don't know. Is human love God? I don't know. Is there a personal God waiting to reward me in a heaven or punish me in a hell? I don't know—but I doubt it.

Bibliography

In addition to works listed in the acknowledgments at the beginning of this book, here are other recommended selections:

Allen, Norm R., Jr., ed. *African-American Humanism: An Anthology.* Amherst, N.Y.: Prometheus Books, 1991.

Bierce, Ambrose. *The Devil's Dictionary.* New York: Dover Publications, 1993.

Bucky, Peter A. *The Private Albert Einstein.* Kansas City: Andrews & McMeel, 1992.

Carter, Stephen L. *The Culture of Disbelief: How American Law and Politics Trivialize Religion.* New York: Basic Books, 1993.

Coupland, Douglas. *Life after God.* New York: Pocket Books, 1994.

Cousins, Norman. *In God We Trust: The Religious Beliefs and Ideas of the American Founding Fathers.* New York: Harper & Brothers, 1958.

Darrow, Clarence. *Why I Am an Agnostic, and Other Essays.* Amherst, N.Y.: Prometheus Books, 1995.

FitzGerald, Edward. *The Rubaiyat of Omar Khayyam: First and Fifth Editions.* New York: Dover Publications, 1990.

Gallup, George, Jr. *The People's Religion: American Faith in the 1990s.* New York: Macmillan, 1989.

Hendricks, William D. *Exit Interviews: Revealing Stories of Why People Are Leaving the Church.* Chicago: Moody, 1994.

Hill, Samuel S. *Handbook of Denominations in the United States.* 8th ed. Russelville, Ariz.: Parthenon, 1985.

Kosmin, Barry, and Seymour Lachman. *One Nation under God: Religion in Contemporary American Society.* New York: Crown Trade Paperbacks.

Kurtz, Paul. *In Defense of Secular Humanism.* Amherst, N.Y.: Prometheus Books, 1983.

Kurtz, Paul. *The Transcendental Temptation*. Amherst, N.Y.: Prometheus Books, 1986.

Lamont, Corliss. *The Philosophy of Humanism*. 6th ed. New York: Continuum, 1988.

McWilliams, Peter. *Ain't Nobody's Business If You Do*. Los Angeles: Prelude Press, 1993.

Marsden, George M. *The Soul of the American University*. Oxford University Press, 1994.

Marty, Martin E. *Varieties of Unbelief*. New York: Holt, Rinehart & Winston, 1964.

Menendez, Albert J., and Edd Doerr. *The Great Quotations on Religious Freedom*. Long Beach, Calif.: Centerline Press, 1991

Roof, Wade Clark. *A Generation of Seekers: The Spiritual Journeys of the Baby Boom Generation*. San Francisco: Harper, 1993.

Russell, Bertrand. *Wisdom of the West*. Garden City, N.Y.: Doubleday & Co., 1959.

Stein, Gordon, ed. *The Encyclopedia of Unbelief*. Amherst, N.Y.: Prometheus Books, 1985.

Thody, Philip. *Sartre: A Biographical Introduction*. New York: Charles Scribner's Sons, 1971.

Turner, James. *Without God, Without Creed: The Origins of Unbelief in America*. Baltimore: The Johns Hopkins University Press, 1985.

Williams, David Allen. *A Celebration of Humanism and Freethought*. Amherst, N.Y.: Prometheus Books, 1995.

Wills, Garry. *Under God: Religion and American Politics*. New York: Simon & Schuster, 1990.

Wilson, R. J., ed. *Darwinism and the American Intellectual: A Book of Readings*. Homewood, Ill.: Dorsey Press, 1967.

Wuthnow, Robert. *The Restructuring of American Religion*. Princeton University Press, 1988.

Index